GESTALT THERAPY

GESTALT THERAPY

Roots and Branches—
Collected Papers

Peter Philippson

KARNAC

First published in 2012 by
Karnac Books Ltd
118 Finchley Road, London NW3 5HT

British Library Cataloguing in Publication Data

A C.I.P. for this book is available from the British Library

ISBN 978 1 78049 072 4

Edited, designed and produced by The Studio Publishing Services Ltd
www.publishingservicesuk.co.uk
e-mail: studio@publishingservicesuk.co.uk

www.karnacbooks.com

CONTENTS

ACKNOWLEDGEMENTS

I would like to thank my journal and book editors over the years for the opportunity to develop and present my views in print, and for permission to reprint here: my friend and partner in *Topics in Gestalt Therapy* (and for over twenty years my co-therapist), John Harris; Malcolm Parlett and Christine Stevens at the *British Gestalt Journal*; Joe Wysong and Molly Rawle at the *Gestalt Journal/International Gestalt Journal*; Joe Melnick and Susan Fischer at the *Gestalt Review*; Dan Bloom, Margherita Spagnuolo Lobb, and Frank-M. Staemmler at *Studies in Gestalt Therapy*; and Teresa Pignatelli at Apertura; and, of course, Oliver Rathbone and staff at Karnac, and Anita Mason and staff at The Studio Publishing Services.

As always, I would like to thank my family for bearing with me while I am caught up with writing, and my colleagues and clients at Manchester Gestalt Centre for helping me develop who I am as a Gestalt therapist.

ABOUT THE AUTHOR

Peter Philippson is a Gestalt psychotherapist and trainer, Member of the Gestalt Psychotherapy & Training Institute UK, a founder member of Manchester Gestalt Centre, Full Member of the New York Institute for Gestalt Therapy, Senior Trainer for GITA (Slovenia) and trainer for training programmes internationally. He is Past President of the Association for the Advancement of Gestalt Therapy. Author of *Self in Relation*; *The Emergent Self*; and many other chapters and articles. He is a practitioner of Aikido.

Introduction

This book is a collection of articles written in the period 1985–2011, mostly for journals. They form both a background for, and an elaboration of, concerns and perspectives in my previous two books (and several book chapters). These perspectives concern the foundations of Gestalt therapy: foundations in philosophy (existentialism, phenomenology, Eastern thought); foundations in psychoanalysis and connections with other therapeutic theories; foundations in its own theory (relational self, field theory, a holistic approach incorporating body, relationships, culture, and politics as well as more "interpersonal" issues). There are two unpublished pieces: writing that was to go into a Gestalt book on the Id, as a counterpart to the classic Groddeck book in psychoanalysis, and a new piece on Introjection.

My experience during my thirty-two years in the Gestalt community has been of an undervaluing of these roots. Trainers speak without embarrassment of never having read the foundational literature, *Ego, Hunger and Aggression* by Frederick (Fritz) Perls, and *Gestalt Therapy: Excitement and Growth in the Human Personality* by Frederick Perls, Ralph Hefferline, and Paul Goodman. It is little comfort to know that this ignorance of our basic theoretical roots was encouraged by

Perls himself in his later years, when he discouraged trainees from theorising. The result has been that the basic contours of a complex theory were replaced by dramatic, yet alien, concepts of emotional "discharge", or catharsis, and a promotion of an extreme individualism that contradicted the relational slant of Perls, Hefferline, and Goodman. This was then compounded by a "reaction formation", emphasising anti-individualism, but at the cost of denying the human capacity to individuate creatively that was so central to the foundational theory, where the self is the "artist of life". The idea of a field-emergent individual who could, at times, transcend and even negate the directions of his/her environment was lost in this polarisation.

What has also often been lost is an understanding of our roots in philosophy and psychoanalysis. Once again, it is of little comfort that this was supported by Fritz Perls as he made his own break from his analytic roots. More recently, there has been a significant attempt to find a rapprochement between Gestalt and psychoanalysis, with people such as my affectionate sparring partner, Lynne Jacobs, being in both worlds. But these tend to be revisionist versions of both finding common ground rather than a finding of our roots in the psychoanalysis of Fritz Perls and the self-in/as-contact expansion of Paul Goodman.

Neither did his sloganising style help his serious ideas to get serious attention. For example, when he said, "If we meet it will be wonderful; if not it can't be helped", he was not saying anything different from Buber saying that I–Thou meeting "comes through grace" rather than being something you can aim for, but it just does not sound as profound.

My background includes a period as a philosophy postgraduate, and I was excited by the philosophical possibilities of the Gestalt approach. I have been fortunate enough to have had a number of philosophy friends to discuss with and be challenged by: my long-term friend and collaborator John Harris (whom I first met when he was a lecturer in philosophy at Manchester University and I was a philosophy student), and Dan Bloom, Sylvia Crocker, Phil Brownell, and Seán Gaffney. My ideas and errors remain my own of course.

So, these twenty-seven papers have a common theme: of taking seriously Gestalt therapy as a meaningful contribution to both psychology and philosophy, with identifiable roots from which it branches in new directions. Of these, the most central is the theory of self arising in contact, rather than being somehow inherent "inside" me (more accurately, the self process and the contacting process are the same process in Gestalt theory). There are two kinds of words. There are "thing" words: table, door. Then there are comparison words: big, small; day, night. Each member of these pairs has meaning only in relation to the other. Gestalt theory says that self–other is of the second kind. If there was no other, there would be no self, and, furthermore, "self" would point to a different experience and significance in relation to a different other. Therefore, therapy requires the exploration of the emergence of self and other in relationship rather than of intrapsychic experience of self, or an "attunement" to an other inherently separate from oneself.

Thus, you can understand the relationship of Gestalt theory to psychoanalytic theory as one of substitution, with relational concepts being "slotted in" as replacements for intrapsychic ones. So, "id" moves from being a reservoir of drives to a void process of self as potential, the ground from which the active functions can emerge. "Ego" moves from being a regulator between the drives and the demands of society to the active identifications and alienations that make a boundary between self and other. "Therapeutic abstinence" becomes "creative indifference", a concept from Friedlander, meaning a stance in the centre around which polarities co-form, rather than seeing the polarities as essentially separate. The "unconscious" becomes a dynamic background to the figures we make, either because the background content is relatively uninteresting or because it is too anxiety provoking. "Introjection" and the related concept of the "superego" are understood as two different processes. "Assimilation" is the work of active contact and growth, taking in what is nourishing and growthful, and rejecting what is not. "Introjection" is a reversal of assimilation, tailoring oneself to fit the convenience of the environment, yet also fighting against that tailoring on another level, what Perls called the topdog–underdog split, or superego–infraego. Rather than the superego being in conflict with the id drives, as in classical psychoanalysis, it is in a conflict for supremacy or survival with the infraego, and the person's desires and needs are lost in that conflict.

Among the articles in this book are my attempts to take this project further, so you will find articles on a Gestalt approach to drive theory, regression, and transference, as well as further discussion of the concept of "introjection", and notes towards a Gestalt version of Groddeck's *Book of the Id* (1949) that so influenced Freud.

Personal identity—the feeling of himself—is natural to man. He is conscious of differing from all things else: he feels his individuality, i.e., that he is distinct from the things external to him. So strong is this innate perception, that man in a state of nature experiences childish wonder when first he learns, that in his physical organization he resembles a vast series of other beings. Having the instinctive feeling of his separateness from every thing external to himself, his existence suffices to satisfy him that he exists. Man is self-conscious; he pre-eminently is.

My great-great-uncle Rabbi Ludwig Philippson, 1847, translated by Anna Maria Goldschmid (Philippson, 1855, pp. 23–24)

PART I
ROOTS IN PHILOSOPHY

CHAPTER ONE

The world according to Gestalt therapy*

It was a joy to rediscover this piece, and its questioning of what we take for granted. Looking at this now, when we know about the banditry of the financial institutions, and the use of the Internet by people in rebellion against their governments in Egypt and other places, as well as by criminals, I feel somewhat smug in my predicting.

A few centuries ago, much of Europe consisted of small villages or towns, with open country in between. There were various lords and rulers who owned the villages, and made rules for the inhabitants. There were usually walls involved. Some towns had walls all round them. Villages were more likely to be overlooked by a castle, where the lord lived, and whose walls they could shelter behind in case of attack.

In open country, there were "outlaws" and bandits. There were wild animals. The law was based on survival rather than the law of the land, or the law of the lord of the manor.

---

*First published in 1996, in *Apertura Magazine*, 1, Luxemburg.

Between the village and the open country there was a relationship. People from the village went out through the countryside to hunt, or to go into the next village, or to join the outlaws. The outlaws in the countryside often had family links with people in the village, although they risked their lives if they came visiting.

Each has its dangers. The danger of the countryside was violent death from wild animals or murderous people. The danger of the village was being destroyed by the lawgiver, or by hunger when the harvest was insufficient to feed the villagers.

Where is our open country, our *wilderness*, now? Certainly not in our tamed and cultivated countryside! We find elements of it in our cities, the "urban jungle". Samuel Delany (1996) writes about the "unlicensed sector" of the city, where normal law does not hold, and about its relationship to the rest of the city. But most of our time, for most of us, is in the villages, where our lives are fairly predictable, and the laws are clear. (I think one of the differences between Europe and America is that America still has open country, complete with wild animals and outlaws, and that this still has some positive place in Americans' hearts: they know what village-dwellers have lost.)

Gestalt therapy, developed in South Africa and America—countries with wildernesses—emphasises the freedom, unpredictability, and risks of the open country. The world of Gestalt therapy is big, lusty, unpredictable, both fulfilling and destroying, and, ultimately, fatal. Whatever I want to find is there to be found, but at a cost, which could be my life. We are part of the wilderness, but it is bigger than us—we cannot feel fully "at home". The prospect is scary and exciting, sometimes too scary or too exciting.

So, we each make our villages, our places where we fully belong, which are not bigger than us. For some of us, the only village we can find is on our own, dreaming our own dreams. For others, we share our villages with other people who live by similar rules, and are willing to give up the same kinds of freedom in return for security. In some places, this is obvious, with estates with walls and security guards like the walled towns of the past. For some, the village is the nuclear family: the English say, "An Englishman's home is his castle". For the isolated, the walls become one small room on their own, or inside their skulls.

There is, of course, nothing wrong with living in a village, of whatever size. The chosen isolation of the hermit has its place as well as more communal options. The question is whether I am making a *choice* about my village, and whether I can fulfil my present wants and needs in this village. There come times in each person's life when we need to expand our horizons beyond the village: adulthood, bereavements, relationships, redundancy, retirement. Each one of these opens for us the excitement and anxiety of the wilderness.

People usually come to therapy when they are living in a village where the harvest has failed. They need support to face the challenge of open country as they seek their new home. They need to be encouraged to contact the reality of the failed harvest, and of the actuality of possibilities and risks in their new decisions.

For the European Union, the wider horizons challenge its citizens with the open country beyond the national villages, and it is inevitable that some will respond by building their walls higher. Those who do this have a point: there are opportunities in the open country, but also bandits and warlords who see the Union as a territory to be conquered or plundered. Part of how the United States of America works is that people are culturally suspicious of central government, and would make themselves ungovernable rather than accept an erosion of local decision-making. Europeans will not usually do that, so there will be little check on the attempt to make decisions for the whole of Europe.

If there is a "global village", where do the outlaws go? Where do we go if the harvest fails? The point I am making is that these questions *will* be answered one way or another. Outlaw enclaves will continue to emerge in cities, extreme nationalism will wall off areas for white people, or people of particular moral or religious viewpoints, people will withdraw inside their homes or their heads with their outlaw dreams. Or the Internet will become the wilderness, or, as a worst-case scenario, the financial markets.

So, we need to balance any move towards the "global village" with respect for, and provision for, the wilderness. We need to avoid "outlawing the outlaw". For all harvests fail sometimes, and we need pointers towards new places to go, and people willing to risk the journey.

CHAPTER TWO

"Let's work seriously about having fun!" Psychotherapists' systemic countertransferences

We all have our blind spots! The areas of our functioning of which we are unaware lead us, as therapists, to messy contact with clients. We avoid areas that we find frightening or uninteresting (because we do not let them be frightening). We call these messy contacts, and the processes behind them, *countertransference*, and bring them to supervision.

But what of the countertransferences which are liable to be shared between therapist and supervisor? Areas where the nature of our profession helps to blind us? In these areas, we can project our life choices on to a client, *and* have the process potentially invisible to a supervisor who has made the same life choices.

I shall go through the potential "systemic countertransferences" that I have thought of. These are not meant to be a fully inclusive list. The areas I have focused on are: relationships, playing, problem-solving, money, work patterns, clarity, and organismic change *vs*. effort. My method will be exaggeration: my picture of the psychotherapist is a caricature, but, I hope, a useful, recognisable one. I want to thank the therapists and clients from Manchester Gestalt Centre, and friends in the Gestalt in Organisations group, for their comments and suggestions.

Deep meaningful relationships

We can be an intense lot, we psychotherapists. Close relationships are important to us, and we gravitate to, and attract, other people who are also quite intense. We enjoy the intense, significant relationships we have with our clients. We analyse our relationships, aiming for the ultimate "I–thou". And we are often not very good at casual friendships, especially with people who are good at casual friendships: often we scare them.

My early experience, and, I suspect, that of many psychotherapists, was of difficulty in making *shallow*, simple relationships, making small talk. My relationships were all or nothing, my boundary tendencies towards confluence or isolation. I have written elsewhere (Philippson, 1990; Philippson & Harris, 1990) about the difficulties inherent in such "oscillating relationships".

And yet, there is a problem here. As therapists, we live in a subculture where this works, after a fashion. Our relationships can be stormy, but we rather enjoy the storms, the drama, the sorting out of the crisis even at the brink of separation. Our clients do not necessarily live in such a subculture. They could come from a more common subculture where the usual path to friendship is via casual encounters: in the pub, club, in leisure activities, or in bed. The pattern of relationship-making in this subculture is, in many ways, more organic than ours, moving from casual contact to fuller contact to intimacy. However, some people, like the stereotypical psychotherapist, find such casual contact difficult. They have not learnt to "fit in", or rather, they have learnt to walk around with a mind-set that they do not fit into whatever environment they encounter. I remember a Groucho Marx quote, "I wouldn't join any club which would have me as a member." In such a situation, the therapeutic method is often not modelling the kind of relationship the client needs to experiment with. Not only do we go for the deep, significant relationship fairly quickly and value it very highly in comparison with casual encounters, we are doing it in a context where the therapist–client relationship says to the client, "You don't fit into my world."

With such clients, I encourage small talk, development of interest in the minutiae of the therapy room, even of my life. We talk about possible contexts where the client can meet people on a casual basis, for example, evening classes, sports activities, social clubs of various sorts, and the importance of deeper contact developing from casual "shallow" contact. However, especially in these days of AIDS, I do not encourage casual sex (and will often discuss the health dangers, and the problems associated with the trivialisation of sexuality). In the therapeutic process, our engagement in more profound work must similarly be based on an ability just to be interested in each other (and certainly not just interest in each other's problems and issues!). The Gestalt approach, emphasising the "surface", phenomenological way that the client presents in the here-and-now encounter of therapy, is very useful here.

Serious and professional

Professional helpers are often not very good at playing in an uninhibited, childlike way. Very often, our childhood experience was of too much responsibility for others too early. We even use the language of play pejoratively: Perls' (1969a) "games-playing" layer, Berne's (2010) use of "games", and the therapeutic use of the term "collusion". Thus, our temptation, when a client comes from a similar background and brings to therapy an inability to play, is to "work seriously" on the "issue". Alternatively, we adopt a split-off, transactional analysis model, and do "regression" work: playing is all right for children/ child ego states, not for adults/adult ego states.

Let us look seriously at what playing is. The infant's first play is a play of arms and legs and facial expressions and sounds, with creating his/her own motion and language and expressing them in the world. This develops into games of contact, noticing the feedback the child gets from the parent, endlessly dropping things so the parent can pick them up. Peep-bo and hide-and-seek: games of developing "object constancy" (what unplayful language for "Are you still there mum?"). Games of "How far can I go?" and "What happens if I . . .?" Games of "mummies and daddies", "doctors and nurses", "cowboys and Indians"/"Americans and Iraquis". Games of "Let's pretend"/ "Let's act as if this box is a rocket". Competitive sports, making and breaking friendships, fighting, making things together: all part of making a culture with others.

As the child gets older, all these abilities merge into a developing ability to be comfortable in many different surroundings, to know what s/he wants, to develop a personal identity, to operate an appropriate contact boundary, and to discover the consequences of various kinds of inappropriate behaviour. We learn to play many roles, and to develop our preferences. We learn to play sexually, both lovingly and by using others as sexual objects. But, in play, we can always step outside our everyday roles, and become anything else, as the ancient Romans (at Bacchanalia) and modern Germans (at Fasching) know.

Looked at this way, one can almost say that neurosis is a work–play split, the loss of the inability to play in a particular area of activity; psychosis is the fixation in a particular kind of play. And yet, we, as therapists, often downgrade play, even in Gestalt therapy, where so many of the ways of working are essentially games (role playing, reversals, non-verbal dialogues).

We need to be able to combine being responsible adult, professional, ethical therapists and being able to play footsie, fighting, painting, clay modelling, yelling, hide-and-seek, dolls and teddy bears, monsters and gorillas with our clients. If we cannot, or if we can only do it by losing our ethical standards, then this is a therapy issue to be worked through with a therapist who *can* play.

Problem solvers

Gestalt therapy, in common with psychoanalysis and Rogerian psychotherapy, is strongly against any attempt to reduce it to the resolution of particular problems in a client's life. Rather, the aim is to facilitate the increasing of the scope of the client's awareness via contact/dialogue and experiment, with the expectation that the sense of the problem changes on the way.

However, most of us therapists originally went into the game (or business, if you do not like playing with serious subjects!) out of a desire to help people with problems. Many of us even find that we can relate better to people with problems who are looking for our help. So, for us, the spotlight of awareness shines on people's difficulties rather than their strengths, even losing the ability to see what the client presents at face value, and, once they become sorted out enough that their strengths and problem-solving abilities are obvious, we kind of lose interest.

And yet, it is through the *client's* strengths and resources that new things can happen, new games can be played, and new experiments performed. They must be a major part of the therapy process. By analogy, the strengths of the therapist must be a major part of the supervision process. An important part of my contract with supervisees is that they bring work that they are particularly pleased with as well as work that causes them concern. I want to see the whole range of the therapist, and model that so that the therapist sees the whole range of the client.

Self-employed

A lot of we therapists are self-employed, many having moved out of jobs to work with people "free of organisational constraints". We can now be more anarchic, choose our work to suit us (see also below), and innovate. And many of our clients (given that we often charge for our services, and might see people at times when employed people need to be at work) are also self-employed. However, I get the impression that we sometimes do not properly understand the world of someone who is employed by others, or is unemployed and wants to work for someone. We assume a kind of superiority of choice in being out of structures, are relatively oblivious to the advantages of working in organisations, and, paradoxically, often lose out ourselves by so doing.

Clients lose out because we can assume that the answer to major difficulties is to leave a job, rather than to struggle on. *Both* are options, and very frequently clients look at all the options, the climate for small businesses, a mortgage, lack of organisational support, loss of friends, pension difficulties, and opt to stay employed. I have come across therapists who are quite dismissive about taking this option.

Therapists lose out, in my experience as a supervisor, because they blind themselves somewhat with the "freedom" of self-employment. Their constraint then becomes lack of money! A therapist is a small business, in a climate that is not good for small businesses (high interest, etc.). We have the advantage that we profit financially from other people's misery, and there is a lot of it around. We have the disadvantage that we tend to be uncomfortable with business realities (as described above). It is a well-known fact among self-employed people (except therapists) that when starting out in business, choice is limited as to what work you take on if you are going to make a reasonable living out of your work. Later on, as the work develops, you can afford to pick and choose more, but still, there are constraints. If you are going to do ongoing therapy with clients, especially the more fragile ones, you are making commitments over a number of years. Trainers will also need to make a commitment to the ongoing development of their trainees. And, often, the therapists who are most interested in the "freedom" aspect of self-employment are also those complaining that clients are leaving —"Where can I find a replacement?"—without making the link between the clients leaving and their own unavailability and invisibility.

Financially comfortable/"You can do it if you really want"

This seems at first to be a contradiction to the previous heading, but is not. The therapists who do not make a lot of money out of their therapy work usually feel all right to do this because they are buffered by a higher-earning partner or by other sources of earned or unearned income. Given the costs of training in psychotherapy, it is rare that people even go into the training without being in the financially comfortable state.

The main countertransference here is the assumption that clients can sort out the money to continue therapy "if they really find it important". Conversely, if they find out the cost of therapy and disappear, then it cannot have been sufficiently important in the first place! This way of thinking means that we do not have to bite the bullet of weighing the cash value of our time and training against the effect of our charging policies on those who might want to become clients. We do not need to think about sliding scales—it is a question of *their* commitment.

The other side of this whole question of money is that we, as Gestalt therapists, become vulnerable to the critique of the psychiatric mainstream that we work with a comparatively easy, self-selected group, who are reasonably well functioning, otherwise they would not be able to afford our services. Far from being an alternative to psychiatric provision, we would find our way of working impossible to sustain if we worked with their client group. We know, of course, that this is not the case: worldwide there are enough Gestaltists work-ing in mainstream psychiatric institutions to put the lie to this, but it is argued quite widely none the less, in circumstances where we have no opportunity to reply. Conversely, some trainings are geared to working precisely with those people well functioning enough to afford the therapist's services, and, in this case, it can be true that they would find working with a wider range of clients impossible.

Respecting oneself more than to take just any job

The question here is: so who *is* going to shovel the shit? The shadowy image, never quite made explicit, is that we, the sorted-out, the "ther-apped", are on a higher, more spiritual plane of existence, where our respect for ourselves is incompatible with a wide selection of the kind of jobs on which our comfort depends. These jobs are to be left to the *untermensch*, the unsorted.

And yet, my understanding of spirituality includes a large helping of humility. True, there have been, and still are, religious hierarchies whose top members are buffered from any involvement in the mundane world, but it is something new to what Lasch (1979, p. 13) calls "the therapeutic sensibility" to tell the followers that this is how one should be, and to (metaphorically) hand the begging bowl to someone else.

So, we need to be aware that, while we have made a decision, based on our own intellectual abilities and often an ability to pay out quite a lot of money, to become professional people, this ability is not open—or even appealing—to many people. In fact, it is often the case that people go into psychotherapy as a job because of quite severe underlying disturbances, along with a pattern of *proflection* (doing unto others what you actually want someone to do to you).

Being clear

We all value being clear: having clear contracts, making clear state-ments, having clear awareness. We have an investment in clarifying the unclear. And, sometimes, we blind ourselves to the problem inher-ent in clarity. Which is, clarity comes from the unclear, and if we avoid the unclear, we limit the new experiences we can become clear about later. What often happens is that clients learn to censor (often without awareness) unclear remarks. They then only get to explore what is almost clear in the first place. This is especially true where the emphasis is on "doing pieces of work", where the "I want something, but I don't know what it is" type of exploration, often the most fruitful in discovering new areas of unawareness, gets lost. In my work, I emphasise the latter: "Make contact, even if you don't know clearly what you want", or "When the issues stop coming, then we are starting the *real* therapy".

Organismic, effortless change

An introject that we, especially those of us who see ourselves as "humanistic" therapists, often hold and project on to our clients is that change is effortless, the result of a new decision by us as whole organisms. We want to distance ourselves from a behavioural model that many of us find distasteful. And yet, it appears to me that many clients benefit from the struggle to learn new behaviours. How can I square this with a theory based on the Gestalt switch, the "ah-ha"?

The way I see the situation is that the power of Gestalt therapy for change lies with two emphases: contact and choice. As we make fuller and more varied contact with our environment (especially with other people), we both discover the *differences* between this environment and our remembered and feared childhood traumas, and the *range of choices* in the environment. However, some people have *never* experienced satisfying relationships, coming from an impoverished childhood to repeating painful relationships in adulthood. Sometimes, even where, on the face of it, the client relates well with other people, there is a frightened, split-off level to which the new information about possibilities of pleasurable relatedness is not allowed access. There is no way (that I know) that someone with this background could get into a different kind of relationship—with a psychotherapist, a friend, or anyone else—without fear and effort. It is at the stage when the client trusts someone (e.g., a therapist) enough to risk opening out that they can become aware of new possibilities and choices open to them. The "ah-ha" experience *follows* the experiment.

First of all, the fear needs to be recognised and acknowledged. The fear, and the understanding of the world that underlies it, can be worked with in fantasy ("What might happen?") and in the relationship between therapist and client (and maybe other group members). The client can be encouraged to look at other people's experience as different from their own, even to read autobiography, and to undertake carefully graded experiments in relating differently: to join a club, or an evening class, to experiment with new ways of relating with present friends, and with me, or with others in a therapy group. If such frightening, effortful experimentation is not tried, my experience is that there is a lot to "work on" in each therapy session, but that not much changes in clients' lives. Sometimes, energisation to do the frightening thing is necessary in order that new contact becomes possible. I tell clients, "There are two kinds of fear. There is the fear of walking along a motorway. The only way to abolish such a reasonable fear is to decide not to do the feared thing. There is also the fear that there are ghosts under my bed. The only way to deal with such a fear is to get a torch, and, with fear and trembling, look under the bed, always wondering whether the ghost will leap out and get me!"

Conclusion

I realise that I have touched quite briefly on a number of different topics, under the general theme of "systemic countertransferences". My main hope is that I have raised awareness of an area that needs further exploring. In the Gestalt therapy community, and the more general psychotherapy community, we have our own culture, and there is much interesting work to be done on how those cultures interact with the often different cultures from which clients come.

CHAPTER THREE

Commitment*

I am quite influenced by the thinking of Christopher Lasch. I like his combining of psychotherapeutic language and political/social understanding, which reminds me of both Gestalt therapy's Paul Goodman and Paulo Freire. I also think it is important for psychotherapists to take on board social critiques of our activities, rather than to assume that we are the "good guys".

> "Even when therapists speak of the need for 'meaning' and 'love', they define love and meaning simply as the fulfillment of the patient's emotional requirements . . . To liberate humanity from such outmoded ideas of love and duty has become the mission of the post-Freudian therapies and particularly of their converts and popularizers, for whom mental health means the overthrow of inhibitions and the immediate gratification of every impulse"
>
> (Lasch, 1979, p. 13)

---

*First published in 1997, in *Apertura Magazine*, 1, Luxemburg.

"Would you tell me, please, which way I ought to go from here?"
"That depends a good deal on where you want to get to," said the Cat.
"I don't much care where –" said Alice.
"Then it doesn't matter which way you go," said the Cat.
"– so long as I get *somewhere*," Alice added as an explanation.
"Oh, you're sure to do that," said the Cat, "if only you walk long enough"

(Carroll, 2000, p. 73)

"Rare is the person who goes for 'treatment' and is in their original 'relationship' – how love is demeaned – a year later. Many is the lonely, anxious, ageing woman – and indeed man – who says, 'but it was my therapist gave me the strength to leave my marriage'"

(Fay Weldon, newspaper article)

Let me start here: what is my stance if I am working with a couple, or with someone unhappy in his or her marriage? Is my stance to try to save the marriage, to facilitate parting from a relationship which causes the person pain, or to be neutral? I have come across therapists who have taken all of these stances. Taking therapy out of it, I know of people who practice "serial monogamy", moving into and out of relationships as these lose their shiny newness; I also know people who have lived together for years, bound together by hate. In the former, there is little space for children to feel secure; in the latter, the children become one of the battlegrounds between the parents. I see as clients the adults both these groups of children become.

The stance I take is one I call "not-quite-neutrality". On the one hand, I am not putting myself forward as the authority figure who will decide what will happen with this couple. On the other hand, I am aware of a silent, but important, third partner in the relationship: *commitment*.

If commitment is not present in a relationship or an undertaking, then there is usually a great sense of insecurity, as any problem, discomfort, or disagreement immediately leads to the question, "Is this the end?" The effort involved in working through these can be avoided by giving up, or giving in. In the latter case, I can go for a superficial agreement, and, while still seeming to be in the relationship, it is no longer the one that fulfils what I wanted from it.

When I work with couples like this, I suggest that they make an absolute commitment to staying together for, say, six months. In doing this, they often find that their relationship changes so that problems are more easily sorted out, and both people's needs are met. This does not mean that they necessarily stay together at the end of the six months: some do, some do not. However, even if they decide to separate, they will be able to do so with a sense that they have first of all really worked to meet each other. A prerequisite for saying a proper goodbye is having said a proper hello!

I now want to widen this, and to look at commitment in society. From my perspective on Britain, where I would part company with Fay Weldon is in saying that the therapeutic culture she talks about is part of a much wider social phenomenon. Looking around me, the emphasis everywhere seems to be on quick answers, lack of commitment to any structure, and an expectation that people will be willing to move at short notice to wherever the next bright idea wants them to be. New structural initiatives on the health service, education, transport, industry, and economics are constantly being brought out. One government department acts to reduce its spending, even though this will increase the spending of another department. Each time any of this happens, a whole group of workers is redeployed or deprived of employment, or told to move to a new location. No sooner are people beginning to sort out the difficulties of one new structure than it is replaced again. Workers face the insecurity of knowing that there is a strong probability that their jobs will disappear at some random time. Similar jobs might even reappear with the next turn of the wheel, but not for them. Employers get the benefit of lower costs, and the more concealed deficits of more social disruption and anger, lower employee motivation (apart from fear), and the insecurity of fluctuations of markets and infrastructure (e.g., suppliers going out of business or supplying more profitably elsewhere, or changes to transportation networks).

At a still more basic level, I come back to the Alice in Wonderland epigraph to this article. If I do not commit to walking in the same direction for long enough, I reach nowhere. My aim becomes survival in the wilderness rather than the achievement of any goal. And my survival will be at other people's expense, as well as that of my environment: we cannot work together, live together, play together, raise children together, make laws together without commitment.

I do not know how this is in the rest of Europe. I am heartened by the EEC Social Chapter, and hope that the UK gets a government which supports it. I do think that the Social Chapter on its own in a "free enterprise" environment will lead to a drain of work to countries which go for low wages and job insecurity, and that some of the directions sponsored by European social legislation goes counter to some of the directions required by the move towards a single currency. Maybe I am wrong here: I am a psychotherapist, not an economist.

So, I am arguing for a value to be given to commitment in and for itself, as a basic building block and cement of society and community. Then we will be in a position to work through our mutual difficulties, and, paradoxically, know when to end commitments and to give due care to the ending.

CHAPTER FOUR

Zen and the art of pinball*

This is, for me, a very satisfying paper. I used to be pretty good at pinball when I was much younger. And I think the application of pinball to philosophy has been underrated. Why does it just have to be archery or motorcycle maintenance? I like how the principle is illustrated by such an accessible means. I am also proud that it was quoted on a website devoted to all things pinball!

"You know the theory of destiny: that we are destined to do what we do? Well I don't agree with that. We are destined to be where we are; what we do with it is ours"

(Said by my younger son when he was eight years old)

S uppose you've never seen a pinball table before, and come across one for the first time. Stripped of all the flashing lights and noises, what you see is a large bagatelle game, most of which

---

*First published in 1996, in *Group Relations Training Association Bulletin*, 1985 and *Apertura Magazine*, 2, Luxemburg.

operates automatically. It seems the only control you have is the spring-loaded plunger and two flippers. If you then try to play the table, you discover that most of the movements of the ball are entirely random and out of your control.

Then you watch a "pinball wizard": the ball moves precisely to the places needed to rack up points and replays. So, what extra control is involved? Purely mechanically, there are three mechanisms involved: precise control of plunger speed, which controls where the ball goes first; precise timing of flipper use, so the ball goes off at the right angle (which would sometimes involve just letting the ball bounce off the flipper rather than being flipped, or trapping the ball at rest with the flipper); and "nudges", where the table is nudged gently to slightly deflect the ball at the moment it hits an obstacle and changes direction (you must nudge gently, or the table registers a "tilt" and penalises you).

All right, now you know! However, if you try to play with this extra information, you will find that you will not score much more. But what you need to know is that you have all the technical information needed to achieve a large measure of control of the ball, just like the experts. So what do you lack? Practice, yes, but practice to do what?

Watch the experts: there is concentration, and more. They seem to be at one with table, controlling the ball with their whole bodies, indeed as part of their bodies, an extra limb. Aiming a ball at a target is now no more calculated than controlling your leg muscles to walk.

Where does Zen come in? In a world that seems to determine our lives, Zen and most humanistic therapies assert the possibility of achieving liberation from the internal and external chains that would bind us. Furthermore, Zen paradoxically says this can be achieved by realising that we are not separate from the rest of the universe; the ego which says "Now I will press the left flipper button . . . now I will nudge the table diagonally up and left . . ." impoverishes both our pinball and our lives. Technically, most of us have more than enough information to control our lives, but it is only as we learn to realise our oneness with our environment that we discover that the small choices we make at each moment can come together into a pattern of life of our own choosing.

There are several traps along the way: first, the illusion of powerlessness we abstract from the smallness of our individual choices (looking at the pinball table for the first time); second, the illusion that the answer lies in amassing large amounts of knowledge (learning about plunger, flippers, and nudges); third, taking enlightenment as a goal in life rather than a recovery of something always available to us (getting addicted to pinball).

Finally, we need to be aware that, for all our skill, the ball will eventually go out of play, and the game will end. If I am desperate to avoid this, I will never push the plunger; I will stop the ball on the flippers, playing "safe" to avoid the end of the game. The life will have gone out of my pinball, and I will fail to achieve anything on the scoreboard. In accepting the game, and knowing that it will end some time, I can play my game at my highest level of skill, and then, when the time comes, withdraw and leave the table to others.

Pinball is not unique: there are many recognised Zen arts (martial arts, dance, painting, calligraphy, etc.). However, you are unlikely to see these practised in the West with as much dedication as I used to give to pinball. Watch a good player on a good table before they all get replaced by video games and you may discover an extra dimension to your life!

CHAPTER FIVE

Gestalt therapy and the culture of narcissism*

I was very impressed by Lasch's book The Culture of Narcissism *(1979) as a Jeremiad for our times. I wanted to introduce the ideas to a Gestalt audience. Part of the idea, which I believe psychotherapists need to consider, is that the things put in place to try to solve the problems of our society, including therapy, are part of the problem and participate in the same blind spots as the problems they are trying to solve.*

Even when therapists speak of the need for "meaning" and "love", they define love and meaning simply as the fulfillment of the patient's emotional requirements. It hardly occurs to them – nor is there any reason why it should, given the nature of the therapeutic enterprise – to encourage the subject to subordinate his needs and interests to those of others, to someone or some cause or tradition outside himself. "Love" as self-sacrifice or self-abasement, "meaning" as submission to a higher loyalty – these sublimations strike the therapeutic sensibility as intolerably oppressive, offensive to common sense and injurious to personal health and well-being. To liberate humanity from such outmoded ideas of love and duty has become the mission of the post-Freudian therapies and particularly of their converts and popularizers,

*First published in 1994, in *British Gestalt Journal*, 3(1).

for whom mental health means the overthrow of inhibitions and the immediate gratification of every impulse. (Lasch, 1979, p. 13)

What is narcissism?

Narcissism is defined in terms of preoccupation with self, coupled with a lack of empathy for others, emotional coldness, and grandiosity. This can be overt—the undiscovered genius (Kenneth Williams: "I could have been a star")—or covert, with rage and sense of injustice hiding behind a superficial humility (like the very 'umble Uriah Heap).

Perls (1948) identified (secondary) narcissism with retroflection. He pointed to the customary usage as being "self-love", but said that this is to miss the point. The narcissist is not capable of love of self or others (but can often simulate love quite well). Think, rather, of the beautiful boy Narcissus looking at himself in the water and believing that he is looking at someone else. He cannot move away from the water without his friend disappearing; neither can the water be disturbed by the slightest breath of wind without his image of perfection rippling away. Under what conditions in the rest of this youth's world will he stay with his reflection as his only friend?

There are many ways of describing the aetiology of narcissism: among the best-known writers are Kernberg, Masterson, and Kohut, all from various parts of the analytic tradition. However, we have in the Gestalt theory of the relational self a particularly good way of understanding narcissism. Self grows by contact: with the other, the novel, the exciting, the nourishing. But what if there is no other to really contact, to be excited by or to be nourished by? Say the parents are sick, or physically or psychologically unavailable to the child. The drive for self-actualisation (in the Goldstein sense: self is made actual by my action/contact, with no normative content as "humanistic psychotherapy" has added to the concept) will often be strong enough for the infant to *project* their desired ideal parent on to the blank screen of the unavailable parent. In order to support this projection, the infant must learn to deflect any sense data that might contradict this image; this would include most real emotional contact! So, the infant develops a sense of self based on retroflection rather than contact.

An infant in contact with a real, human, more-or-less available person learns to deal with the disappointments of those times when the parent does not understand what the child wants or is just not prepared to play with the child in the middle of the night, or any of the ordinary mismatches that happen between real people; any such disappointment to a child in love with an ideal projected image potentially opens the floodgates to an awareness of his/her real abandonment rage, accompanied by a sense of dissolution of the self. As this infant grows up, this will manifest in an inability to show real warmth, an inability to separate image from reality, and rapid alternation from grandiosity (a perfect person from a wonderful family) to rage and feelings of inadequacy (always caused by others!) if anyone truly gets through emotionally. Looking acceptable will be important rather than acting morally; the narcissist is not trustworthy, since his/her commitment is to a fantasised ideal rather than to a real person.

The culture of narcissism

Manchester Area Health Authority has insisted that surgical waiting lists be reduced to a year. This laudable aim has been achieved by closing the waiting list to new people when it has reached a year.

British Rail wants a greater proportion of trains between Manchester and London to arrive on time. They have, therefore, adjusted the timetables to make the journey time five minutes longer.

The doings of characters in television "soaps" are presented as news.

The trend in politics is never to resign, even if caught out in a stupendous misdemeanour.

The common factor in all this is the elevation of images above reality. If there is a disaster, it is someone else's fault, and someone else should do something.

Lasch (1979) cites several areas of narcissistic culture: a sense of doom: nuclear, environmental, culture falling apart. Analogously to the individual narcissist, the culture retrenches and stops looking. A real sense of continuity with history and movement towards the future is replaced either with an obsessive focusing on the present, or an allegiance to an idealised past when everything worked and the trains ran on time. Plans for living turn into plans for mere survival. Compare with the frequent misreading of Perls on the here-and-now as "You should only focus on the present", rather than seeing memory and hopes/plans/fears of the future as being part of the present field.

Success is seen less as achievement of ambition than as achievement of admiration from others because of how successful you seem to be.

In advertising and politics, a cynicism going beyond truth and falsehood to the truly narcissistic NLP ideal: "The meaning of a communication is the effect it has." If the facts are verifiable, so much the better, because that will be more effective.

The "degradation" of sport into entertainment/spectacle rather than part of the fabric of society in another factor.

The school is acting more and more as part of the "new paternalism", "Paternalism without Father", so that parents can have a sense of handing over to the school the responsibility for the child's upbringing. And if that fails, there is always the educational psychologist, the probation officer, the social worker. This goes alongside, is both a reaction to, and promotes, the collapse of authority. The buck stops somewhere else! In the UK, education is full of new programmes to increase the sense of achievement, which militate against actual achievement: school league tables, ill-thought out testing, pseudo-relevance to industry.

Similarly, other bureaucracies, such as the health service, take over the looking after of the old and dying, the disabled, and the brain-damaged. Thus, they both respond to and contribute to the cultural disinclination of families and communities to look after those who need this extra attention.

The trivialisation of personal relations, the loss of culturally approved and agreed methods for signalling sexual interest, the pathologising of commitment "for better or for worse", leads to an intensification of the sex war as men and women look for some ideal of confluent togetherness, and are enraged when they do not find it. They then flip to the other side, either isolation from the other sex or exploitation.

There is dread of old age, with its loss of power, beauty, and health, and devaluation of the old, so that the government can say that we cannot afford state earnings-related pensions, and plans to impose VAT on fuel bills.

In each case, what was previously provided (while often not very wonderfully) in the community is now provided by a bureaucracy or not at all. The solution becomes the new problem by contributing to the decline of mutual commitment and the expectation of someone else providing the contact, or denial of the importance of contact.

Applications to psychotherapy

So, what does this mean for psychotherapy in general and Gestalt therapy in particular? There are essentially two approaches in psychotherapy: problem resolution and self-exploration. Gestalt has been used in both these forms: the original form pointed at by *Ego, Hunger and Aggression* (Perls, 1947) and *Gestalt Therapy* (Perls, Hefferline, & Goodman, 1994) and Perls' verbatim transcripts and lectures (1969a), and a more recent form of "working on issues". It seems to me that if we concentrate on working on issues, we come to facilitate what Hunter Beaumont (personal communication) calls "polishing the ego" rather than the development of the relational self, and thus fit into Lasch's critique of the post-Freudian therapies. However, if we work the other way round, facilitating the exploration and growth of self in action and relationship, we know that the work promotes greater ease in dealing with life situations, for growth in self *equates* to greater flexibility of relationship possibility, and, hence, to greater ability to apply self- and environmental support to difficult situations. The difference would be that the new solutions would be integrated with a more contactful self-process rather than being techniques.

I will sidetrack to a paper by Argyris (1986), titled "Skilled incompetence", where he points out that many professionals are debarred by their interpersonal skills from really resolving conflicts; rather, they learn to deflect from them and either find forms of words, or acknowledge the OK-ness of the other person. This is demonstrated very clearly in a paper by Rogers and Ryback (1984), which outlines their facilitation in the Camp David accords between Begin and Sadat. The process of dealing with the hard and conflictual issues involved was diverted to a process of people discovering their common humanity. Then Sadat was assassinated, the Israelis went on killing Palestinians in their occupied territories, Carter was ousted by Reagan, and nothing had really changed. They had used their skills to answer the wrong question.

One of the points that Lasch and others (e.g., Wheeler, 1991) have made is that the way clients present has changed with the culture. We rarely see over-bounded clients from the kind of strict families that Freud saw, with the clients responding with repression and hysterical conversion symptoms. We are more likely to see the under-bounded client who has no sense of who they are, where any physical abuse they suffered would have been unavoidable and meaningless as opposed to a technique in instilling a particular kind of socialisation. To ask someone to answer the question "What do you want?" is not useful if the client does not know whom this "I" is who might want something! It is very easy to produce a pseudo-solution that makes more problems than it solves.

A second point for Gestalt therapists is linked to the last one: the importance of *dialogic* therapy. Overuse of empty chair and other techniques are part of the issue-orientated approach. However, if self is to be developed, then, as self is relational, the work must centre round relationship. This is *not* to say that experiments are out, but are to be seen as ways of enhancing contact and exploration in the "safe emergency", as Perls put it, rather than the primary focus of Gestalt. It is also well known that two-chair work across the primary split for narcissistic or borderline clients does not work, since an ending of the split plunges the client into depression.

Third, I believe there needs to be a de-emphasis on *regression* in therapy. Hillman and Ventura (1992) have co-written a very interesting book, *We've Had 100 Years of Psychotherapy and Things Are Getting Worse*, which complements Lasch's book well. One of their most telling points is that in focusing on "the inner child", psychotherapy is promoting the identification of clients with a way of being which is individualistic, irresponsible, lacking commitment, or responsibility for others. More here-and-now Gestalt questions are: "What is the process by which we make memories of pain from childhood figural now"; "What ecological function do they have now"; "What are the learnings about the world that we made then which we are still holding to now?" Borderline clients are very likely to "fall apart" in any form of regressive therapy, especially if this includes a lot of physical holding. Narcissistic therapists and clients will enjoy their sense of specialness to each other, but woe betide the therapist who tries to get beyond this and confront the client's manipulation. Rather, the important point is that clients learn to remake good contact with first the therapist and then the world. I also believe that group therapy has a great part to play in this, with its richer environment, with the other group members providing a symbolic representation of the whole world. Will they like or dislike me; will they think I'm good or bad, attractive or ugly; will they accept me or reject me?

Following on from the point about responsibility, we need to be much clearer about the Gestalt approach to who and what we are responsible for. In its Gestalt formulation, "response-able", I am response-able for myself *and* for my environment, and, since the meaning of me is inseparable from the meaning of my environment, I cannot be one without the other. If my life is totally dependent on the air that I breathe, then I am response-able for the state of the rain-forests which produce most of the world's oxygen. If my life is here in the UK, then I am response-able for the social, political, and cultural situation in the UK, which is vastly important for my own existence. Read some of the political and educational writings of Paul Goodman (e.g., 1971) to see how central this was to the foundation of Gestalt therapy. The point is that the Gestalt concept of response-ability is not additive: if someone else is 100% response-able for herself, it does not mean that I am 0% response-able for her. In fact, I am 100% response-able for her as well. I am response-able for the client, and the client's family and environment. If my client is discovering anger, it is my responsibility to encourage her not to practise on innocent civilians (like the assertiveness training course which was thrown out of a hotel after *all* the members sent their wine back!).

Beneath the façade

I want to end with an expansion from my own and others' experience of what I said about the kinds of clients we encounter. There is a very large number of people about who manage to hide psychotic and close to psychotic symptoms behind a well-functioning façade. Our culture of narcissism presents us with many ways of creating this façade. A standard psychiatric assessment is to ask someone to count down from 100 in sevens. Patients know this and have been frequently observed on the wards practising together. A large percentage of clients will, at least temporarily, function *less* well during therapy as they come to terms with issues of abandonment, rage, their

carefully constructed retroflective self vanishing. Some are at immediate risk of breakdown, or of being *perceived* as having had a breakdown. I remember working with a mental health professional whose
new-found ability to feel emotion was looked on with such suspicion
by the consultant psychiatrist that he was required to undergo a
psychiatric assessment! Our work must take this into account,
together with the ethical question: "Do we work with someone whose
job, status in society, sanity, primary relationship, or parenting could
well be permanently adversely affected?"

We must rediscover the human function of *thinking*. So many
people have flipped to the other side of Perls' equation, feeling but not
thinking or using their senses, so that, as well as being told "Lose your
mind and come to your senses", they need to be told "Distrust your
feelings; what do you think?"! So many clients' feelings have so little
connection with here-and-now reality: on body image; on how they
are perceived; on how others are relating to them and their motivation for criticising them; on the consequences of their actions. A huge
number of people has simply lost the knack of making friendships
and committed relationships—and this includes many therapists! A
huge number of people has lost the knack of enjoying themselves
without looking over their own shoulders at the image they are
presenting—also including many therapists. People's feelings are
based on their own aggression projected out on to the environment
and then seen as attacking them, the victims. They need to think about
how they know what they know—the question Bob Resnick (personal
communication) is very keen on asking. What are they actually
perceiving and what is projection?

Conclusion

Shorn of narcissistic grandiosity, therapists cannot really change the
world. Therapy is neither the new form of politics nor the new religion. What we can do, however, is be aware of how our cultural
assumptions relate to the assumptions of the world we live in, and
whether we are, in our focus on the individual, reinforcing cultural
assumptions which are at best not conducive to mental health and
destructive to human relatedness, and at worst could be fatal to the
human race.

CHAPTER SIX

Requiem for the earth*

This is a rather bleak piece. I do not know if I would put it in this fairly extreme form now, but sometimes I would, and I think it is a viewpoint very much worth expressing.

The death of the human race

My sons have T-shirts saying, "Why should I tidy my room when the earth's in such a mess?" I believe that we all know that several factors are coming together which, together or separately, could spell the end of the human race and many other species within the lifetime of people (especially children) who are alive today. Further, I believe that we cannot understand many of the clients who come to us except with this awareness. This is because many of the "problems" we see are manifestations of people's responses to this situation. Many of the stock ways of working with these "problems" are manifestations of therapists' denial of the situation.

---

*First published in 1994, in *Topics in Gestalt Therapy*, 2(2):17–22.

The illness

We know about the hole in the ozone layer and the increase in skin cancer, and that what is being done about it is too little too late.

We know that the greenhouse effect is causing major climate changes with more on the way. For example, the Gulf Stream flows from the more dilute Pacific Ocean to the more concentrated Atlantic. The melting of the polar icecap is diluting the Atlantic with the possibility of the Gulf Stream reversing—and God knows what this would mean.

We know that the forests which replenish the earth's oxygen are being felled.

We know about AIDS, Dutch elm disease, falling male fertility (in humans and other animals) connected with many pervasive chemicals that act like oestrogen.

I know that there is a possibility that any or all of these are part of a process that could end the human race in my children's lifetime. And I know that the power I have to change this situation is limited, probably to a less than effective level. How do I relate to this?

Another illness

Twelve years ago, I developed testicular cancer—incidentally, another illness whose incidence is rising to the point where it is the most common form of cancer in young men. During the course of the treatment of the illness, which involved an operation to remove a testicle, radiotherapy, and two lots of chemotherapy, there were times when I believed that I was going to die soon (and, in fact, due to the amount of spread, it was touch and go), and I met people who were dying. I know from personal experience and the experience of others that there are many responses to awareness of closeness to death.

I can deny the fact or the significance of death. To quote an anonymous poet (Quiller-Couch, 1939, p. 95): "Is't not fine to dance and sing / When the bells of death do ring". I can go into desperation: either desperately fight death, with the result that I survive longer, often in great pain and with no quality of life, locked in the battle with death, or I can desperately cling to another person or a belief in the hope that he/she/it can save me. A third option, and the one I took in my own illness, was to accept both the possibility of my death and my desire to stay alive. In a sense, this stance is a negotiation with death. "If you must take me, I will go. However, I will not go willingly. I want to live, and will work towards staying alive."

Analogously, these responses are the same ones made towards the prospect of the ending of human life on earth. Some people deny that there is anything to worry about. "We've had weather change before, science will come up with an answer to the problems. Meanwhile, we've never had it so good." And, in some ways, they are right. We are at a cusp in the Western world, where many of us can visit places that were never available to any but the very rich or very brave in the past, and which are, as yet, little enough eroded that we can ignore the cost to the places we visit, and the cost to ourselves in, for example, the bewildering variety of illnesses that sweep the world. We can eat food from all round the world, and ignore the fact that we are part of a system where food is exported to the UK from countries where many of their people are dying of starvation, because the price has risen to what we will pay rather than what local people can afford. The advantages of our world are extolled while the costs are kept low-key enough to be ignored most of the time.

There is another form of denial: to say there is a problem, but to minimise its seriousness to a level at which we can believe that fairly simple actions can cure it. This "liberal" response is to agree that something needs doing, and organise "Green" events, use recycled paper, plant trees, while denying the minimal, or even harmful, effect of these efforts in isolation. For example, recycled paper manufacturers can be major polluters because of the way many of them use bleaching chemicals. Or they can focus on one aspect because it could particularly affect them. For example, nuclear power is dangerous to people, and it is easy to forget that coal-mining is also dangerous, causing many slow lingering deaths, but of people in self-contained mining communities with which most of us have no contact. I am not saying here that this sort of activity is wrong or useless, but that we know in our heart of hearts that it will not, by itself, prevent any of the disasters that face us.

Another response to the danger facing us is to fight for the survival of the human race and other endangered species by any means necessary. There are two versions of this. One, the "survivalist" option, is to say "The world as we know it is doomed. All I can hope for is personal survival. When the crunch comes, I will be the best-armed, the most ruthless, with the largest supply of canned and dried food. I will adapt to live in the world of 'Mad Max', not for pleasure, but just to survive."

The other version of fighting for survival can be called radical, or revolutionary, or deep ecology. This approach says "The unwelcome truth is that we are on the brink of destroying the human race and countless other species by our actions, not just individually, but by a collective denial of the consequences of our actions. The people in power know that what they are doing is harmful, and will continue doing the same things unless they are stopped. There is not the collective will to stop them, so we will do what we can. In doing this, any effective actions are justified, even violence and destruction of property, because unless we stop this madness, we are all doomed anyway." So, we get everything from Greenpeace's non-violent direct action to the eco-terrorists attacking people and property implicated in particularly bad environmental damage. At one level, this is actually a more realistic response to the scale of the problem. Put simply, things are that bad. Simply altering my lifestyle will not suffice, and the economic and political forces against change are not going to be swayed by appeals to better natures. However, neither are they going to be swayed just by action, even violent action. The guerilla movements that have succeeded have, in general, been fighting against a foreign aggressor rather than a national political system. The radicals thus become a polar opposite to the environmental destroyers, sharing some of the same values: short-term planning, denial of long-term uselessness, the end justifying the means. Also, my own experience from my time in radical politics is that many of the radicals in this sense have lost their sense of the joy of life in much the same way as the cancer sufferer who fights death to the death or the survivalist. They both lose sight of what they are wanting to preserve. They lose humanity to save humanity; or they lose themselves to save themselves.

Or we can find someone or something to cling on to as things fall apart around us. Whether this is a person or a religion or sex or drugs or rock and roll, there is a frenetic quality about it. As John Lennon sang, "Whatever gets you through the night".

The remaining response to potential eco-disaster, and the one I am arguing for here, is acceptance. I need to accept the possibility/likelihood of the end of humanity and much more besides, and mourn for the loss. Goodbye to humans, goodbye to whales, goodbye to many forms of animal, fish, and plant life. Goodbye and I'm sorry. It is only through this acceptance that I can live with joy what life is left to me, and act in ways which hold the possibility of avoiding disaster—but with humanity and pleasure in the world rather than desperation. Now I can be a member of Greenpeace or write to newspapers or even deny what is going on as a normal part of the mourning process. I can want to act through my attachment to life rather than through my attachment to short-term survival or to a political programme, however worthy.

If the encounter group that is the earth is ending, will we make a good ending?

Maybe human intelligence is ultimately fatal. Our very ability to stand back from our situation or environment, to make part of that environment our tool, to engage in I–it relationship with that environment, predisposes the human race to the role of destroyer of balances. Other animals are much more immersed in their environment with many more feedback effects, and can be said to relate on the level of I–Thou even with their prey. We can look at this from the level of the theory of dissipative structures (Prigogine & Stengers, 1984). This theory, which is related to chaos and complexity theories, explores situations where the entropic rundown of the universe powers a local increase in complexity. A simple form of this would be a water-wheel powering an irrigation project. The flow-down of water to its lowest level, as required by the second law of thermodynamics, actually powers the distribution of water to higher levels in a localised area. Life is an anti-entropic process, producing increasing complexity, and intelligent life even more so. The theory of dissipative structures also says that this has a price: entropy is exported outside the localised area and decays even faster. We have seen this in business, which has often embraced chaos theory. Smaller stocks are held, fewer workers are employed, structures change continuously. The business is more efficient and exciting to work in. However, customers wait longer to receive goods, there is more unemployment, and contact with the needs of the environment (as opposed to the needs of the business) goes to zero. Of course, when the environment becomes too impoverished, the business suffers too, and then there are real problems at finding outlets for all that energy, often with disastrous consequences: the lemming effect!

Why be so morbid?

I hope those who know me realise that I am in fact quite a cheerful person! So, why write about death and destruction?

I believe that, without having some awareness of this background, it is impossible to understand the society we live in or the clients who come to us. We are in a society where politics has ended because there is no sense of polis, a society which is extreme because it is in extremis, where "The words of the prophets are written on the subway walls" (Paul Simon) and they say "No future", where a Prime Minister (Margaret Thatcher) can say "There is no such thing as society". So many of our clients cling desperately (and we call them "borderline"); or they deny the real world and live in some kind of a fantasy world (and we call them "narcissistic"). Parents are ambivalent about having children, children are not interested in going to school and "preparing for the future", the images in which we are bathed are violent or sickly sweet or sexual-but-disconnected.

Our therapy must take into account the despair behind these manifestations, and, as Gestaltists, we must see it in terms of the field of the client in relation to the whole environment, including the social situation. We must avoid contributing to the culture of privatisation, internalisation, amorality, taking without giving. I want to particularly note, as an example of good practice, the contribution theory of the Pellin School of Gestalt, where they ask not only "What do you want or need from the environment?", but "What do you contribute to the environment?" We must be able to distinguish between surviving and living; between introjects and values; between guilt (when we disobey introjects) and shame (when we deny ourselves, including our core values); and (as Perls, 1969a reminds us) between using therapy to work on our self-concept and using therapy to work on ourselves. Then there is a possibility to move through despair to acceptance and then to living: not just for the present, but in our becoming—including the coming of death.

CHAPTER SEVEN

Cultural action for freedom: Paulo Freire as Gestaltist*

I have liked the work of Paulo Freire since the days of being a student activist, and I had the pleasure of attending seminars with him in Britain in about 1975, and loved the way he worked. Later, as I became involved in Gestalt therapy, I realised the similarities between the two sets of ideas, in both the theories and the methodology. Part of our holistic heritage as Gestaltists is an interest in the social and political aspects of being a human being, and Freire brings that in a manner similar to our Paul Goodman, who was, after all, author of one of the first radical critiques of education: Growing Up Absurd *(1960). The writing is experimental, trying to capture some of the essence of Freire's approach in the linear format of a paper.*

I would particularly like to thank here the participants in my Cleveland workshop of the same title, in particular the participants from Brazil and the Philippines, who brought their own experience of Paulo Freire and his work.

---

*First published in 1999 in *Gestalt Review*, 3(3), based on a presentation to the conference of the Association for the Advancement of Gestalt Therapy (AAGT) in Cleveland, Ohio in 1998.

I am caught in a paradox. If I present the approach of Paulo Freire here, I contradict his approach, and my workshop. As a participant in my Cleveland workshop pointed out, if I tell you *why* this is, I already pattern your response.

So, let us dialogue, as best we can on paper.

Why do you read this article? Is it the next page of the *Review*, which you read through? Is there something particular that catches your eye: the names "Paulo Freire" or "Peter Philippson", or the words "liberation" or "education"? Can you refine this "why"? What are you on the lookout for? Do you seek an "assimilable novelty" (Perls, Hefferline, & Goodman, 1994, p. 6) or an accumulation of "facts" to introject?

Is your intent to engage with this article actively: as a "subject . . . who acts" (Freire, 1996); or passively, as an "object . . . who is acted on"? Whence does my authority arise? Is it based on my status as a conference presenter, or a writer, or a trainer? Is it based on editorial acceptance? Or is it based on *your* decision, in dialogue with me, that there is something nourishing you can get from me?

Can you see the paradox? These questions are Freire's questions as well as mine. Thus, while asking you pertinent questions about your relation to me and to this article, I am also sneaking in information about Freire. I am manipulating you.

You can not trust me in my role as teacher. I cannot be value-free. Either I present "facts": Paulo Freire, who died in May last year aged seventy-five, was a Brazilian educationalist who revolutionised the teaching of literacy in Brazil, Chile, and other countries, and profoundly affected the understanding of education for many people worldwide from the 1960s onwards. He envisioned education as either domination, "banking" facts in order to get them back with interest, or as liberation, a dialogue in which the educatee's awareness grows of her/himself as a problem-solving being in the world . . . have you grown from this? Have you found yourself slipping into a familiar, comfortable configuration of "recipient of information"? Do you find your ability to creatively engage with the world activated or pacified?

So, to finish my sentence, either I do what I did above, or I try to engage you as an active participant in this interaction. I cannot avoid manipulating you by my style of interacting with you. At least, through my making it overt, you can make an informed choice of whether to accept the way I encourage you to be. I would insist, however, that a "straight, factual" presentation of Freire's work would also be a manipulation, but more invisibly, because our respective roles fit within a shared cultural introject about the nature of learning. Freire is saying that this introject is particularly problematic in a society characterised by forms of domination.

Having said this, I now continue in more "factual" mode. I shall provide more "information" on Freire's work, and my understanding of its connection to Gestalt therapy. My hope is that I have done sufficient above to facilitate the deconstruction of this mode, and to invite you to continue engaging with what I write as an active participant.

Freire's distinguishing characteristic of human beings is that, alone among animals, we are *problem solving*. We are capable of posing our position in the world as a problem to be solved rather than acting on it as a given. By doing this, we are not immersed in reality, but can see reality as something we can shape by our "cultural action". It is in our interaction with the world, and in our dialogue with other people mediated by the world, that we make meaning, we "speak our word" in the world.

In this emphasis on creative dialogic–dialectic action in the world, achieving both meaning and transformation, Freire is absolutely in line with both the theory and practice of Gestalt therapy. To quote Freire,

> If it is in speaking the word that people, by naming the world, transform it, dialogue imposes itself as the way by which they achieve significance as human beings. Dialogue is thus an existential necessity. And since dialogue is the encounter in which the united reflection and action of the dialoguers are addressed to the world which is to be transformed and humanized, this dialogue cannot be reduced to the act of one person's 'depositing' ideas in another, nor can it become a simple exchange of ideas to be 'consumed' by the discussants . . . It is an act of creation; it must not serve as a crafty instrument of domination of one person by another. (Freire, 1996, pp. 69–70)

Compare Gestalt therapy:

> Often, it must be said, the therapist tries to impose his standard of health on the patient, and when he cannot, he exclaims: 'Be self-regulating, damn you! I am telling you what self-regulation is!' (Perls, Hefferline, & Goodman, 1994, p. 59)

> Speech is good contact when it draws energy from and makes a struc-
> ture of the three grammatical persons, I, Thou, and It; the speaker, the
> one spoken to, and the matter spoken about. (ibid., p. 101)

Thus, I am not making good contact with you now unless there is something in "the matter spoken of" which is energising our communication, and we are both willing to put our energy and interest into our mutual theme (here something about Paulo Freire). If I were to write this only because I want my name in print, or you were to read this because it is the next page or out of politeness, we would not be in good contact.

Both Gestalt therapy and Freire's liberating education are support for people to challenge the limits in their lives, whether self-imposed or imposed by others. They are, therefore, support for a *risky* under-taking. Living freely in this way is more anxiety provoking than finding a familiar niche, whether it is one of domination or of being dominated. The method is termed, in one, "awareness", and in the other "conscientisation". In both cases, it means more than receiving sense data. Awareness/conscientisation is a creative act, an act of culture-making. I bring myself to the world and engage it based on both what is in the world, and on my own interests and needs. I "speak a true word" (Freire, 1996) in this world and in dialogue with other people. In speaking it, I "transform the world" (ibid.).

This emphasis on dialogue follows from the emphasis both Freire and Gestalt therapy place on the relational nature of self. For Freire (1996), "*I* cannot exist without a *non-I*. In turn, the *not-I* depends on that existence. The world which brings consciousness into existence becomes the world *of* that consciousness" (ibid., p. 63, original italics). For Perls (1978, p. 55), "The self is that part of the field which is opposed to the otherness".

What Freire (1996, p. 69) adds is the political dimension:

> Dialogue cannot occur between those who want to name the world
> and those who do not wish this naming – between those who deny
> others the right to speak their word and those whose right to speak
> has been denied them. Those who have been denied their primordial
> right to speak their word must first reclaim this right and prevent the
> continuation of this dehumanizing aggression.

That is, in order to dialogue, I must risk stopping being subjugated, and deny the power of the other to subjugate me. Conversely, in order to be a dialogic educator or therapist, I must have no wish to subjugate my students or clients, but, more than that, they must be willing to put aside being subjugated, and be willing to fight me to prevent me being the dominator. I cannot give up my domination on my own; it must be taken from me. If I hold back from expressing my own power in order to "empower" the client or student, paradoxically I am proclaiming myself as the powerful one in the encounter, the one with the power to empower or disempower, the benevolent dictator. If I act from my own power, I can invite my client or student to engage with me from his/her power.

One of the controversies in the Cleveland workshop links to this point. I began the workshop by asking the participants to divide into small groups to share their interests in attending: why were they at the workshop? (I did a similar thing in this paper.) But how could they answer, since many of them did not know anything about the work of Paulo Freire, and were expecting me to give them that information? I eventually clarified, as I did here, that I was aiming to encourage a specific relationship between myself and the participants. Some participants objected that this was manipulation of them, and that I should have made clear that I was doing this from the outset.

The simple answer to this was that I had been clear in my introduction to the workshop in the conference programme that I intended "using some of Freire's own methodology" in my presentation. However, as I wrote above, there is a deeper philosophical point here. According to both Freire and Perls, there is no neutral stance. For Freire,

> We simply cannot go to the labourers – urban or peasant – in the banking style, to give them 'knowledge' or to impose upon them the model of the 'good man' contained in a program whose content we have ourselves organized. Many political and educational plans have failed because their authors designed them according to their own personal views of reality, never once taking into account (except as mere objects of their actions) the *men-in-a-situation* to whom their program was ostensibly directed. (Freire, 1996, p. 75)

For Perls (1969a, p. 77), "People have to grow by frustration—by skillful frustration. Otherwise they have no incentive to develop their own means and ways of coping with the world".

Thus, in both Freire's and Perls' approach, there is a need to frustrate the initial assumption that the expert is going to give the answers. In seminars I attended with Freire in the 1970s, he refused to say anything until the discussion had started, after which he agreed to have his say where he felt it was useful. He later commented that he knew little about the interests of the British participants, and wanted to let the discussion find a level that fitted for us before speaking himself. But would it not have been more egalitarian to have explained this earlier? Once again we discussed this in the workshop. My assumption, which was shared by a number of workshop participants, was precisely the opposite. If I had started the workshop by saying that I wanted them to start the discussion, and then I would join in, the focus would have been on explaining to me so that I could join in. There is a similarity here to the thinking of Bion (1961), which underlies the practice of the Tavistock model of T-group, where the leader waits for a process to begin, and then relates to that process, and to the psychoanalytic approach of exploring the transference by therapeutic neutrality.

There is another aspect to the power theme if we take Freire's perspective: that of *shame*. I support the awareness that some ways a psychotherapist, might act towards a client can lead to the client suppressing her/himself in order to comply with the therapist. The client can experience this as shaming. (See, for example, Lee & Wheeler, 1996.) However, in my discussions at conferences, it seems that shame is often, *in practice*, equated with *vulnerability*. If my starting point is that my clients are more vulnerable than I am, then I will always be pulling back from a full-blooded encounter with them. A client with a background of compliance with important others, who has developed an ability to pick up how the other person sees a situation, will read two invitations here. First, that the client should fit into my projection of vulnerability; second that s/he should see me as stronger, and easily capable of hurting her/him. That is, I believe that many of the expressions of shame by clients are induced by the expectations of shame-sensitive therapists. This process can then become invisible, and, indeed, reversed, as it is assumed that the different experience of more robustly dialogic therapists is because they do not notice that they are shaming the client. (This is, of course, sometimes the case. I do not want to deny the potential for a therapist to ride roughshod over a client.)

The perspectives of Paulo Freire and of the people from Brazil and the Philippines who attended the Cleveland workshop are important, since the experiences they bring are of domination, hardship, and violence beyond anything most of our clients have experienced, and of the strength and robustness of those who experienced these. Freirean educators relate to the oppressed through politics, philosophy, and awareness rather than through trauma. For Freire (1996),

> The oppressed, who have been shaped by the death-affirming climate of oppression, must find through their struggle the way to life-affirming humanization ... In order to regain their humanity they must cease to be things and fight as men and women. This is a radical requirement. They cannot enter the struggle as objects in order *later* to become human beings. (p. 50, original italics)

The danger of adopting any other approach with those who have been dominated is that it is a form of *noblesse oblige*, configuring the other as the object of our altruism.

Put in Gestalt therapy terms, the dominated need to re-own their capacity for *aggression*. Their assumption will usually be that, if they do this, it will be by making the other powerless: this is how power has always been used in their experience. It is, therefore, important for me, as therapist, to stay centred in my own power and capacity for aggression, so that we can meet each other in a different way. (Robert Resnick, workshop presentation, describes the dominator/dominated mode as a "one-power system" and the horizontal mode as a "two-power system".) This was part of the power that Fritz Perls brought to therapy: he was a therapist you could fight with, and who would show his appreciation of the fight.

Summary

Both Freire and Gestalt therapy face the issue that the former calls "dehumanisation" and Gestalt calls "loss of ego function" through an approach based on dialogue and phenomenology. Both resist providing answers to the educatee/client's difficulties. Both challenge models that encourage the other to accept their place in society. Both are based on the assumption that the world is a risky place, and that true engagement with it takes courage.

Freire adds the political perspective that no dialogue is possible until the dominated are ready to risk rejecting domination. Human beings have the capacity to be problem solving, and to become a "subject" requires a person to face the culture of domination as a problem to be solved.

The therapist or educator cannot be neutral in a culture of domination. The client or educatee will expect (and wish for) the therapist or educator not to act in a horizontal manner. In psychotherapy, this is called "transference". The therapist or educator needs to avoid taking on the role of dominator from the beginning of the relationship. "Dominating" and "acting powerfully" are different (although the difference is difficult to see in a culture of domination). The therapist or educator can only avoid dominating through an exercise of her/his own power.

For both Freire and Gestalt therapy, self is relational, and emerges from our action in the world, rather than as an "inner" reality. Growth arises from dialogue and interaction.

CHAPTER EIGHT

Response to "Intercultural aspects of psychotherapy"*

I pondered whether to include this. In some ways it is not fair to include a critique of a paper that people have not seen. However, the subject of the invisibility of assumptions about race, class, sexuality, and culture is an important one. Where therapists take for granted that our professional assumptions of openness to diversity are to be imposed on clients as the only acceptable cultural assumptions, we are paradoxically losing our openness to diversity. Yet, otherwise, we are facing people whose life choices, while valued in their community, are uncomfortable for us to face. The act of defining those whose ideas run counter to ours as psychologically disturbed has a long and dishonourable history.

I have been sent a copy of the above paper by the Intercultural and Equal Opportunities Committee, and I want to raise with readers of *The Psychotherapist* some concerns I feel about it.

Essentially, while I am very glad this paper has been produced, I would hope from an organisation committed to psychotherapy something less standardised, and more willing to face some of the really

---

*First published in 1999, in *The Psychotherapist*, 12, Spring.

difficult questions round "equal opportunities". I do not see this here, particularly in writing about class, race, culture, and sexuality. Rather, I see some culture-bound assumptions being treated as if they were objective.

To take the section on "class": in many ways, this is a necessary statement of the obvious. However, the invisible assumption is that it is written by someone from a more privileged class to someone else from that class about people from the working class. It might be fairly inevitable in UKCP that this would be the case. I am querying the *invisibility*. Furthermore, I believe that the statement "Remarkably little has been written about working psychotherapeutically with people from socially disadvantaged backgrounds" is more a statement of what writings are visible. Much has been written in reports of community mental health projects, Richmond Fellowship, People Not Psychiatry, and Mind, but many of these are not written from the perspective of the professional, rather from the perspective of the recipient. There are also classic works about the psychological development of the impoverished from *within* their communities: Fanon's *The Wretched of the Earth* (Fanon, 2001) and Freire's *Pedagogy of the Oppressed* (Freire, 1996). Much of this writing would offend many psychotherapists' assumptions about violence and the place of politics in mental health. As Sartre says in his introduction to Fanon's book, he is speaking to the oppressed, not to the professional.

Similarly, in writing about "race and culture", it seems invisible that the relativism emphasised in, for example, this document would not be valued by many cultures, and that the *act* of assenting by a patient/client or by an aspiring psychotherapist to the idea of free choice in relationships or sexuality would be an act of cultural self-exclusion (in some cases leading to extreme violence). Unless people are willing to embrace such a relativism, which they might not see as a social good, they cannot with integrity train as psychotherapists within the models we have. Many communities have approximately parallel provision with more consonant cultural assumptions, for example, pastoral counselling in black churches. Once again, Fanon (*Black Skins, White Masks*, 2008) is not mentioned.

In talking about "sexual orientation", there is even more of a minefield if the assumptions are invisible. To see this, let us take the second paragraph and make a small addition: "Particular difficulties arise for gay, lesbian, bisexual or trans-sexual people *or paedophiles*." Continuing: "Acknowledging minority sexuality to others carries a great risk of losing family, friends, jobs – even children." I want to make clear that I am not arguing for the normalisation of paedophilia! I am saying that we still do have boundaries of what is acceptable, and need to make those visible. Or take transsexual people: there can be two different takes on this. Either it is a valid part of the psychosexual spectrum, or it is an accommodation to a family or society that pushes a child to disown his/her gender, even to the extent of surgical mutilation. If it is ever the latter, should we, as a profession, be discouraged from facing this with a client because of a commitment to non-discriminatory practice? We need to be clear that we are not being open to all viewpoints and lifestyles, and that we make cultural choices which need to be visible. To sum up, we are a profession based on facing difficult issues with clients. We need to be able to face our own discrimination, and I honour the members of the UKCP Intercultural and Equal Opportunities Committee for doing this work. We need, however, to take this commitment to equal opportunities at a level as multi-layered as the work we are using it to underpin. This is, unfortunately, much more difficult and painful than appears in the present paper.

PART II

ROOTS IN PSYCHOANALYSIS AND CONNECTIONS WITH OTHER THEORIES

CHAPTER NINE

Gestalt and drive theory*

This article reflects two of my ongoing concerns. First of all, to acknowledge our roots in, and commonalities with, the psychoanalytic community. Here, I point to the lack of acknowledgement that our founders used the language of drive theory within the Gestalt approach. Second, I raise a concern that the very popular language of dialogue has been used in a way that disembodies us, and takes away from a sense that, on a bodily level, we have needs and desires that are not focused on a specific relationship. Such an approach to dialogue seems to me to import a mind–body dualism that is antithetical to the Gestalt approach.

My thesis in this paper is that the uncritical rejection Gestaltists of Freudian drive theory is part of the ground of the histori- cal neglect of the body and sexuality in much therapeutic thinking. This neglect has more recently been written about in a number of articles in the *British Gestalt Journal* and elsewhere (see, particularly, Latner, 1998; O'Shea, 2000; Roberts, 1999, and responses

---

*First published in 2004, in *British Gestalt Journal*, 13(2).

in the same issue; Kepner, 2003, and other papers in the same issue; Cornell, 2003, and responses in the same issue).

It is the drive theory that states that the body, the physical being, has its own requirements for survival, contact, and procreation and that these, while being object-seeking, are more geared to the satisfaction of a hunger than to the specificity of the object. I need to eat, even if the food is not tasty. I need parental attachment, even if the attachment comes at a high price. I need people to connect to, even if the only people around me require me to submit to pain and frustration. I lust for sex, and gravitate towards those who might provide it, though I might conceal that attraction behind moral condemnation and other sublimations. In both individual and group psychotherapy, sexual drives are activated in both the client and in the therapist, or are suppressed for fear of what might happen, which has its own implications for the therapeutic relationship.

The above, I would contend, is so obviously true in experience that we could wonder how the existence of such body drives ever came into question. Why do we need to recover this aspect of our existence in a holistic therapy? In search of an answer, I propose a historical sketch of the rise and fall of drive theory in Gestalt therapy.

Perls

For the Perls of *Ego, Hunger and Aggression* (1947), there are three central drives: hunger, disgust, and aggression. Hunger is the wish to assuage a lack; disgust is the wish to throw back to the otherness or annihilate what is not wanted or is toxic; and aggression is an active engagement with otherness to make it nourishing. The whole psychology of *Ego, Hunger and Aggression* is based on movement towards and away from, accepting and rejecting, the embryo idea of the "ego functions" (identification and alienation) of *Gestalt Therapy: Excitement and Growth in the Human Personality* (Perls, Hefferline, & Goodman, 1994).

It is important to note that in this early work (Perls, 1947), Perls downgraded sexuality as the basic drive (as psychoanalysis would make it), and turned it into an example of the hunger drive. As such, it is to be assuaged without any sense of a long-term relationship, but as it arises. When we realise this, we can become aware that Perls, far from being a very sexually driven person, was willing to engage in sexual contact with clients precisely because, for him, sexual contact was not significant beyond the satisfaction of an immediate hunger. The relationship aspect was secondary. This explains why Fritz Perls the therapist would (from my viewing of films of his work) hardly ever touch clients in therapy sessions or explore themes of sexuality much: that was not his hunger at the time.

When Perls (1978) expanded his theory of development (in a lecture he gave in 1957, and which prefigured Stern's work (1985)), his first level was what he called "animal self", the physical, organismic wants and needs, which then had to interact with the other layers of selfhood: the playing of socially required roles; the development of a parallel cognitive/fantasy world (mind); the abstraction of fixed tools, including language, from the field; and the organisation of tools into systems. So, this hard-wired, instinctive, need-satisfaction level—basically, the drives—is present in the system as Perls then envisaged.

Perls, Hefferline, and Goodman (1994)

Above all, we must remember that where the contestants are natural drives—aggressions, special gifts, sexual practices that in fact give pleasure, etc.—they cannot be reduced, but their manifestations only deliberately suppressed, bullied or shamed out. When all the contestants are in awareness and in contact, a man may make his own hard decisions; he is not a patient. The hope is that in such a case a difficult drive will spontaneously find its measure in a new configuration, by creative adjustment and convalescent organismic self-regulation. (p. 138)

Gestalt Therapy, the book, does indeed speak about the drives in several passages such as the one above. And, as in psychoanalysis, the ego—here defined as the active identifications and alienations of the self—engages with the drives and makes the "hard decisions". The difference between the Gestalt and the psychoanalytic picture is in the status of the superego. For Freud, the id drives conflict with the demands of the superego, with the ego acting as mediator. For Perls, Hefferline, and Goodman, the drives and desires compete with each other, with the ego orientating and creatively adjusting. The superego (top dog) is in an uncontactful and uncreative fight with another artefact, the infraego (underdog). This is a fight for supremacy or survival, and soon loses any sense of the underlying organismic wants and needs.

One major limitation of Perls, Hefferline, and Goodman's work is the confusion between the physical boundary (primarily, as they state, at the skin surface and the sensory organs) between organism and environment, and the boundary between self and other, which is non-geographical, fluid, and choiceful (see Philippson, 2001). It is the latter that should accurately be called the "contact boundary", since that is where contact, in the Gestalt therapy sense, occurs. While every organismic need is in relation to the environment, it does not require an ongoing relationship to that environment. Human beings began as nomadic hunter-gatherers, eating what was to hand, and only later settled to the more intense, "objectivised" relationship with a bit of land that allowed cultivation. If there was a spiritual connection to the earth, it was to the whole earth, or to places that became significant (where the food was, or where they buried their dead) rather than to a bit of land called home, or to a nation.

Self in relation to other is very different. Self, involving choice and will and identification with the physical experience ("I am experiencing this"), emerges in relation to whatever aspect of environment (or even of the organism) I take as other, and allows for interests and creativity to develop beyond the scope of any immediate hunger, even allowing the hunger to become secondary to the development of interests. I can deny my hungers in order to further relationships—to people, communities, and interests, commitments and morality.

Gestalt therapy must relate primarily to the boundary of self and other, but also recognise that this boundary is settled on a base of the sensitive boundary between organism and environment, where experience (rather than fantasy or cognition) occurs. Yet, this level has become less acknowledged in some recent Gestalt therapy, and this is what I will now look at.

Buber and "dialogic/relational Gestalt therapy"

More recently (Hycner & Jacobs, 1995; Yontef, 1993), there has been a wish to re-engage with the ideas of Martin Buber (Buber, 1965), making the dialogic relationship between two human beings central to life and therapy. There are many positive aspects to this shift in emphasis. It is certainly true that some ways of understanding the Gestalt concept of the "here-and-now" made it difficult to talk about ongoing relationships and commitments, and some ways of looking at hungers gave the sense, quite alien to Gestalt self theory, that human beings are disconnected, individualistic bundles of hungers—merely organisms. Sexuality becomes, in the dialogic approach, an expression of a relationship rather than an immediate bodily hunger.

However, having said this, it is important from the perspective of this paper to note that a dialogic approach, relatively speaking, down-grades the kind of "animal appetite" of the organism in its environ-ment that we have been looking at here. For the (possibly uncomfort-able) fact is that sex-in-relationship is a modification of a primary physical hunger, an evolutionary necessity for the survival of the species. In terms of Perls' developmental layers outlined above, this hunger is overlaid with, first, society's rules for mating and the roles assigned to men and women; second, fantasy such as romance and cognitive considerations such as the wish to have someone to look after you; third, the ability to "objectivise" a single person as "hus-band", "wife", or "partner" to commit to, an ability entirely different to an animal's instinctive mating patterns; and fourth, with the place of such relating in the fabric of our social systems (a consideration different from the individual's fear of society's disapproval of rule breaking, which I mentioned above).

Thus, in the attempt to make a more human and humane Gestalt therapy, there is a loss of the primacy of the body, and of relating that is not part of an ongoing relationship with a human other. And, with this, some of the specificity of Gestalt therapy also gets lost. For exam-ple, the "Paradoxical theory of change" (Beisser, 1970), which states that the best stance from which organismic change can emerge is acceptance and ownership of what is, depends for its validity on a reasonably good and immediate sensory contact with the world (a function of the body-organism in its environment). Someone who is paranoid, for example, might accept and own their belief that the world is hostile to them as an individual, and act in a self-regula-ting manner in relation to that belief, but will not grow from that acceptance. The same consideration applies to other Gestalt tags: "organismic self-regulation" and "creative adjustment". These are only possible (indeed, are only meaningful) when based upon physi-cal experience in the world.

Integrating the two boundaries

The need, then, is to integrate these two levels: the physical boundary between organism and environment and the human boundary between self and other; in the terms of this paper, between a drive theory and a relational theory. If we have only a drive approach, based on the boundary between organism and environment, the theory becomes mechanistic in ways described by Hycner and Jacobs, and Yontef. If we have only a relational approach, based on the boundary between self and other, the theory becomes disembodied.

Apart from Gestalt therapy, these issues have been wrestled with by Kohut (1971) and the self psychologists:

> [Kohut] introduced his theoretical and technical innovations *within* the framework of classical drive theory by positing a division of libidinal energy into two separate and independent realms: narcissistic libido and object libido. Both types of libido cathect objects, but the objects are vastly different. Object libido cathects 'true' objects, experienced as truly separate from the subject. Narcissistic libido cathects selfobjects, in which the object is experienced as an extension of the self, serving the functions of mirroring and idealization. (Greenberg & Mitchell, 1983, pp. 357–358, original italics)

What this means, potentially, is that the object of sexual desire can be merely an object "experienced as truly separate from the subject" (and, thus, satisfy a physical drive), or a selfobject, who sustains our sense of selfhood through an ongoing and internalised relationship.

Gestalt therapy does not make quite this distinction. Self is always in relation to other, which can be human or non-human. Neither is this necessarily about "mirroring and idealisation", but about the *ego* functions of both identification and alienation. It is important to realise that Kohut understood the self as an "inner" event, though supported by the introjection of selfobjects, while for Gestalt therapy self is at the contact boundary, which both joins and separates. It is not self that we explore, but self–other.

Personality and drives

When we look for a Gestalt therapy correlate to Kohut's concept of the "selfobject", we are essentially looking to the assimilations to what

Perls, Hefferline, and Goodman call "personality function", "the system of attitudes assumed in interpersonal relations" (1994, p. 160)—and, I would add, in all relations with the world, not just with other people. The person who has assimilated love and acceptance from others is capable of both relationships and drive fulfilment, though both of these will be modified by introjects and assimilated values. The person who has assimilated hate and rejection from others is incapable of both relationships and accurate awareness of drive needs, and this time it is their isolation that is modified by introjects and values. For example, I think of clients who make and stay in loveless relationships because that is what they are supposed to do; or who look for sex or food or drugs as an immediate but inaccurate "fix" of a hunger that they do not know how to regulate contactfully.

It is worth looking carefully at Perls, Hefferline, and Goodman's chapter on "Human nature and the anthropology of neurosis", and especially section 9, on "Symbols":

> He lives in a world of symbols . . . All this has given an enormous increase in scope and power . . . The dangers in it are, unfortunately, not potential but realized. Symbolic structures . . . become the exclusive end of all activity, in which there is no animal satisfaction and may not even be personal satisfaction . . . Emotionally a few artists catch from real experience symbols of passion and sensory excitement; these symbols are abstracted and stereotyped by commercial imitators; and people make love or adventure according to these norms of glamour. (ibid., pp. 94–95)

In such a society, therapists must be willing to go back to basic "animal hungers", bodily urges and sensory awareness, before going on to the more symbolised connections of relationship and dialogue. The therapy must involve touch, taste, hearing, smell, sexual awareness—whichever of these is missing.

Drives and body

We now have more conceptual tools to understand the body. In the Gestalt world, Frank (2001) shows how assimilation of parental contact occurs on a somatic level, in the support or inhibition of relational movements. Thus, an early change in patterns of reaching into the world will affect how sitting up, and later walking, develop. These developmental bodily patterns can be worked with directly in the present on a somatic level.

In the world of neuroscience, Schore (1994) shows how, through basic neurology, the early environment with care-givers affects (or even prevents) the maturation of the brain. The human infant is not born with full neurological development, unlike other animals. In particular, there is a need for further connections between the mid-brain and the frontal lobes after birth, and this is vital for such things as impulse control and delayed gratification. This maturation requires the oxytocin released through physical contact with the parent, and, if this is lacking, the connections will not happen. Thus, if there is disrupted development of the neurology, no psychological methods or techniques will allow the development of impulse control (normal retroflection and egotism, in Gestalt therapy terms). The work has to involve the physical contact that will finally allow the release of oxytocin and the maturing of the client's neurology.

This work requires a relationship with the therapist, and, at the same time, attention to fully physiological needs/drives, and very little in the way of technique.

Working with drive needs

In working with all these drives, it is not the primary aim of the therapy to satisfy the needs, but to bring them into full awareness. It is even possible for the touch that some clients require, coming from a background of physical neglect, to be provided by someone other than the therapist. For example, massage can often be a useful adjunct to therapy in these situations. Yet, I will usually bring exploration of touch into therapy. If a client does not want to be touched, this in itself can become a primary focus of therapy, in a way graded to be assimilable to the client. Remember that some changes simply cannot happen without the neurological development facilitated by touch. There is no replacement. There is no paradoxical theory in this area: the paradoxical theory presupposes adequate neurological development to allow full organismic self-regulation.

The area that raises the most questions for many therapists is, as I have written above, the work with sexual drives and needs, and here it is most useful that our theory does not require the therapist to satisfy needs, just to bring them into awareness. Hence, it is not ethically problematic to work with sexual drives. However, it does require good contact with the client and sensitivity on the part of the therapist. Again, if the sexual area is specifically excluded by the client, this can be a focus of therapy. For example, with a female client who was abused as a child:

> Client: I'm scared that you will want sex with me; so many men have only wanted me for that. Of course, I know that can't happen here.

> Therapist: Slow down. It is true that I will not have sex with you, but you have raised the possibility, and I want to acknowledge that we could have sex, and can explore this possibility. We will not have sex because I make that choice, not to exclude the subject but so we *can* explore it. It sounds like the theme of sex between us is here.

For clients with painful associations to sex, this is a frightening dialogue, but one that they, in my experience, always come to value, holding out the possibility that they can acknowledge themselves and be acknowledged by others as sexual beings. This kind of exploration often leads to the client's recovery of her (or his) sexuality and the development of a satisfying sexual relationship in the world outside therapy.

Conclusion

In this chapter, I have argued that relational Gestalt therapy must be both dialogic and embodied, and that the discarding of the awareness of basic human drives makes the therapeutic relationship less real and meaningful. I have speculated on how this splitting of mind and body has occurred in current Gestalt therapy, even though it is centrally a holistic theory and such a split is alien to the approach. I have indicated how it is vital to be open to exploring issues round touch and sexuality within the therapeutic relationship.

CHAPTER TEN

A Gestalt approach to transference*

This is another bridge between Gestalt therapy and psychoanalysis. It has a particular importance for me in that it raises questions about the place of regression and the character of the therapist–client relationship. If I were writing this today, I would add something about "mirror neurons" in the section on "projective identification".

The question that I want to pose in this paper is: what is the meaning of transference in Gestalt therapy?

The originators of Gestalt therapy, trying to distance themselves and their approach from their psychoanalytic roots, emphasised the here-and-now relationship between therapist and client rather than transference. More recently, there has been a rapprochement to psychoanalysis in many parts of the Gestalt community, and a rediscovery of transference, countertransference, and projective identification. Often, there is a sense of two relationships going on simultaneously: the real relationship and the transferential one (see, in particular,

---

*First published in 2002, in *British Gestalt Journal*, 11(1).

Clarkson, 1992). Yet, there are still questions about what these words mean in a Gestalt context.

One approach would be to reduce the concept of transference to that of projection of an introjected parental figure on to the therapist, but this reduces it to an instance of such a wide phenomenon that it says nothing particular about the therapeutic encounter, which it must do to have any connection to the psychoanalytic meaning. Similarly, it can be viewed as an instance of a fixed Gestalt, an unfinished scene that is pushing for completion with the therapist. Once again, however, such a replay would be happening in a wide variety of settings, and says nothing about the therapeutic encounter. If transference is to mean anything particularly significant about therapy rather than life in general, there needs to be something more specific than these.

Requirements for a Gestalt approach to transference

Recall that "self", in Gestalt therapy, is a *field-relational* term, so that what we are exploring in the therapy situation is the moment-by-moment co-creation by and of therapist and client. This is a very different image of the therapeutic encounter to the analytic one in which transference has its normal meaning:

> A patient in psychotherapy tends to transfer into his relationship with the therapist the sometimes intense feelings he experienced at an earlier stage in his life, in his relationship with his mother or father or other important figure. (Davis, 1987, p. 781)

So, the classical theory presupposes a possibility of the therapist being a blank screen on to which some other historical relationship can be projected. This cannot be true in a Gestalt theory. The therapist's action cannot be separated from the client's experience. If such intense "transferential" feelings and attitudes to the therapist are a specific aspect of psychotherapy, as I believe they are, there must be something in the therapeutic relationship itself that lends itself to such a response.

Furthermore, Gestalt therapy is a *phenomenological* approach, so the idea that we can ever fail to transfer our expectations on to our present experience is inconsistent with the approach. Yet, neither does Gestalt phenomenology support the idea that all is transference, that the world is just what we make of it. As I have written above, Gestalt theory always points to a co-creation in a field context: organism and environment, or self and other. The most we can achieve is some degree of "bracketing": having some sense of our own bias, and what this might mean in terms of the "spin" we put on our experience and consequent ways in which we limit our being in the world. That is, what is the therapist's experience in the present situation that links to the client's transferential experience?

Third, there are presuppositions about the nature of memory, childhood, and developmental theory concealed in the word "transference" that are quite different from the present-centred emphasis in Gestalt therapy. Developmentally, the theoretical groundwork was consistent with the classical theories of Mahler, Pine, and Bergman (1975), where child development was understood to proceed in completed stages, with a "developmental arrest" if a stage is not able to be completed satisfactorily. The meaning of "transference" was caught up in the idea of "regression", conceived as a wholesale return to a historically previous way of being. The more recent work of Stern (1985) has questioned the empirical and theoretical basis for this approach, and the whole idea of "regression" as a return to a past state has been questioned in the Gestalt world (Philippson, 1993b; Staemmler, 1997). In Perls, Hefferline, and Goodman (1994, p. 70) we read, ". . . it is not by inertia but by function that a form persists, and it is not by lapse of time but by lack of function that a form is forgotten", and "For the purposes of therapy, however, only the present structure of sensation, introspection, behavior is available; and our question must be what role remembering plays in this structure" (ibid., p. 69).

Thus, it seems clear to me that no theory of transference can be integrated into Gestalt therapy which does not take into account field theory, phenomenology, and attention to the present moment (including memory as one of the functions of that moment).

I shall look at all these considerations in turn, and propose how we might understand transference and related phenomena in a manner consistent with them. I shall then suggest how this might inform the work of the Gestalt therapist.

Transference and co-creation

If the client experiences the therapist in ways that could be labelled (by client, therapist, or observer) as resembling childhood relationships to significant others, how does this come about? It is often simplistically assumed to be inherent in a relationship where the client is looking for help, or where the therapist is offering help, but this is not true in my experience. The client is equally likely to expect some arcane procedure from the therapist (analogous to what might be expected from a doctor) that will make things better; or to expect to talk to the therapist and be listened to with little other input. It rather depends what has been shown on television most recently, or how a referring agency has described the therapy. It is true that clients are often ready to pick up therapists' assumptions, but it is unclear to me as a parent that this is a defining aspect of what children do with parents.

If something recognised as transference develops in a specific way in therapy (which I agree it does, in a sense), then it must emerge from something the therapist brings to the encounter. This might be an assumption that transference will emerge, which is then passed to the client. If so, it says something about the therapist, and very little about the client. It might be a response to the therapist's refusal to take the role the client does expect—the understanding I favour—but then there is a need to explain two things: how do the actions of the therapist connect with the client's "transferential" responses, and how is this therapeutic?

Let us begin with some Gestalt fundamentals. I will primarily use a Perlsian formulation of psychopathology, as it is most directly easy to understand, but it is not formally different from the descriptions of "loss of ego function" in Perls, Hefferline, and Goodman (1994). Perls spoke of "manipulating the environment for support" instead of "self-support". Note the choice of words. He was not polarising "self-support" and "environmental support", as he has often been taken as saying, but never said. For Perls, consistently, "self" is located at the boundary of a person and the person's environment, so such a polarisation would have been meaningless. To self-support is to orientate yourself creatively and contactfully in the environment so that the ever-changing environment supports you. This is the theory of "creative adjustment". To manipulate the environment for support is to act in a way that is familiar rather than creative, to adjust *oneself* in such a way as to pull a familiar outcome from the environment, and to avoid any contact that cannot be pulled into such an outcome. It was a creative adjustment when the person first did it; now it is a fixed Gestalt. There will, then, be areas of the person's life that are repetitions of familiar relationships, often beginning in childhood. It is when these are seen as problematic that the person comes to a therapist, but the "problems" are now disowned, alien "things" to be solved rather than what the client does.

The fundamental assumption of the Gestalt therapist, though, is that there is no alien problem, but the action of the client. If there is to be change, it will come through the client's re-identification with his/her own actions, and this awareness will be part of the ground of the therapist's presence with the client. Yet, this will not be an abandonment ("You're on your own"), but a statement by one who stays in contact. (Notice how powerfully this happens in classical psychoanalysis, with the silently present therapist.) In this situation, the client will experience a number of things: anxiety, confusion, and powerlessness (and a wish for the therapist to take on the powerful projection). Those, like me, who like the five-layer model can see in this the impasse and the implosive layer. Then comes the next layer, which Perls calls the explosion: the suppressed needs, desires, emotions, and contact wishes. Notice that it is not these desires, etc., that are archaic, but the sense of how the world reacts to me, and how those desires can or cannot be met. As Perls, Hefferline, and Goodman point out:

> It is not the old image that has released the feeling, but the relaxation of the present inhibition. *The old scene is revived because that happened to be the last free exercise of the feeling and gesture in the sensory environment, trying to complete the unfinished situation.* (1994, p. 72, original italics)

Phenomenology

One of the problems with the whole theme of "transference" is the assumption that it is a replay of childhood in some sense. Rather than exploring phenomenologically the meaning of this desire or emotion *now* as part of the process between the therapist and the client, it is seen in analytic psychotherapy as a provider of information on the past, to be interpreted and understood. In some forms of post-analytic psychotherapy, the transference is seen as a regression to childhood behaviour, to be re-enacted with the therapist explicitly taking a parental role to provide a corrective developmental experience to the client's "inner child". In either case, the emotions and behaviour assumed to be "childlike" are love, hate, fear, dependency, or desire for nurturing, but I would not see these as being inappropriate adult responses.

Thus, rather than bracketing assumptions, and looking for what is particular in this moment, the whole process is looked at through a fixed lens based on the past. The therapist acts (and encourages the client to act) as though this lens is the present reality, and as though the client's phenomenology cannot belong to the present. Then, clients will often become confluent with this sense of themselves as "regressed" children. This can be a way of mutually understanding psychotherapy, but it is very different from the paradoxical theory of change in Gestalt therapy, where what the client brings in relation to the therapist is accepted and explored in aware relation to what the therapist is bringing to the relationship, so that it can be fully owned by the client as her/his own choiceful activity. In terms of the extract from Perls, Hefferline, and Goodman, above, the chronic inhibitions can be relaxed precisely because the person is now not in the childhood situation, the therapist is not the parent, and, thus, the emergency is safe.

Phenomenology fits best with the Gestalt theory of the "here-and-now". Phenomenologically, what is available to us as the "past" is memories, reconstructions, myths, etc., while the "future" is available to us as expectations, hopes, fears, myths, etc.

The present moment, history, and memory

The classical theory of transference assumes that the meaning of the client's response belongs to the past, and, thus, that the past is accurately reconstructable from such responses. In Stern's (1985) terms, the "clinically reconstructed infant" is synonymous with the actual infant. Stern and many other researchers working with memory make it clear that this is not how memory works. Memory is always a construct based on the person's present state. Neither does recent research, notably by Stern (1985) support the idea of developmental stages as sequential and needing to be completed before the next stage can begin. Rather, there are several "domains of relatedness", which may start sequentially, but which continue as ways of relating and experiencing selfhood throughout a person's life.

Phenomenologically, what is the difference between childhood and the client's present adult state? Is there anything to be gained therapeutically by trying to "recapture" the childhood state? The differences, as I understand them, are:

1. The child is physiologically not fully developed. This means lack of mobility, physical dependence on carers, and brain function (especially in the field of memory and understanding of consequences) not fully developed.
2. The child is smaller and weaker than parents for most of childhood. This is supported by the fact that parents and schools are supported by law in their control of the child. The child cannot just leave home, for example.
3. The child has limited perspective. The way things happen in his/her limited world is how the world is. Even that is only understood in a limited way.

There are also aspects that do not conform to the "regressed" view of the child. Children can feel secure and powerful, relate to other children and adults with pleasure and skill, enjoy experimenting and learning about the world, even if aspects of their lives are difficult. They often look forward to growing up and having more possibilities in their lives, rather than trying to stay little.

Taking all these aspects into account, I do not understand how it can be helpful to encourage a regression to a position that emphasises lack of resources. It is true that clients sometimes go to such a place, usually as part of an avoidance of choicefulness (loss of ego function), as described above. The experience of being with a therapist who is being encouraged to act in the complementary parental way will then seem familiar and intense, but the meaning will be very different from the analogous experience in childhood (even if this was an accurate depiction of the client's own childhood), where this could have been an experience of an inescapable reality.

Transference, countertransference, and projective identification

Much of what is called transference is an enactment of a fixed Gestalt of smallness and powerlessness, a projection of the largeness and power on to the therapist, and an avoidance of facing the reality of present freedom and choice. We could call this "defensive transference". The therapist's countertransference is either a confluence with the client's fixed position, or something of the therapist's own process (a wish for a powerful position, for example), and these two are not mutually exclusive. Unless there is an underlying theory of the need to complete developmental stages, there is no possible therapeutic reason for the therapist to encourage the development of such a state.

As I have written above, another aspect of the transferential experience is the re-owning in the relationship with the therapist of intense emotions of love, hate, fear, shame, rage, and sexual arousal, long denied as overwhelmingly dangerous, either to the client or to those around him/her. We could call this "expressive transference". The therapist's countertransference here could be fear and withdrawal, or a wish to exploit the client's experience by, for example, engaging in inappropriate sexual activity (sometimes in the guise of physical nurturing).

For example, let us take the situation of a man severely beaten in childhood for the slightest infraction of parents' wishes. The immediate organismic responses to the beatings were fear and rage, which the boy did not dare to express. I have described the consequences of this in my paper on shame (Philippson, 2004, p. 87):

> An energetic, emotional expression of a vital boundary function [disgust] does not merely disappear, however: it is retroflected. To be more precise, the boundary identifications and alienations of the ego are altered, so that the child identifies with the force-feeder and alienates her/his disgust response as an 'other', whose disgust is then aimed at the 'self' that is the source of the poisoned food.

In this way, the boy retroflects his outward aggression, regards the world as too dangerous to look at directly, and himself as both weak and the object of his own retroflected aggression. He projects this aggression on to other significant figures, who are seen as dangerously hostile towards him, once more justifying his avoidance of contact. Thus, he never has to face the fear of risking his outward aggression, but at the cost of a greatly diminished capacity for spontaneous existence.

This makes very clear what the "defensive transference" of this boy-become-man would be with a therapist: "I am weak and he is powerful, and will hurt or reject me if I show myself." If the man is supported to risk moving beyond this avoidance, this will be replaced by the "expressive transference": the fear and rage appropriate to the full expression of the unfinished situation, expressed to the therapist, who ". . . according to his own self-awareness, declines to be bored, intimidated, cajoled, etc.; he meets anger with explanation of the misunderstanding, or sometimes apology, or even with anger, according to the truth of the situation" (Perls, Hefferline, & Goodman, 1994, p. 25).

Projective identification, the experiencing by the therapist of emotion that is being denied by the client, I would understand in Gestalt therapy terms as a more technical (although interesting and clinically useful) event. Notice that the therapist is trying to practise inclusion, an understanding of the experience of the client, while maintaining separateness. Part of this is a close observation of the client's psychophysical state, using a refinement of the knowledge all human beings (apart from a few described as autistic or similar) have about the "body language" of others. Thus, the therapist notices the beginnings of the feeling (tensing of shoulders, reddening of eyes, clenching of fists, etc.), and becomes ready for the full expression. When this comes, it represents for the therapist—and of course for the client—an unfinished Gestalt, which pushes for completion. Just as "I wandered lonely as a . . ." brings up the word ". . . cloud" in most people who know the poem, an incomplete emotional Gestalt brings up the emotion in the therapist. This can be very useful as a guide to what is happening for the client, but for me does not need any mystical explanation.

Implications for therapy

The therapist must face the defensive transferential enactment in full understanding that this is a present action in support of a fixed Gestalt, avoiding the risk and anxiety of choicefulness. As Perls said to Gloria, "Are you a little girl?" The therapist needs to avoid becoming confluent with the client's wish for a parent. At the same time, the therapist must be aware that the client can only move beyond this by facing a high, and seemingly overwhelming, level of anxiety. It is like imagining there is an intruder in a room: the only way to remove that fear is to turn on the light and check—but this is frightening because the intruder might actually be there and attack you. What the therapist provides at this point is the support that the client is not alone.

In terms of our example client, the experiment towards moving out of the defensive transference might be to look the therapist in the eyes, to sit more upright, to say an uncomfortable truth, to show an interest in some aspect of the room, to breathe more fully, or similar. If there is no increase in anxiety or agitation, the situation is still in some way avoiding the real issue.

The expressive transference needs to be met by the therapist as a present moment experience: with acceptance and presence, neither exploiting it nor pulling away from it. For this client, the transference is likely to be rage, fear of rejection, fear of exercising his own power and becoming like father, or of killing the therapist. It is very tempting, but not very useful for the therapist to avoid facing this by exploring the defensive transference rather than encouraging the client to move beyond it to such an expression.

The significance of groups as an important way of working thus becomes clearer, precisely because it discourages the viewing of the therapy horizon as limited as childhood. The other group members can be a support in challenging the therapist, and a support for the therapist in facing the client's rage. The client can see other group members denying their power in ways that they cannot see in themselves. Kindly feedback from group members is often more easily believed than the same feedback from the therapist, who can be dismissed as saying what s/he thinks the client will like. The power of an individual therapy to encourage a "childlike" transference is a potential problem to be avoided by the therapist rather than an advantage. (Even in its own terms, there is a contradiction: is an only child generally more psychologically healthy than one with siblings?)

While it is easier for a client to mourn and mature from a "good enough" parenting experience, the need to be able to move on and become adult is common to all. For example, a child who has been sexually abused by father needs to reclaim her/his own sexuality from him and apply it to the adult situation—and so does every maturing adolescent. It is, in this case, more anxiety producing and needs more support, but the process is not inherently different.

Conclusion

In this paper, I have endeavoured to produce a Gestalt theory of transference and countertransference consistent with our approach based on field theory, phenomenology, and attention to the present moment. I have distinguished between defensive and expressive aspects of the experience usually described as transferential, and proposed that neither of them benefits from being understood as a regression to childhood. I have described ways of envisaging the work with each of these aspects. I have proposed a mechanism from Gestalt psychology to account for the phenomenon of "projective identification".

CHAPTER ELEVEN

Gestalt and regression*

Once again, I am exploring territory opened up by psychoanalytic thinking, and wondering what it might become from a Gestalt perspective. I was aware, in writing this piece, that "regression" has taken on many different meanings in different approaches: "reparenting", "past life regression", "inner child work", "hypnotic regression", etc. Some of these have justified very questionable or even abusive practices. I decided this was a minefield worth stepping into. It is also one where I received angry feedback from people who did not want me to allow any meaning to the term at all, having had bad experiences in their own therapy.

Introduction

A t the time of writing the first draft of this paper (30 September 1991), there was a controversy raging in the national media about "regression therapy". There was particular concern that there had been occurrences of abuse within this kind of therapy. At

---

*First published in 1993, in *British Gestalt Journal*, 2(2).

the same time, there are a number of different attitudes to the meaning, usefulness, therapeutic approach to, and even existence of, "regression" within the field of Gestalt therapy. This paper is intended to give my particular perspective on the subject. I will argue that "regression" can mean a number of different things, some of them wholly alien to the theory and spirit of Gestalt, some of them therapeutically invalid. However, there are ways of seeing regressive phenomena that fit well with the Gestalt theoretical and clinical approach.

Part of the problem is that "regression" has been defined in many different ways since Freud's first definition (1916–1917): ". . . a return to the first objects invested with libido, which we know to be incestuous in character, and a return of the whole sexual organization to earlier stages". Lewin (1951) differentiates "regression" and "retrogression", defining the former as "The return to a type of behaviour characteristic of a previous stage of the life history of the individual"; and the latter as "A change to a more primitive behaviour, regardless of whether such behaviour has actually occurred within the life history of the individual". Stern (1985) makes the distinction between *observed* developmental processes in children, and clinically *reconstructed* developmental processes, theorised to underlie the behaviour of adults seen in psychotherapy. Clarkson (1992) sees "the developmentally needed relationship" as one of the useful types of therapeutic relationship. Schiff and Day (1970) base their work with schizophrenics on a radical and controversial approach to "reparenting", where the line between useful therapy and abuse is difficult to draw. Unfortunately, it is quite easy for Gestalt psychotherapists to assume we all know what is meant by "regression", and use the term without having a clear sense of what this would mean from a Gestalt (i.e., a present-centred, relational) perspective, and, therefore, to follow a therapeutic path which is at variance with their general theoretical perspective.

My own understanding of "regression" from the point of view of Gestalt therapy is that the client enters therapy still enacting a *fixed gestalt* from childhood. In the *safe emergency* of the psychotherapeutic encounter, two things happen: the client, who has *introjected* his/her parent figures, *projects* this half of the internalised interaction onto the therapist, while playing the other (child) half; at the same time, the client has decided to *trust* the therapist to the extent of showing his/her vulnerability and fear, even to the extent of allowing the therapist the power to reenact the traumas of childhood with them. So, in both these ways, the client's actions are based on the encounter with the therapist. At the same time, a third event can happen. By the client's *projective identification*, the therapist can find him/herself *becoming* one of the sides of this drama: either a parent, as actually experienced by the client (abusing, over-protecting, discounting), or the client's fantasied ideal parent (nurturing, ever-present); or the child (abused, helpless, anxious, angry).

Thus, there is no real distinction between "regressive work" and other aspects of Gestalt work with clients. The client brings inner conflicts, and conflicts between his/her ways of perceiving and contacting the world and the demands of the present environment. These conflicts are externalised in dialogue and through experiment, so that the client finds some completion of "unfinished business".

Clinically, the question for therapists is whether to work with the client in that regressed state directly or whether to "call back" some more adult functioning. For example, in a psychotherapy session, the client curls up, looking like a very frightened child. Do I provide an *experience* of holding that the client missed as an infant? Do I act as *witness* to his fear and sense of abandonment? Do I *remind* the client that s/he is now an adult, and has wider resources available, checking out how she continues to replay that remembered abandonment in her adult life and what s/he might believe s/he gains from this? The first of these I would understand as an *experiment* in awareness, the other two as essentially a *dialogic* approach.

Different Gestaltists have preferences for each of these approaches. Certainly, Fritz Perls did not work with clients who went into a "regressed state" in any way that could be called regressive, and made the centre point of his work the idea of *self-support*. A central concept here would be the *fixed Gestalt*: the client would be seen as hanging on to "unfinished business" from infancy and childhood via a process of introjection and projection, hoping to resolve it in the present. The aim of Gestalt therapy would be to confront the fixed Gestalt, and, in the "safe emergency" of the therapeutic encounter, to use the here-and-now resources available to close the Gestalt, and give up the quest for the unattainable.

Some Gestaltists believe that this process is not always possible for clients. In Marcus (1979, p. 87), John Stevens takes a footnote to protest that the author has written about playing the "ideal nurturing parent" for a client, saying that he "is putting the responsibility on someone else and . . . not staying with the bad situation till she deals with it fully". The author replies that in her present psychological state (experiencing herself as a scared eight-year-old) she is not able to get past the impasse directly.

The question of how to understand and work with regression is also linked to the different views within the Gestalt community about whether a developmental theory is needed, or even useful, since part of the aim of "regressive therapy" is to enact important developmental stages that might have been missed out on or failed in during the client's infancy or childhood. Examples could be: to provide an experience of safe physical contact to someone who has never experienced it; to provide boundary-setting for someone whose childhood was unbounded and chaotic; to provide protection from potentially dangerous situations where the client's experience was of being in danger and unprotected.

Another important strand for me is the latest research about "state-dependent memory, learning, and behaviour" (SDMLB) (see Rossi, 1986). This shows that memory is intimately linked with a person's psychophysical state at the time of the event to be remembered. Thus, for example, if I experience something when I am drunk, I am less likely to be able to remember it sober, and more likely to be able to remember it if I become drunk again. Similarly, if I experience an event in a very stressful state (which is likely if an event is a traumatic experience of, for example, violence in childhood), that memory will be associated with the stressful state, and will begin to be evoked by stress. Conversely, when remembered, stress similar to the stress of the original event will be experienced as part of the memory. Under this approach, regression is about accessing a particular *state-bound* memory–behaviour pattern, associated with childhood experience. This fits well with a Gestalt holistic approach to memory.

So, with a client, I am faced with the situation that s/he moves into what I perceive as a stressful, state-dependent memory of childhood. My understanding of the aetiology of this is that the client is experiencing a demanding memory of some hurt, of a time when some event or series of events altered the child's sense of the world, which s/he nevertheless fears to allow fully into awareness. Furthermore, it is central to my understanding of Gestalt therapy that this SDMLB state is evoked *in the context of* the client's here-and-now contact with his/her environment: specifically, hopes and fears in her/his relationship with me as therapist and potentially significant other. In these circumstances, I bear in mind the great advantage of Gestalt over many other approaches: that we can work both with the impulse to remember and the impulse to repress, and we work with both in the context of the *dialogic encounter* with the therapist. We know that these two impulses are being acted out in the here-and-now therapy situation. We are not limited to "bringing the memory out". Thus, we are a long way away from an approach based on "regress the client to the traumatic situation and then reparent them". In fact, it seems to me rare that single scenes traumatise the child; rather, the *gestalt* of a number of scenes, each confirming a particular understanding of the world, are symbolised by a particular event. Even a particularly painful scene, such as physical or sexual abuse, is remembered in the context of whether the child felt able to talk to parents, whether the parents took protective action, whether the child has been taught to accept violence as their due, and so on.

How does my work relate to methods that can be seen as "regressive" or "reparenting"? The most important clinical distinction for me is between (1) the client's "acting out" a role—clinging, tantrum, "not fair", naughtiness, adolescent sexuality—in contact with me, and (2) the much more difficult situation of a client caught in an inner nightmare of childhood, maybe projecting this on to me or group members, but without looking or otherwise making contact.

In the first situation, the client is re-enacting an incomplete Gestalt with me, in the *expectation* of a repetition of the childhood scene, and in the anxious *hope* that it will be different this time. In this situation, my responsibility as a therapist is to ensure a non-repetition, being sensitive to the number of skilled ways the client can encourage just such a repetition. There are certain polarities here that I find useful to think along, where either extreme of the polarity is limiting to the client in isolation from the other pole. One of the tasks of the therapist is to ensure a balance of the polarities from the list that follows, These are: over-bounded/insufficiently bounded; over-empathic/under-empathic; encouraging playfulness/encouraging seriousness; affirming sexuality/affirming there is more to the client than sexuality; that the client is safe with my power/that the client is safe if I refuse to run the show; the client is in a SDMLB pattern where words and verbal thinking about behaviour is possible/the pattern was established preverbally, and we must communicate all the above by voice tone, eye contact, careful touch, sensitivity to distance, and movement. This can look like "reparenting", but the assumptions are very different. I am not acting the parent and not seeing the client as an infant. I am responding *from myself*, flexibly, and in the knowledge that my task is to be sensitive to the possibility of repeating abusive or unbalanced patterns from the past (fixed gestalten). As in all Gestalt therapy, I have available the widest range of modes for contacting and communicating with clients who might have, at any moment, limited modes available to them.

So, to go back to the Marcus–Stevens controversy, I would not act the "ideal nurturing parent", but I might praise or hold a client if that warmth comes from me, *and* after checking out that this eliciting of praise and physical contact by distressed childlike behaviour is not the *precise* fixed Gestalt that I need to avoid. On the other hand, Stevens' concept of self-support seems to me to be insufficiently flexible to take into account clients whose fixed Gestalt *is* to support themselves, as they perceive environmental support to be unavailable or dangerous. My guess is that this isolationist approach to self-support was developed by Perls in response to his belief that the only safe way to live was to be radically self-supporting in this way.

The client out of contact

In this second situation, whatever is happening *internally* for the client, the contact between client and therapist is minimal or absent. The client might be sitting hunched up, silent, or projecting dislike on to the therapist or the group, not checking the projections because s/he can see the group/therapist in fantasy, and has lost the distinction between the fantasy and reality, inside and outside. At extremes, the client might be catatonic or autistic.

My understanding is that these clients are in *terror*, perceiving the world as so terrifying and/or painful that they shut themselves off from it, making, at most, the minimal contact to stay alive and healthy. This does not mean that they are necessarily perceived this way; their emotional disconnectedness or lability and their ability to work things out for themselves can be seen as positives and rewarded, so they can become computer programmers or actors, psychoanalysts or Gestalt therapists or counsellors, businessmen or artists. This way of being is very common, not just in clinical practice, but in psychotherapy and counselling training groups. The work of Lasch (1979) is based on the assumption that these narcissistic and borderline manifestations are as central to our society today as hysterical manifestations were to Freud's time. This fits with my clinical experience. In fact, it does represent a good first step when the therapist recognises that this terror is there, and develops sufficient contact that the client is willing to show his/her terror.

So now what? The client has put me in a tricky double-bind. If the door is shut, I can either wait until it opens, knock, or push my way in. Gendlin (in Rogers and Stevens, 1973) demonstrates the waiting approach beautifully—standing in virtual silence with a schizo-phrenic man twice a week for nearly six months—while Schiff and Day (1970) push in with their radical re-parenting approach. The double-bind for therapists is that the client would often perceive both waiting and knocking as invasions or demands. I believe that some aspects of all three approaches are, at times, necessary, and the choice of which to take demands of the therapist very fine judgement, good contact skills, and awareness of countertransference issues around power, abuse, pain, and infancy. Once again, I would not role-play a parent with these clients: they need to meet me in *reality*.

Situations where primarily I wait

When the client remains passive, slowly checking me out, not pulling further and further in or acting self-destructively, then I am willing to wait, and have waited, for years. What then often happens is that I become the focus for the out-of-contact behaviour, and while the client continues to sit silently with me for long periods, s/he finds her/his contact improving in everyday life. As the client slowly allows the possibility that I will not repeat past hurts to percolate, we will make slow progress towards contact, with many episodes of the client pulling back. From a Gestalt perspective, I would see these episodes very positively, as my understanding would be that, in each case, the client would be checking out and working through different fears, and integrating different state-dependent Gestalten. From my own part, I negotiate with the client that I will not guarantee to keep looking and interested when they are showing me nothing for long periods, so that I will look out of the window, think my own thoughts, and if they want contact I will be there. This saves me from having to pretend to keep interested in a situation where nothing of interest to me is happening most of the time.

Situations where primarily I knock

I do this in two situations. First, where the client is rather less terrified than the ones I wait with, so that they can respond to a knock and still keep thinking. I knock by telling clients that I am guessing they are holding in large aspects of themselves (with evidence from their behaviour), that to show these aspects may be frightening for them, but that I am here and available if they want to show them, and they are safe to do that here.

The other situation where I knock is where my sense is that I will end up pushing. My knock then is more a minimal push to check if the door really is locked. My knock here may take the form, "Where do we go from here? What do you want from me? I am here with you and yet I see you pull away inside. I'm not sure you even see me— maybe you are putting someone else's character on to me." It is hoped that this is enough to start making contact.

Situations where primarily I push

This is the most difficult and demanding, and the one where the dividing line with abuse is most shaky. I would only go into this work if a number of conditions are met:

1. A client has a support network available or has built one up with my help.
2. My client will be more terrified by what they project on to my waiting or knocking than by the reality of my pushing.
3. I am not in angry or impatient countertransference with the client. To prevent this, if the other conditions are met, I would rather push early than later.

4. Postponing this work until the client has learnt more contact skills is not a feasible option: likelihood of suicide, severe self-harm by active self-injury or by neglect/self-starvation, etc., severe damage to others, especially children (and here hospitalisation is another option, but is also going to be seen by the client as abusive or invasive), clients where the pulling-in has turned into or contributed to a major physical problem: multiple sclerosis, colitis, heart disease, asthma (although here, again, pushing has its own dangers, and maybe learning biofeedback or doing Tai Ch'i would be a better initial approach: I am talking about a progressively worsening condition, where, on balance, conservative measures would be more dangerous than the risks of intervention).

5. I have sufficient knowledge of the client to be able to assess that contact is likely to be achievable.

6. I have the grounding and energy available to work through to a contactful relationship.

7. I have good supervision available.

My push then might be (in a firm but not angry voice), "Hey, come out here, I want to talk to you. I'm not willing for you to use this therapy to hurt yourself, and I see you doing that by . . . I know it's frightening for you if I talk like this, but I am also pretty sure that the reality of me is much less frightening and dangerous than your fantasies of me and others. I want you to think about what I'm saying and to respond, because my bottom line is that what is happening between us now is harmful to you, and I respect you too much to allow it to continue. I'm not willing to drop this for the same reason. We must get out of this trap or end the therapy." I might not need to say all of this, of course, and would not say it as one continuous monologue, but would provide time to get my client's reactions, verbal or non-verbal. Sometimes the client will open up more, sometimes we' will end therapy: I, personally, am not prepared to say, "You must continue", although I might say in other circumstances that I think it would be a bad idea to stop. Sometimes the client chooses to continue with, say, a woman therapist.

Whichever of these approaches I choose, it seems to me vitally important that I am clear that I am not a parent but a therapist, that my time with my client is limited, that when I finish a session my client is not asleep in a cot but going out into a world in which s/he has lived for many years. This is all reality as well.

The ethical dilemma

There is one more thing to be said: there are some people who would not cope with the world, who would normally spend their lives in and out of institutions, continually drugged. If they were sent to a therapeutic community, made to undergo "re-parenting", and it could be shown by independent research that this could well mean that they could function in the outside world without drugs, then what? I think I would still not want to work in that way, wanting to keep firmer boundaries on consent. But, given that the lives of many schizophrenics are full of experiences of coercion, I am aware that something could be lost if no one did the work. It could be too easy to produce a quick defensive reaction, "No ethical therapist could work like that." Can we produce a psychotherapeutic equivalent to the cytologist's decision to give chemotherapy that is more likely to cure and less likely to kill a patient than cancer, or a surgeon's decision to operate under the same circumstances? I have no replies, just a mistrust of easy answers.

Conclusion

Gestalt therapy, with its concepts of fixed Gestalten, Gestalt completion, the primacy of contact and awareness in therapy, and the emphasis on the real person of the therapist, allows for a number of fine distinctions to be made which are not possible in other psychotherapies with a less flexible range of options for the therapist. One major distinction is that while the therapist might be *seen* by the client as a parental figure, the therapists keeps a sense of the *reality* that s/he is not a parent, but a therapist. The lack of here-and-now reality testing and the potentially demanding transferences, countertransferences, and projective identifications are important enough in these situations that the therapist needs to keep this perspective in mind.

CHAPTER TWELVE

Notes for a book on the id

This is an unpublished fragment of a book I never wrote! Many years ago, I read the original Book of the It (Groddeck, 1949), which so strongly influenced Freud's view of the unconscious, and found it fascinating, sometimes thought-provoking and sometimes mad (and sometimes both). I enjoyed Groddeck's free-wheeling, unstructured approach in a series of letters (signed, for some reason, "Patrik Troll"). I thought that I would like to do a Gestalt version of the book, rambling and edging into taboo areas, but did not get very far. I think there are some interesting ideas in this fragment.

"I assume that man is animated by the It, which directs what he does and what he goes through, and that the assertion 'I live' only expresses a small and superficial part of the total experience 'I am lived by the It'"

(Groddeck, 1949, p. 11).

"What a toilsome business it is to speak about the It. One plucks a string at hazard, and there comes the response, not of a single note but of many, confusedly mingling and dying away again,

or else awakening new echoes, and ever new again, until such
an ungoverned medley of sounds is raging that the stammer of
speech is lost"

(ibid., p. 26)

This book is my confused mingling of many echoes: things I have
noticed in fifty-one years of being a human being and eighteen
years of being a Gestalt therapist; things I have thought about
while writing *Self in Relation*, discussions I have had about therapy
and philosophy since the publication of that book, and my continuing
reading and thinking in the field.

Fortunately for me, and maybe also for you, the reader, this is a
very different book to the other one. There, I was trying to be as coherent as possible, to make as much sense as possible, and to back up
what I am saying with accurate referencing. Here, I am trying to point
to something, and to use my reading as Fritz Perls used it, for the sake
of the echoes it raises in me rather than as a faithful record of the other
person's views.

Rather than adopting the original format that Groddeck used,
letters to a friend, I shall start with a theme, and follow the echoes
wherever they lead me.

No-self

Mostly, this is a book of balancing: my last book was about the Self,
this one is about no-self. However, in this introduction I need to talk
about Self to give any sort of sense of what I mean by "no-self". For
this is a curious project; in fact, an impossible one for a world-view
where Self is a continuing agent: nothing is just done—there is always
an "I" doing it, and every "I" is separate from every other "I". Every
verb in English has a subject, and, just as the subject can move
between different verbs, the "I" (the soul or spirit, the essence of a
person) can be understood to move between different bodies, and still
be the same "I".

Gestalt Therapy views self in a very different way, and this was
the subject of *Self in Relation*. Put simply, there are two kinds of words:
words that have, more or less, an object they refer to (such as table,

computer), and words that are comparisons and only have meaning in relation to an opposite (such as big, small; light, dark). Gestalt therapy says that "self" is the second kind of word, only having meaning in relation to "other", so it can only be the ongoing emergence of self and other that we engage with. "I" (and "other") coalesce round experience rather than experience coalescing round an "I". (This position is now very much accepted among modern researchers in infant development, for example, Daniel Stern, and in neuropsychology, for example, Antonio Damasio.) Thus, it is meaningful to explore the world of experiencing without a prior "I" to experience it. (I am going to drop the quote marks round "I" from now on, except where they are needed to make sense of the text, distinguishing discussion of self from talking about myself.)

Chaos and complexity

It is important here to make a distinction. For Groddeck, "I live" is an illusion of agency, and the reality is the play of the It. This is not the position I take, although it is a position taken by some of my critics, for example, Jacobs (2003), in her review of the book. For these critics, my approach is "individualistic", with its therapeutic emphasis on differentiation and choice. Yet, there is a set of assumptions here which were, in the past, taken as self-evident, but are now known to be wrong: that if the I emerges from the It (which I agree to), then the I is *reducible* to the It, the It is real and the I is illusory.

However, let us consider a system much simpler than a human being: a running car engine. Now it is clear that the "life" of this system emerges from the engine. Yet, it is not inherent in the parts of the engine: neither the carburettor, the cylinders, the distributor, nor the camshaft make it run. Neither is it inherent in the putting together of the parts: all the parts are present in my car, yet it is not currently running. We could say that the running engine is one of the *states* of the engine, and that the parts are engineered so that this state can be started, stopped, and maintained.

Let us go a stage further. Since it is the running state that is wanted, not the engine, once the running has been achieved, the physical engine becomes secondary to the running state. If a part wears out and cannot carry out its function in allowing the engine to run, it is replaced, or its form is altered (e.g., adjusting the points) to keep the car running. We could even imagine a time in the future when *all* the parts have been changed but the running state remains. So, is the running state an illusion? Well, if you take a purely materialist view that things only exist if they have dimensions and weight, then you can say that the running state does not exist, it is an illusion caused by the engine. On any other reading, something that can be harnessed to take me across the world, or that can propel a car into me and kill me, must be granted a reality. In fact, it is the primary reality, to which all the other parts of the engine must give way. The running state determines the shape, size, weight, and material of the engine parts, whether they stay or whether they are replaced.

Then, in order to run a car, you need roads and traffic laws, driving technique and driving lessons. Once again, though these are not in conflict with the physics of the engine, they cannot be derived from the parts or from viewing a car with its engine not running.

In the same way, while self and other arise out of a field, it does not mean that self is an illusion. It can act to change the field, can make unexpected choices, however hostile the field is to such choices, and it is governed by laws and patterns which, while not in conflict with patterns of the field, are not predictable from the field.

This kind of understanding is the perspective of chaos theory (Gleick, 1987) and complexity theory (Lewin, 1993; Waldrop, 1993). The most exciting perspective to arise out of these disciplines is the idea coined by Stuart Kauffman (quoted in Lewin, 1993, p. 28) of "the crystallisation of order out of massively disordered systems. It's order for free". If a system is at the "edge of chaos" (Kauffman again), but with lots of feedback possibilities, then order spontaneously arises in the system.

An initial look at properties of the field

What can we say about a field from which selfhood can emerge as a spontaneous order? I want to look at some very basic properties at this point. And I want to start very far back in history, to the Big Bang, where the universe came into being. From the perspective I am using in this book, this could be seen as a spontaneous state-shift to a new form. Scientists have raised the question of *symmetry breaking*. If I explode a bomb, different parts of the bomb will move in different directions at different speeds, as the air currents they encounter, the collisions between different bits, would vary. At the Big Bang, none of these varying environments existed, so you could expect the matter emerging to come out symmetrically. Yet, the universe we know is not symmetrical. More than this, it is one in which clumps of matter with shapes arise: stars, planets, trees, animals, people.

Back to no-self

The reason I want to go into this theory here is that it clarifies what I am trying to do in this book, which distinguishes it from the last one. In *Self in Relation*, I looked at the emergence of self from the field, and the meaning of the individual in a field understanding. In this book, I want to explore the characteristics of the field that allow it to be the "engine" from which self emerges. I want to look at patterns of field relatedness in which people participate, rather than at the people who do the participating. If you put a piece of paper on top of a magnet and then sprinkle iron filings on the paper, you will see a pattern formed by the iron filings that follows the contours of the magnetic field. If you turn the magnet, the filings organise themselves into four separate circles of movement. So, while we might be looking at the iron filings, or the people, it is the contours of the field that we are looking for here.

I try to find a middle path between saying that everything is biologically or culturally determined, and that choice is an illusion, and saying that I can be whatever I want to be if I act right, so that chance is an illusion. For me, choice can only appear at the edge of chaos, but where the chaos is accompanied by feedback loops. However, simple feedback loops can support very rich patterns. We will find that the same developmental, evolutionary, and cultural patterns are used in a variety of different ways: in the family, in politics, in the workplace, and elsewhere. The same magnetic field animates all four circles of filings.

I take as basic that, somewhere in the evolutionary past of human beings, a new factor emerged: the ability to separate oneself from the field, observe it, and make meaningful choices about how the person wanted the field to be and how to act to achieve this. Further, these choice-making human beings are significant players in the development of the field around them. I am not going to try to prove this assertion. I realise that there is a more mechanistic way of seeing this: that the sense of choice is an illusion; my actions are determined by the field as a whole, and what I believe is a choice is not, in fact, in my ability to change. There is no way to disprove this. I will just point out that it would be ridiculous to try to prove this to be true, since the act of proving it and people's responses to the proof would lack any significance!

It is important to note that, although I am basing a lot of human capacities on these comparatively simple patterns, I am also trying to avoid being reductionist. That is, I am not trying to say that these patterns *cause* the capacities. The magnet does not cause the patterns: there is something also about the iron filings, and even the paper. Change the nature of any of these (e.g., use aluminium filings or emery paper), and the pattern either would not happen, or be different.

This is a controversial and difficult area, with many pitfalls. It is inevitable that I will see or project those patterns that fit my beliefs or blind spots. I could easily ignore the effect of my own and my clients' culture on the patterns I see, though there are advantages to the fact that my family of origin are immigrants to the UK (so my cultural environment inside and outside the home were different), and that I also work with people from many countries. However, I hope there is something here to get you thinking, and maybe clarify for yourself what you believe, whether it is what I believe or not.

Threads: Stockholm syndrome, religion, attachment

Human beings are social animals. Our being is bound up with family, tribe, and culture. Our evolutionary history is not that of solitary hunters, like the cat family, though we can act in this way also, especially (and paradoxically) if there is a cultural and social valuing of such individuality. Yet, we also take individual initiatives, and separate ourselves at times from our social milieu. In this chapter, I will speculate on the factors that lead to both identification and alienation. I hope that this will help to clarify the perspective I am playing with, of general patterns and feedback loops that support the action of the individual in a variety of different ways.

The first thing that I want us to notice is that human beings are born very physically underdeveloped (we have to be, or our large heads and brains would not be able to travel through the birth canal). For a very long period, we cannot walk, run, hide, clean ourselves, find our own food. We are reliant on carers for our survival, in a way and for a period that is well beyond that of other mammals. And carers also have an evolutionary drive towards caring for children, or the human species would not survive.

But notice, here, there are two seemingly different stories. There is a story of attachment as a survival trait, a necessary evolutionary adaptation to larger brains and their effect on the birth process. Then there is the psychological story about attachment, bonding, love between mother and child. Can they be seen as aspects of the same story?

I have been thinking about the Stockholm syndrome. This occurs in the situation where someone is kidnapped or taken hostage, and, over time, comes to identify totally with the kidnapper or hostage taker. The most famous example occurred when Patti Hearst, the daughter of an American newspaper magnate, was kidnapped by the Symbionese Liberation Army. She soon progressed from hostage to participant in their actions, including a bank raid where she was photographed.

The pattern seems to be that people come to identify with, and surrender themselves to, and even come to love, someone on whom their life depends, who is seen as willing to make that choice either way, and who demands compliance in return for keeping the person alive, and, in fact, can be quite benevolent if the person is compliant. This makes sense: any expression of separateness is seen (by both captor and captive) as life threatening to the captive.

It seems to me that this response brings together the two stories. In infancy, the dependency will trigger the attachment. Where this goes well, the attachment is both ways. The infant and the parent both feel the loving intimacy that keeps the child protected and nurtured. In the tribe, as in other mammal groupings, the member attaches to the leader, while the leader feels responsibility for the members. When the parent or leader cannot fulfil their function, a different pattern is triggered, which I shall explore later. At the moment, I want to stay with the patterns round a powerful, vital, but dangerous leader or parent, and the powerful feelings of dependency felt towards such a person.

For this triggering of deep feelings leads to very dangerous possibilities. If it is a standard human response to a particular kind of situation, then it is a very useful way of manipulating people, whether knowingly or unknowingly. We can see elements of this in many totalitarian political situations, with personality cults based round a leader who is loved and feared, and who does not have the inhibitions about protecting and nurturing the follower that a parent usually has for a child.

In the personal arena, it is common to see relationships where the man is violent towards the woman, and the woman comes to feel intense love for, and attachment to, the man, including, significantly, the thought "I can't live without him". Norwood (1989) has coined the term "women who love too much" for this situation.

The same behaviour can be found in cults, where the leader also adopts such a combination of benevolence and love, on the one hand, and punitiveness for any independent thinking or action, on the other.

Unfortunately, this does not only happen in cults. It is very common for religions to say that their god loves those whom they have created, and yet will damn to eternal punishment those who do not do as they say. In such a religion, people will experience a loving and faithful attachment to the god, irrespective of the existence or benevolence of the god. In fact, the more powerful and potentially threatening the god is, the more love the followers will experience. The hellfire-and-damnation people have got their psychology right! (I am not arguing here for or against the existence of a god. I am saying that the powerful emotional responses experienced in fundamentalist religions can be explained by, and are even expectable from, a normal developmental response, and are nothing to do with the actions of a god.)

Religions that act in this way are likely to get recruits from two sources. They either come from families or cultures where the existence of such a god is taken for granted, and is passed to all the children from an early age, or they are looking for someone or something to be dependent on, and are vulnerable to those who offer this dependency. It does not seem to me that it is often both: in a stable, ordered society, people might accept the culturally supported religion, but do not usually look for religion. It is important to notice here that the theology of such a religion does not need to be simplistic, or to require such primitive dependency: the primitive response is inherent in the situation. This often happens with cults, whose leaders can start off well meaning and providing an experience that is quite positive for their followers. They are then faced with the massed attachment response from their followers, and, usually, things go from bad to worse.

For there is also danger from the other side of the fence. The attachment response in the carer is also triggered in situations of dependency. Rutter (1990) has written about the strong temptation of powerful figures (therapists, teachers, priests, etc.) to break sexual boundaries. But where *is* this powerful emotional urge to go between two adults? The powerful are emotionally vulnerable to the display of dependency by the powerless. Unless they are aware of this, and have a number of different kinds of support, professional, personal, and cognitive, it is very easy to fall into accepting the dependency fantasies of clients and followers.

Even within families, there are powerful sexual urges to be dealt with. It is a common experience, for example, that brothers and sisters (and other close relatives) brought up separately, when they meet, get involved with each other sexually. They recognise their kinship on a level of smell, appearance, ways of movement, and other similarities, and this is a very powerful pull. It is as if one of the tasks of the attraction is to hold the family together, and one of the tasks of the family dynamic is to discourage such pairings. So, it is developmentally important, for example, that brothers and sisters annoy each other!

We are here getting close to the other side of the coin: the inbuilt developmental, evolutionary, and cultural factors that counter the closeness. Let us look at the situation in the wolf pack or the primitive tribe when the leader, often through old age, no longer exercises the powerful role he (usually a he) used to exercise. In this situation, a challenge arises from another pack or tribe member. There is a conflict, which might involve the death of the old leader, or of the challenger if he has misjudged the powerlessness of his opponent. Either way, the one who is leader at the end of the challenge has publicly shown some power and dangerousness, and so the role of the powerful leader can continue.

Look at the similar pattern in the family. As the child gets older, there comes a time when the power of the parents over the children reduces as the child becomes older, bigger, and less dependent. The child then challenges the parents: same basic pattern, different outcome. Usually the outcome is for the child-becoming-adult to form its own family, replacing the parent as the new parent of children rather than directly defeating the parent. The defeat is built into the ageing of the parents, rather than having to be fought for. However, we can see shadows of the wolf-pack pattern in royal dynasties and family businesses, where there can be vicious battles between generations. We can also see families where the child has to fight to leave home against parents who will do anything to stop them leaving. Sometimes the child loses the fight, and ends up as an adult still dependent on, and resentful of, the parents.

CHAPTER THIRTEEN

On yelling and bashing cushions*

This article also comes out of my interest in the place of emotion in our actions, and in therapy. There was a lot of "bashing cushions" in 1993! I realised that I had never seen anyone change as a result of this kind of cathartic work. Somehow the (melo)drama of this way of working supported its continuation, though it was not an approach that fitted the original theory, which always emphasised that emotion was a means of orientation in the world and was not to be wasted in "discharge". I emphasise to trainees that, if there is to be drama in therapy, it has to be good drama of believable human characters, drama that you would want to see in the theatre, not melodrama with a wicked uncle twirling his moustache.

"Emotion, considered as the organism's direct evaluative experience of the organism/environment field, is not mediated by thoughts and verbal judgements, but is immediate. As such, it is a crucial regulator of action, for it not only furnishes the basis of awareness of what is important but it also energies

*First published in 1993, in *Topics in Gestalt Therapy*, 1(1).

appropriate action, or, if this is not at once available, it energies and directs the search for it"

(Perls, Hefferline, & Goodman, 1994, p. 343)

A stock image of Gestalt therapy (apart from talking to mother on an empty chair) is of someone doing "Anger work", that is, yelling and bashing cushions (YABC), maybe with the hands, maybe with a tennis racket or other implement. Somehow or other, this is connected with "discharging" emotion.

Compare this with Perls, Hefferline, and Goodman's description of emotion as a "gestalt of exteroceptions and proprioceptions" (ibid., p. 327), the "regulator" that moves us all the way from sensation to awareness to energisation to action, and their insistence that work with the emotions

> must employ a unitary method which concentrates *both* on orientation in the environment . . . and on loosening the motor blocks of the 'body'. Undue emphasis on either side can produce only pseudo-cures . . . if the therapist works with the 'body' alone, he may get the patient to simulate and express in the therapeutic session various feelings, but these, unfortunately, will not match up with or will be actually irrelevant to what he experiences his situation to be when he is away from the therapist. (ibid., p. 346)

In other words, the primary aim is *not* to facilitate the client to feel more relaxed or comfortable in the therapy session, but to enable the client to reconnect his/her emotional response with contact needs and wants from the environment, both in the therapy session and outside. This integration of the situation external to the client and the client's emotional response in turn leads to the client taking action in the external environment to change it. The work must, therefore, involve both attention to the variety of physical sensations, impulses, and tensions that the client experiences and produces, and to the field context of the client's interactions with the environment.

Enright (1980) has added another basic dimension to the emotional equation: *comparison*. To what do I compare my present experience? More pleasant or less pleasant experiences of my past, other people's more or less pleasant experience, a fantasy of the experience I "deserve"?

> The quality of experience in life depends less on what happens to you, than on what you compare it with. I often comment to clients . . . that if they want to feel consistently bad, just make sure they regularly compare 'what is' with something better; if they want to feel good, compare 'what is' with something worse. (ibid., p. 55)

In contrast, the discharge model comes from the early writings of Freud, for example, Breuer and Freud (1895d), and is based on what Freud called the *constancy principle*: that human beings seek for maximum quiescence and to avoid excitement, but that sometimes it is necessary to discharge stored-up affect in order to get back to that quiescent state. It is also implicit in the *drive theory*, where the environmental object of the drive is secondary to the energy dissipation of the drive itself. The associated clinical method of promoting abreaction of repressed affect later travelled, via Reich, into the body therapies, like bioenergetics. "Discharge of distress" is also an important part of the theory of co-counselling, and here the association with "distress" makes a further distinction: the emotion that is to be "discharged" is a "negative" emotion, which causes "distress". This is taken to be anger, fear, grief, but not joy, vitality, excitement, which are all regularly denied expression.

So, in keeping with our unitary method, we need also to avoid evaluating some emotions as "positive", some as "negative". Let us look at the meaning of the main emotional clusters in terms of energisation for action.

Joy: My response to my environmental contact is of attraction, wanting to deepen contact. My energy rises and flows to the boundary and out to meet the environment.

Sadness: Once again, my wish is to make contact with a part of the environment that attracts me, but here contact is not possible. The person I love has died, the opportunity is not available. My energy rises, flows to the boundary, and then outward in expression of grief or sadness, inward in communing with the memory or fantasy of the denied contact. Physiologically, unusable adrenalin is released in my tears.

Fear: Now the form of contact that is available to me is (or appears) dangerous to me. I energize, but that energy is to be used in my escape from the dangerous contact possibility.

Anger: Again, the form of contact is one I do not like, but I perceive the situation as different to the one where my primary emotional response is fear. Either I have a sense of commitment to the environment (a person I want to keep contact with, a mountain I want to climb) or I am in a position where I assess that I can neither run nor hide, so I need to find a resolution with the dangerous environment. In a way, my energy moves in a similar way to that of joy, outward to the environment and beyond, but the aim is, in some sense, to overpower the energy of the other and, thus, to neutralise the disliked contact: "I will not let you do that even if you want to".

This can be simplified (and slightly falsified) by saying: *joy* moves *towards* an *attractive* environment; *sadness* moves *away from* an *attractive* environment; *anger* moves *towards* an *unattractive* environment; *fear* moves *away from* an *unattractive* environment.

Of course, we often feel a range or mix of emotions. We can fear our anger, or enjoy a fight. We can project ourselves into a fantasy where we can experience emotions—both ours and other people's—without relating to the present environment. We can move rapidly from one emotion to another, for example, from love to hate.

Implications for Gestalt therapy

We need to get away from a conception of work with emotions as a "vomiting out" process (with the therapist as the sick bowl). If the pressure cooker is under pressure, we must help the client to explore the flame under the pressure cooker, and also the weight that prevents the steam emerging. Emotion can arise from present concerns, from "unfinished business" from the past that we are reliving in the present so as to try to complete it, from energy deflected from another emotion (men often deflect energy from sadness or fear to anger, women from anger to sadness), or from conditioned emotional responses learned from families ("I must look happy") or therapy ("I need to find something to be angry about and shout about it"). We need to arrive at understanding the client's conception of the world, the comparisons s/he is making, the expressive urge (the flame) and the repressive urge (the weight). By shuttling between them, a dialogue (either verbal or non-verbal) can take place, leading to resolution.

We need to ensure that the client has enough energy left for this resolution. This means that the energy expended in expressing emotion must not be so much as to exhaust the client. To return to the pressure cooker analogy: if we ignore the flame and suddenly remove the weight, pressure will be released explosively, along with most of the liquid in the cooker, and there will be insufficient left to do any more cooking!

We need to be clear what the client is learning about the world in experimenting with emotion, particularly anger. Is the *meaning* of anger with a work colleague or a parent really to energise us to smash somebody to pulp with fists or a blunt weapon? If somebody wanted to do that, I would at least want them to look at the pulped remnant in fantasy and explore what that is like for them. More likely, I would ask the client to explore what s/he is asking from this person, or, alternatively, to say "I have nothing more to say to you". I tell clients that to say "I am angry with you" is meaningless unless they add ". . . and I want of you . . .". It demands mind-reading ability on the part of the other person. Or, rather, the meaning is usually tactical: to put the other person off balance as they struggle to make sense of the anger. This is often useful to clients whose childhood experience (where they first learnt about anger) was precisely of this keeping off balance. I will also introduce what for me is the most exciting bit of the much maligned "Gestalt prayer": "You are not in this world to live up to my expectations". Much of therapy seems to me to be about telling parents how to live up to the grown-up child's expectations!

We also need to bear in mind that it is not unknown for people who are, or have been, in psychotherapy to kill or seriously injure other people. If someone talks to me about fear of anger or fear of love, I would want to know if they have injured people, and if so what were the circumstances. We must also consider our ethical and legal responsibilities: what if a client expresses anger in a psychotherapy session, then goes off and actually bludgeons someone to death? Has the therapist colluded with the client's equation of anger with violence or behaviour without concern for consequences?

Joy is also often repressed by a learnt comparison: "How can you be happy when everything is so awful/I'm so unhappy etc.?" It can even be redefined as a weapon, gloating at others' misfortune.

Fear can be repressed by fear of fear: "If I show my fear, it'll be used against me/I'll look unmanly, etc." Culturally, sadness is often repressed by fear of pain, because sadness is painful. If I deny my connection, I will avoid that pain. Many people become involved in Buddhism and meditation for that reason. Others adopt a shallow, uncontactful optimism. For me, sadness and pain are part of life, and worse pain is involved in avoiding them.

In all these situations, Gestalt therapy encourages us to explore both the expressive and the repressive energies, allowing for dialogue to develop across the splits, leading to resolution, not primarily intrapsychically, but via contact with the environment and, particularly, contact with the therapist. Sensing, feeling, thinking, and acting.

CHAPTER FOURTEEN

Gestalt therapy and Morita therapy*

This is an early paper, written when I was less critical of the "cycle of experience" model, so I would not have written it in quite the same way today. However, I think the perspective on emotion and action that comes from Morita therapy is a useful one, and it is good to look at connections between Western and Eastern psychological thought, especially a form that has historical connections with Gestalt therapy.

> "Neuroses may be quite subtle these days; they fail to respond to a process of sitting and talking about how we came to be the way we are. They come less from what we have hidden from ourselves than from what we know quite well about ourselves. They come from what we do and don't do as much as from the ways we think and feel. To be cured, these modern forms of suffering require being honest with ourselves not only in thought - but in behaviour, as well. Pulling oneself together is a difficult and demanding task in these times. A behavioural commitment is necessary. Insight alone is not enough"
>
> (Reynolds, 1985, pp. 11–12)

---

*First published in 1991, in *British Gestalt Journal*, 1(1).

Some time ago, I was browsing through Changes bookshop in London, where I discovered a book on Morita therapy (Reynolds, 1986). Being involved in the Japanese disciplines of Aikido and Zen, the idea of a Japanese psychotherapy intrigued me. This turned to excitement when I read on the back cover some principles of Morita therapy, which spoke loudly to me about what seemed to me to be missing in much Gestalt practice. I had long felt disturbed by some—as I see it—misconceptions within the Gestalt community about emotions, actions, and the relationship between them. Examples of the kind of remark I am reacting to are "What do you choose to feel?", and "Follow your feelings."

This paper is based on these principles:

- feelings are not controllable by our will;
- we have no responsibility for what we feel;
- but we are responsible for what we do no matter what we are feeling;
- we can accomplish many of our purposes in life in spite of our feelings;
- we must pay full attention to the details of the world around us, in order to determine the proper actions to take;
- every moment is a fresh one, we are all changeable;
- the real world responds only to our actions, not to our will or emotions.

Morita therapy is a Japanese form of psychotherapy, founded by Morita Shoma (in Japanese, the family name comes first) in around 1917. Morita was a psychiatrist, department head of a medical university in Tokyo. He was particularly influenced by Zen Buddhism and the work of Binswanger.

Morita saw his work not as medical therapy but as re-education. That re-education was to be aimed not at changing the past or the emotions, but at affecting the student's action in the world. Unlike much behaviourist therapy, however, Morita's aim was "a technique that would change the fundamental responses of his clients to everyday circumstances. It was not enough to work on the symptoms of the moment" (Reynolds, 1986, p. 83).

Students (not clients or patients) of Morita therapy undertake exercises to develop purposeful, aware action in the world. Energy is to be used in these externally directed activities rather than on trying to analyse inner problems or in feeling emotions unconnected with external reality.

The kind of exercises a Morita therapist could set include:

- keep a daily journal of feelings and actions;
- write letters of concern or gratitude;
- prepare meals;
- work in the garden;
- explore unfamiliar places or time-structuring;
- talk with someone;
- clean the streets in the neighbourhood;
- write a journal of the sounds you hear.

A person who is depressed could be asked to commit him/herself to getting out of bed on the first ring of the alarm clock, concentrating on which foot steps out first, how the floor feels to his/her feet, etc., thus avoiding the cycle of "I don't feel like doing anything", "It's not worth it", and suchlike internalised activities.

Interestingly enough, there has been quite a bit of crossover between Gestalt and Morita: Perls writes (1969b, p. 106) about his stay in a Morita hospital in Tokyo: "I stand it for two days, then throw a temper tantrum, run out and buy cigarettes". A recent book on Morita therapy (Reynolds, 1985) has a whole chapter on "Gestalt therapy parallels". The principles Reynolds sees underlying both Gestalt therapy and Morita therapy are: self-acceptance, paying attention to one's environment, emphasis on experiencing life rather than conceptualising, experiential learning, here-and-now focus, discrimination of reality from fantasy through contact, client responsibility for their process and the paradoxical futility of deliberate change.

My purpose is not to write a full statement of the theory and practice of Morita therapy (I suggest that you read Reynolds' books to find out more), but to explore how the principles underlying Morita therapy can usefully be assimilated into the Gestalt therapy framework, and, specifically, how these principles illuminate the place of action in the therapeutic process.

Gestalt and the principles of Morita therapy

I shall explore the principles stated above in the light of Gestalt theory and practice.

Feelings are not controllable by our will

In terms of the Gestalt cycle (Zinker, 1977), emotion is in the *energisation* phase, between awareness and action. We know from the work of the Gestalt psychologists that we organismically energise towards certain aspects of our environment: the novel, those that complete unfinished Gestalten, those that accord with our physical or psychological needs; we know from the work of Selye (in Rossi, 1986) of the psychobiological response to stressful situations: ready for fight or flight. Notice that in both examples, the feelings are our organismic energetic response towards or away from aspects of our environment—they are not chosen. Our feelings, and how we relate to these feelings, are essential clues to our understanding of our world and our place in it. However, we can get into a terrible twist if we do therapy to change feelings:

> *Therapist*: What is it you want right now?
> *Client*:   I want to be happy.

Morita therapy says that the above statement is meaningless: happiness is an organismic *response*, not an action. To work towards being happy actually prevents us from reaching out to the environment in ways that would make for happiness. A Morita response to the above client might be "How does your tea taste?"

We have no responsibility for what we feel

From a Gestalt perspective, this is only half true. In a direct sense, it is true that, as I have said above, feelings are a response rather than a chosen action. However, we know that on the Gestalt cycle, energisation follows withdrawal, sensation, and awareness. If we do not withdraw effectively from organismically completed tasks, we dissipate energy available for emotion into uncentred, uncontactful actions. If we deny ourselves sensations (either from the environment or from our internal sensors) or the awareness of such sensations, we will not feel emotions based on these emotions or awarenesses (as in depression). We can also retroflect the emotions at the point where we begin to experience them. Our emotions are also, as Enright (1980) points out, based on *comparison*: whether they compare the present moment to something better or something worse. However, the basic point of the principle is accurate: our feelings can be changed, but the point of choice, and, therefore, responsibility, is elsewhere, in our relation to our external environment.

Client: I feel murderously angry towards my father. I know that's wrong and feel guilty.

Therapist: (Getting beyond the feelings of rage and guilt.) What is it you actually experience? What do you want to say to your father? What would I see you do if your father was here right now?

And where does responsibility come in? Read on!

We are responsible for what we do no matter what we are feeling

This is the heart of it. Morita makes a strict separation between *what we feel* and *what we do*. Yes, on the Gestalt cycle, action is based on energisation/emotion. However, the energisation stage and the action stage are separate, and the energisation stage is itself based on the awareness stage via other factors that affect how we move from awareness to energisation to action.

Comparison: As I mentioned above, our reaction to a situation depends to a great extent on what we compare it with, so that the same "stimulus" will produce a different "response" in different people, or the same person in different situations.

Discrimination: A word much used by the Polsters (1974), and that they identify with the infant's development of the ability to chew. In particular, they speak about the fear of madness: "The fulcrum discrimination to be made is whether the fear is mere anachronism or whether it is tuned to the present chanciness" (Polster & Polster, 1974, p. 203). I would particularly place discrimination as a stage between energisation and action on the Gestalt cycle, to clarify that there is a need to *contextualise* any awareness and emotion: is this to do with an *external process* (e.g., someone is acting in an obnoxious fashion, so I want to move away from them) or an *internal process* (they remind me of my father/I don't want contact with anyone today/etc.)? Depending on the discrimination I make, my action will be different. Similarly, is what I am aware of something nourishing that I want to mobilize *towards*, or something noxious that I want to mobilize *away from*?

The particular client group I am thinking of in discussing this are the *Women Who Love Too Much* (Norwood, 1989), and all the women and men who act similarly, some of them labelled multi-impulsive or borderline personality disorder (American Psychiatric Association, 1987). The central thinking disorder/introject here is "To feel is to do". If I feel an attraction to someone, not only must I act on it, but the action is *part of* the feeling. Three days ago, I read, in a pamphlet on "Co-counselling and sexuality", "I have a right to act on my feelings". This unconsidered statement is also often heard in Gestalt therapy under the heading "Be spontaneous". It is, of course, the rallying cry of child abusers and unethical therapists throughout the ages, as well as of women (and men) who regularly get into destructive relationships.

> I went back late that night. Dr. Noren asked me this very well-thought-out question about whether I would like to go to bed with him. He presented it purely as a matter of choice for me. It had been absolutely the last thing in my mind, but I had no objection when he brought it up. In fact, I was very flattered and thought this was a wonderful idea. *So* we slept together on the spot. (Rutter, 1990, p. 122, my italics)

To people with the introject "To feel is to do", the statement "Whatever we *feel*, we have full choice about what we *do*" comes as a welcome relief: the only choices they have usually given themselves are to feel and to act immediately on the feeling, or to suppress the feeling in order to suppress the action. Instead, they could accept their emotions and fantasies, knowing that they can still make appropriate choices in their actions.

> Because (Mary) is working on taking care of herself . . . when it began to get late and Tom hadn't come home, instead of allowing herself to get nervous and worked up about it, she called a friend in her support group. They talked about her mounting fear, which helped to calm her. Mary needed someone to hear how she felt, and her friend listened with understanding but without giving advice. (Norwood, 1989, p. 219)

We must pay full attention to the details of the world around us, in order to determine the proper actions to take

The Gestalt therapy concept of human psychological development is that it is always a function of biological maturation, environmental influences, interaction of the individual and the environment, and creative adjustment by the unique individual. In Freud's drive theory, the emphasis was only on the biological factors and there was a very negative viewpoint on the human potential for growing. (Yontef, 1988b, pp. 20–21)

In order to resolve the sort of issues I presented above, we need to be very conscious/discriminating about what belongs in our intrapsychic processes and what belongs in our dealings with our environment. For example, to feel frightened to speak is an internal event; to say to someone "I feel frightened when I speak to you" is an interaction with my environment. It has been cogently argued (Lasch, 1979, 1985) that the mixing up of these two areas is the central issue for our time, both psychologically and socially:

Even when therapists speak of the need for "meaning" and "love", they define love and meaning simply as the fulfillment of the patient's emotional requirements. It hardly occurs to them—nor is there any reason why it should, given the nature of the therapeutic enterprise— to encourage the subject to subordinate his needs and interests to those of others, to someone or some cause or tradition outside himself. "Love" as self-sacrifice or self-abasement, "meaning" as submission to a higher loyalty—these sublimations strike the therapeutic sensibility as intolerably oppressive, offensive to common sense and injurious to personal health and well being. To liberate humanity from such outmoded ideas of love and duty has become the mission of the post-Freudian therapies and particularly of their converts and popularizers, for whom mental health means the overthrow of inhibitions and the immediate gratification of every impulse. (Lasch, 1979, p. 13)

One of the first Gestalt "exercises" I learnt in my training was the version of the awareness continuum, where I alternate awarenesses, first from internal processes, then from external sensing. When Gestalt therapy is viewed in its original sense, as an exploration of the action of the contact boundary in the person/environment field, we have a therapeutic approach which is exactly right for working with this lack of discrimination between internalised activity and contactful activity.

Morita therapy, as usual, puts this very succinctly: "We must pay full attention to the details of the world around us, in order to determine the proper actions to take". We must make sure we are seeing, hearing, communicating, touching as well as feeling, rather than acting from an isolationist sense of self. Otherwise, our actions can never lead to full contact, but to a repetition of previous disappointments and hurts.

*We can accomplish many of our purposes in life
in spite of our feelings*

Morita therapy is less radical in a sense than Gestalt therapy:

> Perls' solution to the tendency to run from pain seems rather Western, bold, and even counterphobic. He recommends diving into the troublesome dilemma. I am not sure that such an aggressive approach is always necessary. Moritists share with the Gestaltists the opinion that avoiding and fleeing from symptoms only leads to increased difficulties. However, acceptance of myself along with my limitations is sufficient to permit facing unpleasant feelings. So, rather than telling sufferers to rush headlong into distress, Moritist guides suggest doing what can be done to alleviate the circumstantial pressures that cause discomfort. We believe that acceptance and realistic action are sufficient, without attacking the dragon, as Perls advises. (Reynolds, 1985, p. 78)

While Gestalt therapy has something extra to contribute to this discussion in terms of entering the implosive layer and working through the impasse, we should also bear in mind what Reynolds is saying here. True working through can only occur on the basis of *acceptance*. The paradox is that, for many people, entering psychotherapy is based on non-acceptance, even active dislike, of themselves. These are the people who will quickly switch from pain avoidance to pain seeking, and use the pain of working through as a penance for their shortcomings. These are the clients whose work is often to come to therapy and not W-O-R-K, but just to BE! Put otherwise, it is good for people both to have experience of attacking those dragons that turn out not to be so fearsome after all, and to have experience of living alongside those dragons that will swallow the attacker. It is also good for the therapist to be aware that both exist, and to have sufficient contact with the client that s/he can get some kind of sense as to which is which.

Every moment is a fresh one; we are all changeable

I like this one. For me this is saying, "There is no last chance, now-or-never. Tomorrow is also the first day of the rest of your life." The client can mess up until s/he acts contactfully; the therapist can lose contact over and over until s/he does not. (Of course, if I keep on losing contact with a particular client, I need to be checking out what is happening to me in relation to that client!) As a therapist, I can communicate this acceptance to the client, making the therapy more comfortable for both of us. Further, by not activating the underdog, the therapy usually goes quicker!

The real world responds only to our actions,
not to our will or emotions

Put otherwise, my environment responds to my relationship with it, rather than to my relationship to myself. If I am bound up in my internal processes, even if these are "about" processes in the environment, my relationship to my environment is withdrawal or isolation, rather than contact, and my environment will respond accordingly.

A marvellous counter to magical thinking, this one, full of memories of people in groups looking surprised when a co-member tells them something so important that s/he expected them to know without having to say, and my sense of relief when thinking "So that's what it was all about!"

This is not to deny that synchronicity sometimes happens, and that the intention to make a change (e.g., to contact someone) can be fulfilled in a surprising way (say, by that person unexpectedly contacting me). However, my guess is that that rarely occurs if I wish and feel and intend (all internal activities) and also tell the universe that I am not going to act whatever gifts the universe brings or does not bring.

Postscript

Moritist thinking is an unusual but reasonable view that reminds us that the world doesn't create problems; we invent them with our imaginations. The world only creates things that need to be done. If I drop a pen in front of an audience, it merely falls. It needs to be picked up. I can make a problem of dropping the pen by focusing on my clumsiness and embarrassment at dropping it in front of others, revealing my awkwardness to them, tarnishing the image of competence that I hoped they might have. Just as there are no psychological, sociological, or chemical events in the world (only our mental templates or ways of looking at them—no events at all except as we choose to divide the stream of awareness into segments we define as "events"), so there are no problem events except when we define them as such. (Reynolds, 1985, p. 172)

PART III

ROOTS IN GESTALT FOUNDATIONAL THEORY

CHAPTER FIFTEEN

Gestalt in Britain: a polemic*

This paper has been one of the most controversial ones I have written. I decided that there was a need to support the foundational Gestalt theory with the same strength as those who want to support revisions. The first Journal to which I submitted it held an editorial group meeting to decide whether to publish it (they did not), but I have also had warm support for it. Some things have changed very much for the better since then. There is far more interaction between people from different institutes and theoretical "schools" and more international conferences where people meet and discuss, and people do not hold the same views as they wrote then, but the point remains that their original writings are still uncritically viewed by people who are not aware of the debates that have taken place or the full issues involved.

T he theme of this paper is that there is widespread misunder-standing in British Gestalt of the original theory as expressed in Perls, Hefferline, and Goodman (1994), and ignorance of the

*First published in 1995 in *Topics in Gestalt Therapy*, 3(3), reprinted in 2001 in *Gestalt Journal*, XXIV(1).

debates that have taken place over the past twenty years round this theory, mainly in the pages of the (American) *Gestalt Journal*. Thus, Gestaltists in Britain have noticed (accurately) a dichotomy between "old-style Gestalt", which is identified with Fritz Perls, and a "new-style Gestalt", more identified with the writings of the Gestalt Institute of Cleveland. However, the issues at stake, both theoretical and clinical, are, in my opinion, often not understood, and the value given to "new-style Gestalt", whose American proponents also often do not understand the original theory, leads to a dilution rather than an enhancement of the power of the original. So, I want to make a bold statement: my Gestalt work is based squarely on the theory (particularly the theory of self) in Perls, Hefferline, and Goodman (1994). I work with clients who can be classified as growth orientated, neurotic, character disordered, self disordered, and exhibiting psychotic symptoms. I have worked in a number of different ways within the Gestalt spectrum, and, across the wide range of clients I have worked with, this way of working is by far the most powerful and effective. Furthermore, the latest thinking in science and developmental studies supports the assumptions of Perls, Hefferline, and Goodman better than they support the "revisionist" thinking. Thus, I am concerned when it is assumed that "new-style Gestalt" is an improvement on the original. It is certainly an improvement on what some of the revisionists believe the original is, and an improvement on the work of those who, while they misunderstand the theory in the same way, work in line with their misunderstanding of the theory: lots of shouting and bashing cushions. I also do believe that Gestalt needs to grow methodologically and not slavishly copy Perls or any other Gestaltist. There are inconsistencies in Perls, Hefferline, and Goodman, some of which I have written about elsewhere (Philippson, 1990). However, no Gestalt writing so far is as complete a statement of the subtlety of the approach.

An American history

Gestalt therapy was developed nearly fifty years ago by a group of theorists based in New York: Fritz and Laura Perls, Paul Goodman, Paul Weisz, Elliot Shapiro, and Isidor From. Fritz Perls wrote the first book, *Ego, Hunger and Aggression* (1947), detailing his movement away from psychoanalysis in the direction of Gestalt. (There is a story originating with Isidor From (1984) that Laura Perls wrote some of the book, and received the dedication in the first British edition for this, but not in the American edition. However, the first British edition was dedicated to Wertheimer, and we will never know how much truth there is in the story. In some ways, it is irrelevant.) The other major text to come from this group is *Gestalt Therapy: Excitement and Growth in the Human Personality* (Perls, Hefferline, & Goodman,1994), whose theoretical section was written by Paul Goodman, apparently from original text supplied by Fritz Perls. It is important to realise that the reason why the complex ideas in these books received any notice at all, let alone the widespread acceptance they did find, is that Fritz Perls was widely seen as the most effective psychotherapist working in America in his day. Walter Kempler, the family therapist (quoted by Bergantino, 1993), said that the only therapist to whom he would refer people was Perls, "Because he worked at such a level that each time he worked he either did or had a chance to move someone's life". This is important for our heritage: Fritz Perls was not a nice person, or an ethical therapist, or a systematic writer or trainer; he was a showman and an inveterate producer of "soundbites", and he was also, by his skill, the guarantor that the theory had practical significance. Many of those who now criticise Perls' approach to Gestalt only came to Gestalt because they were attracted by the power of his approach.

Early in the history of the spread of Gestalt, a group of mental health workers from Cleveland, Ohio, went to New York and trained with Perls, Jim Simkin, and others. They then set up the Gestalt Institute of Cleveland, which is known in the UK through the comparatively large amount of literature it has produced, in a field where many people do not write books. However, many in America widely believe that the Gestalt that comes through from most of the Cleveland literature diverges widely from what they would understand as the Gestalt approach. This has been most centrally stated by (Cleveland graduate) Latner (1983) and in the review by Yontef (1992) of Wheeler's (1991) book *Gestalt Reconsidered*, making very similar points to the present author's review of the same book in the *British Gestalt Journal* (Philippson, 1991). A vital part of the equation, as I understand it, is that Cleveland (strangely for an Institute which expounds "open systems theory") is almost totally isolationist! It is rare for any Cleveland book to reference anyone outside Cleveland (except Perls, often disparagingly). There is no mention of, or involvement in, any of the *Gestalt Journal* debates by Cleveland writers. So, Wheeler does not mention the extended debate round the "interruptions to contact", which took up one and a half issues of the *Gestalt Journal* (Fall 1988 and Spring 1989), which covers many of the points he raises. See in particular Yontef (1988a). Similarly, British Gestaltists are not aware of the debate between Davidove (1991) and Polster (1991) on "Loss of ego functions, conflict and resistance", or the debate between Jacobs in Alexander, Brickman, Jacobs, Trop, and Yontef (1992) around the former's case presentation at the 1991 Gestalt Conference on the themes of Gestalt and self psychology.

I want to list several items, most of which have been very fully discussed in Perls, Hefferline, and Goodman (1994) and the *Gestalt Journal*, but where the debate is widely unknown or oversimplified in Britain.

1. The theoretical and clinical adequacy or otherwise of the Perls, Hefferline, and Goodman theory of self. Does it only deal with well-functioning self process? Does it need to be supplemented with inputs from analytic writers such as Kohut?
2. "Resistances"/"interruptions to contact" or "contact styles"? Do Perls, Hefferline, and Goodman view these as necessarily patho-logical?
3. Working with "structure of ground" (Wheeler, 1991). Is this a new approach?
4. The Gestalt experiment: is it a behavioural tool, as Zinker (1977) suggests, or is this a misreading of the place of the experiment in Gestalt therapy? How is Gestalt a "paradoxical theory of change"? The relative place of dialogue, experiment, and the therapist's suggestions and interpretations in Gestalt.
5. The debate over the Cleveland "Cycle of experience", the "Five layers", and the "Gestalt Prayer".

I shall go through these in turn.

Theory of self

Every psychotherapy is fundamentally based on a particular view (or non-view, in the case of behaviourism) of the "psyche", and the methodology and aims of the psychotherapy need to be in line with these. Gestalt is fundamentally a field theory, where "self", far from being an encapsulated thing inside someone, is an emergent process. Perls (1978, p. 55) wrote a beautiful explanation of this concept:

> . . . the field is, like in modern physics, the basis of Gestalt therapy. We are here in a field . . . The self is that part of the field which is opposed to the otherness. You see, you can look for the self. Does the 'self' exist? Does the 'I' exist? Can you dissect the brain and find the 'I', or the 'super-ego', or the 'self'? Definitely not . . . Now the 'self' cannot be understood other than through the field, just like day cannot be understood other than by contrast with night . . . the 'self' is to be found in the contrast with the otherness. There is a boundary between the self and the other, and this boundary is the essence of psychology.

In other words, it is a mistake to look for "self" as arising "inside me", but as a relationship process at a boundary of interaction. This is the Gestalt, and the original Goldstein (1939) concept of self-actualisation: self actualising at a contact boundary. That boundary is not created by some "self" and some "other" coming together; rather, the boundary is prior to both "self" and "other". And there are some quite particular requirements for that contact boundary to be the birthplace for the statement "I am". As I write this, there are several terrible conflicts taking place in the world, which have as a major factor the habit of the former imperial powers of drawing fairly random lines on the map of Africa, Asia, and the Balkans. These boundaries have never been able to carry out the function required of them. In some cases, other factors, such as a politician of great charisma or repressive power (or both), have managed to weld those inside the random boundary into a coherent state. When the charismatic leader dies, or the repressive regime is toppled, the state fragments. Either "other" is inside the boundary—"I am not part of the same nation as them"—or "self" is outside the boundary: "Those across the border are also my kin".

The process that we could call "selfing" consists of two factors: an identification "This is me", and an alienation, "This is not-me". Notice that I am here talking about a polarisation of experiences, whereas, in self-concept, what is identified and alienated is a polarisation of concepts. In Perls, Hefferline, and Goodman, these functions of identification and alienation are called the ego functions.

A number of Gestaltists have written of the "inadequacy" of this formulation. In particular, Tobin (1982) has written (I shall quote this at length, since it contains the core of the objections of "new Gestalt" to the theory of self *though I want to add that Tobin no longer holds these views*) of

> serious problems with this description of self. First, it seems to imply that each person has an equally effective, well-functioning self. Second, it makes the self a function only of conflict and fails to touch some of the important self-functions of stability, groundedness, confidence and flexibility that I think should be subsumed under the concept of self. Third, in their definition Perls and his co-authors do not consider the fact that, for some people, conflict results in a fragmenting of the self rather than a mere diminution, which is less rather than more self. (ibid., pp. 5–6)

He, therefore, advocates the introduction of concepts from self psychology (Kohut, 1977) into Gestalt therapy.

Each of these statements is inaccurate, as Yontef and Tobin (1983) have pointed out. Gestalt theory nowhere assumes that all selves are equally well functioning. Perls (1948) wrote about narcissism, and stated that the customary understanding of narcissism as "self-love" was to miss the point, which is that the narcissist is not capable of love of self or of others (he was not always so clear). Rather, the defining concept is narcissistic retroflection, where the person splits, and provides the contact and continuity for him/herself rather than getting contact from the environment. The point about the Gestalt theory of self is that it is non-normative, unlike psychoanalytic theories. It is much more true to say that Gestalt conceptualises all neurosis as self-disorder. The processes involved in a fragmented self are based on the same capacities for creative adjustment as those involved in a more unified self process. In fact, paradoxically, it is Tobin, in his second objection, that identifies "self" with stability and groundedness! This is similar to the "humanistic psychology" rewrite of the concept of "self-actualisation": an "actualised" self is somehow better or more whole than an "unactualised" self. This is certainly not Goldstein's or Perls' view of actualisation.

Our experience of self as stable and continuous in the (non-neurotic) situation of good contact is viewed in Gestalt theory in terms of three aspects of the selfing process: ego, id, and personality. Ego is essentially the process of making figure (identification) and ground (alienation). The ego process can also involve identification with my own acts of choice: values, interests, and avoidances. In fact, when this happens, it is what Perls, Hefferline, and Goodman (1994) call the "autonomous criterion for health"; when it does not happen, self is fragmented and unstable. Id is the relaxation of deliberateness in the absence of any particular interest or need. It is "unified only by the looming sense of the body" (ibid., p. 160). "Personality" is the verbal analogue of self, a statement of "This is who I am." It can (but might not) provide another kind of continuity. In healthy functioning, ". . . the Personality is a kind of framework of attitudes, understood by oneself, that can be used for every kind of interpersonal behaviour" (ibid.). Neurotically, however, it "consists of a number of mistaken concepts of oneself, introjects, ego-ideals, masks, etc." (ibid.).

For me, this is far more profound and far closer to my own experience of the varieties of self-functioning than any other theory of self. It is most definitely not a theory of just a well-functioning self, or one that leaves our sense of continuity of self unexplained.

Tobin's third objection, that Gestalt theory fails to account for fragmentation of self resulting from conflict in narcissistic people, also cannot be upheld. What Tobin does not take into account is the very basis for psychopathology in Gestalt theory: the fixed Gestalt, which repeatedly looks for closure, and recycles its own chosen method of frustrating itself. In the case of someone whose understanding of the world is that it is barren or overwhelming, and who has withdrawn into a system of splitting and false identifications, any demanding approach by others immediately makes this splitting obvious, and simultaneously terrifies the person by exposing the falsity of the retroflective pseudo-world that s/he has projected on to the environment. So, the id process of relaxation and withdrawal can never take place, because then the person's (fantasy) world would disappear. And, of course, the body never then "looms" via proprioception, but is replaced by a visual, conceptual, or fantasy image of the body.

Later in Tobin's paper, he underpins his and Kohut's approach with the infant developmental theory of Mahler, Pine, and Bergman (1975). However, the later researches of Stern (1985) fit much better with orthodox Gestalt theory than with Mahler and colleagues:

> [Infants] never experience a period of total self/other undifferentia-
> tion. There is no confusion between self and other in the beginning or
> at any point during infancy. They are also predesigned to be selec-
> tively responsive to external social events and never experience an
> autistic-like phase.
>
> ... There is no symbiotic-like phase. In fact the subjective experiences
> of union with another can occur only after a sense of core self and a
> core other exists." (Stern, 1985, p. 10)

Interestingly, Perls himself (1978) proposed a very similar model of
human development, involving five stages that begin sequentially but
do not end (see Philippson, 1995).

In other words, separation comes before joining in Stern and
Gestalt, rather than joining before separation, as in Mahler and Kohut.
The former is also the position taken by Buber:

> ... Buber asked himself, 'What is is that makes the I–Thou and the
> I–It relationship possible?' He decided that it was a twofold human
> movement that the animals do not have that makes possible both of
> these relations. He called it 'Urdistanz und Beziehung'—the primal
> setting at a distance and then entering into relation. (Friedman, 1990,
> p. 13)

This, of course, must have implications for clinical practice: the possibility of joining between therapist and client must be based on a prior
separateness, rather than the possibility of separateness being based
on prior empathic joining. As an aside, I am concerned that a number
of people identify with both Buber and Kohut, not noticing that, both
theoretically and clinically, they are incompatible. Kohut's method, by
systematically downgrading the therapist's presence and commitment
to dialogue and by its emphasis on empathy, is not compatible with
dialogic relating.

There is often, in British Gestalt circles, a lack of understanding of
the dangers of working from a developmental theory. These are:

● Cultural bias: Developmental theories tend to assume the patterns of child upbringing favoured in the society from which they
stem. In a different cultural situation, it may well be that different ways of bringing up children are more valuable.

- Loss of the "autonomous criterion of health": This is replaced by the assumption that certain ways of being are in themselves pathological (for example, homosexuality).
- Dependence on shaky theories: Whether these are the theories of Mahler, Pine, and Bergman (1975) or of infant feeding by the clock, one era's "proven" theory is contradicted in another era. If psychotherapy is based on a particular developmental theory, it is difficult not to fit the client into it.

So, we have the strange situation that the Gestalt approach has been backed up by observational evidence, but some Gestaltists still look to theories that both fit less well with Gestalt and are not supported by the latest evidence. I would go further: almost every new theoretical approach in science has backed up the Gestalt approach! Chaos theory (Gleick, 1987) and complexity theory (Waldrop, 1993) are based on the idea of emergent order, which is central to the Gestalt concept of self emerging from the contact boundary. Land's (1977) "retinex" theory of colour vision states that we cannot see any colour except in relation to our whole visual field.

The issue for orthodox Gestalt theory in working with people with fragile self-process is one of grading contact to keep the level of the encounter within a sustainable anxiety range for the client. I am happy to integrate Masterson's (1981) suggestion to interpret to the client my understanding of the disappointment and rage behind any withdrawal and acting-out (although I must own that it is more out of previous experience and cognitive understanding than out of empathy that I can make the interpretation). I am available for contact and I do not force contact. With borderline clients, I find that the contact skills that have come out of my Gestalt training (and personal psychotherapy) greatly enhance the effectiveness of the therapy, and I would see Gestalt as treatment of choice with borderline clients. Further elaboration about how to work from a Gestalt perspective are beyond the scope of this paper, but see Yontef (1988b) and Greenberg (1989, 1991).

Resistances?

> ... if the awareness is creative then these very resistances and defenses—they are really counterattacks and aggressions against the self—are taken as active expressions of vitality, however neurotic they

may be in the total picture. Rather than being liquidated, they are accepted at face value and met man to man: the therapist, according to his own self-awareness, declines to be bored, intimidated, cajoled, etc.; he meets anger with explanation of the misunderstanding, or sometimes apology (cf. Masterson on working with narcissism), or even with anger, according to the truth of the situation; he meets obstruction with impatience in the framework of a larger patience. (Perls, Hefferline, & Goodman, 1994, p. 25)

Much has been written in "new Gestalt" about "resistance" as a form of contact (see, in particular, Wheeler, 1991). This seems to have become, for some British Gestaltists, a touchstone of difference from "old Gestalt". However, as this quote (chosen from among many) shows, the connection between resistance/interruption and creative adjustment was there explicitly from the beginning. It was, in fact, the basis for Perls' critique of Reich: that understanding tension as "character armour" was to alienate it. Rather, both impulses—to express and to repress—need to be acknowledged, owned, and worked with. As I understand it, Gestalt adds something to the "There is no such thing as resistance" model: yes, a communication is always being made; sometimes the sole content of that communication is "I am resisting you; I am interrupting our contact". There is another theme here around confluence, which I shall come to after talking about "structure of ground".

"Structure of ground"

Wheeler (1991) has made the major thrust of his book the "fact" that previous Gestalt was "figure-bound", and that we need to "pay attention to the structure of ground". But how can you explore ground without making it figure? To quote Yontef (1992, p. 106), "In Gestalt therapy theory, when one examines something from the ground, including structure, it becomes figure". The submerged point of all this is that there is absolutely no reason why the client and the therapist need to make the same things figural (and many cogent reasons why not!). When you look at things this way, it becomes obvious that Perls, with his interest in the "holes" and "what is not there in the dream", would have absolutely agreed with this. I think every statement about being "figure-bound" *which we must be by definition*, or about "structured ground" should be ritually expunged, lest trainees stop understanding the basic concept of "figure–ground", that is, gestalt formation! Of course, the therapist must not be "bound" by the client's figure: this would be confluence.

So, we come to what, in Perls, Hefferline, and Goodman (1994), is called the "contextual method", that is "Fundamental theoretical errors are invariably characterological, the result of a neurotic failure of perception, feeling, or action" (ibid., p. 20). The fundamental error in both the discussion of "resistance" and of "structured ground" is the assumption of confluence between therapist and client. Let me clarify this. The assumption is that "resistance", or "interruption to contact", or "figure", or "ground" will have the same meaning for two people who are sitting together: therapist and client. So, while it might be true for the client that s/he is resisting, it is not true for the therapist that s/he is being resisted against, since, one hopes, the therapist is not avid to push the client into doing what s/he does not want to do, but, rather, is ready to be interested in the client's hesitation. The client's image of the therapist as pushing for a particular result should be a projection (although, granted, this would not be the case with Zinker (see below)). Similarly, when a client interrupts contact, the therapist can note the interruption, but not feel interrupted. Wheeler's assumption that we can "pay attention to ground" only has the possibility of being meaningful in relation to an assumption that what is figure for the client is figure also for the therapist. This might be true for Rogerian practitioners (although not for Rogers himself), but should not be true for Gestaltists. It certainly was not true for Perls. (Please take a moment to check with yourself whether this is accurate, or just me being rude.)

Yontef (1992, p. 107) has written that "Structures are slowly changing processes that organize other processes". If part of the ground is structured, that part of the process is slow moving. This could include my family, cultural and national identifications, my memories, my "representation of interactions that have been generalised (RIGs)" (Stern, 1985, p. 97)—that is, a generalised picture that I create of interactions with a particular significant person ("self-regulating others"). Gestalt theory is a well-balanced theory in recognising both the advantages and the disadvantages, the neurotic and contactful uses of this. The advantages are in not having to reinvent the wheel each time, in having sufficient Yontef-structure to organise our process of contacting (= self). What is gained is autonomy. What is lost is spontaneity.

Autonomy must not be confused with spontaneity. It is free choosing ... But the middle mode of spontaneity does not have the luxury of this freedom, nor the feeling of security that comes from knowing what and where one is and being able to engage or not; one is engaged and carried along, not in spite of oneself, but beyond oneself. (Perls, Hefferline, & Goodman, 1994, p. 161)

I orientate myself on the spectrum leading from confluence with a particular view of myself (with all the implications for my creativity) to surfing the wave of my creative encounter with my environment, each moment fresh, without commitments (with all the implications of this for myself and my family or society). The question for Gestalt therapy is whether the identifications are chosen with awareness or whether they are unawarely introjected, and whether the choice is made with awareness of the implications for contact with the environment. Thus, clients generally come into therapy (of any kind) when their identifications are not adequate for the environmental situation in which they find themselves.

I also want to be clear that Gestalt therapy is flexible enough to operate through ongoing individual or group therapy and also through weekend or longer workshops with good results. People have found their lives transformed in intensive short-term Gestalt therapy, not least in workshops as part of training programmes. People have found their neurotic manifestations (phobias, work or relationship problems) changing very quickly, not because the Gestalt therapist is aiming to solve the problems, but because the problems are part of a larger Gestalt that can sometimes move very quickly. Short-term workshops will not deal with deeply ingrained self or personality disorders, but can make them more obvious to the client and the therapist, and be the route by which the client moves into more long-term therapy on the advice of the therapist.

The experiment

... a unique quality of Gestalt therapy is its emphasis on modifying a person's behaviour in the therapy situation itself. This systematic behaviour modification, when it grows out of the experience of the client, is called an experiment. (Zinker, 1977, p. 123)

Sonia and I began to notice . . . that we had developed and meticu-
lously followed an aesthetic process . . . [Zinker then outlines ten
steps, of which some are:]

6. After some further discussion, proposing to the family that they
    need to learn a skill that is not fully developed.

7. Teaching them how to do an experiment intended to enhance
    their functioning in the underdeveloped area.

8. "Selling" the experiment to the family and making sure they
    understand its purpose.

9. Watching the family work the experiment and occasionally
    coaching them if they get stuck.

10. Asking them what they learned from the experiment and how
    they could practice their new skill at home. (Zinker, 1994:
    xxx–xxxi)

I am sorry, but I cannot recognise any similarity between this and
what I understand as Gestalt therapy, and really worry that Zinker is
seen as the theorist of the Gestalt experiment. In pushing couples to
change in particular ways to get away from "problems", Zinker is
truly "figure-bound" (that is, confluent with the client's wish to
change). Clients can only understand or name their difficulties in relation to their own perspective, which is, in itself, part of the problem!
The impasse inherent in their perspective is why individuals and
families come for therapy in the first place. When a client is at this
impasse, s/he is profoundly suggestible, looking for a way out to be
given from outside. Any suggestion then will be taken as the therapist's advice. The sequence of the Gestalt experiment, as I understand
it, is, rather, experimenting with new possibilities, or with an exaggeration of the old pattern, leading to the impasse, where the therapist
stays with the client until s/he risks moving through to implosion/
explosion, whereupon s/he will autonomously find new possibilities
for him/herself. This is the same as what Erickson (1980) calls "indirect suggestion": the suggestion leads to a place where the gate to
wider choice is open, rather than in any way suggesting the choice, or
even requiring the client to enter the gate.

    This is a true experiment rather than the kind of "experiment" that
children do in school, where they have done it wrong if they get the
"wrong" result. It is truly based on the paradoxical theory of change,

where the client is supported and challenged to say "I own this as my existence now", and, in this owning, is aware of choicefulness— including the choice to disown and to stay where s/he is. Even to say, "I own that I don't want to look any further" must be acceptable here. Again, Zinker (1994, p. 102) subtly changes this theory: "We encourage the couple or family to see and to experience the goodness, the usefulness, the creativity of what they discover when they examine themselves". The point is not that it is good, or useful, or creative (it might be, or it might be a weary accommodation to a situation that only exists in the family's imagination), but that it is theirs! They do it. They will keep doing it until they stop doing it or are stopped by the environment. And that is the reality that must be affirmed by the therapist. I think some ways of doing Gestalt have introjected a "humanistic" sense of "All clients are good really". From the point of view of creative indifference, we might as well say, "All good clients are evil really". The existentialist perspective is merely "They are."

Means and ends

The paradoxical theory of change also has implications for the therapist's stance. In some other systems of counselling/psychotherapy, it is assumed that the stance of the therapist will be consistent with the desired end result. Specifically, if the end result is to be that the client experiences themselves as empowered or as being equal in power to the therapist, then the therapist is expected to be careful not to advise or suggest anything to the client, or to act powerfully in relation to the client.

In Gestalt therapy, which combines a paradoxical approach with a methodology which distinguishes direct and indirect suggestions and an emphasis on boundary conditions, the logic of the therapist's stance is very different. If the therapy is paradoxical, it is to be expected that the means will differ qualitatively from the ends. It is only if the therapist is powerful that the client can take her/his own power. Paradoxically, if the therapist "empowers" the client, that, in itself, affirms the therapist in a "one-up" position, from which s/he can hand over some power. The implication is that "in the real world", where people do not hand over their power, the client is no better off than before. What the Gestalt therapist provides is a safe but strong boundary in relation to which clients can experiment with developing their own strength. The therapist can be active, suggesting experiments and giving feedback, and simultaneously be providing a graded experience of firm contact in relation to which the client can take her/his own power. Along with these active possibilities come a number of considerations of which the Gestalt therapist must be aware. With a compliant client, is the activity of the therapist pointing towards the "safe emergency", or is it providing a series of exercises that the client can compliantly go through the motions of carrying out, without touching their real growing edge at all? Much "Gestalt" done by people copying Perls without understanding the basis of what he was doing can end up this way. With a frightened or ashamed client, is the contact offered by the therapist graded right, or is it so overwhelming that the client must leave therapy or dissociate, and again go through the motions, while cordoning off their vulnerability? The opposite problem would be to work so hard at trying to avoid "shaming" clients that they do not experience the shame linked with their "response-ability" in abusive situations. It must be recalled that one of the distinguishing features of Gestalt is that there are no passive victims.

Thus, a Gestalt dialogic approach has a very specific character. Gestalt shares with other approaches from the analytic tradition an emphasis on therapeutic abstinence, coupling this with a de-emphasis on the verbal. Gestalt dialogue does not presuppose a great deal of verbal self-revelation by the therapist. The therapist invites contact, but not with the partial, neurotic self of the client; rather, by owning his/her strength and frustrating such contact, the therapist offers a relationship with a more authentic integrated self at the highest sustainable level of honesty. This is also what Buber and his followers did (he called it *confirmation* of the client's becoming as well as the client's being), and is inherent in the existentialist tradition. It is not a "nice" approach!

"The cycle", the "five layers" and the "Gestalt Prayer"

In the past, Gestalt therapy was identified with the empty chair. Then it became identified with yelling and bashing mother on a cushion (which was not at all what Perls did), or lots of touching and holding clients (which Perls also did not do). Now it seems to be becoming identified with the "Gestalt cycle" (Zinker, 1977). This was developed as a teaching aid in the Gestalt Institute of Cleveland, where, to avoid introjection, it was drawn in many different ways. I want to state why the cycle as conventionally drawn (withdrawal–sensation–aware-ness–mobilisation of energy–action–contact–satisfaction–withdrawal) is incompatible with Gestalt theory, and how the way it is used takes it even further away from that theory.

> ... in act, in contact, there is given a single whole of perception-initi-ating movement tinged with feeling. It is not that the self-feeling, for instance of being thirsty, serves as a signal that is noted, referred to the water-perception department, etc., but that in the same act the water is given as bright–desirable–moved toward, or the absence of water is absent–irksome–problematic. (Perls, Hefferline, & Goodman, 1994, p. 36)

That is, there is no necessary separation between sensation, aware-ness, mobilisation of energy, action, and contact. In the complex situ-ation, we can make separations, which slow down or block contact, but the cycle, as described, describes a particular situation of complex-ity rather than basic theory. I suppose, like "Mind", it might be an unavoidable illusion in the "low-grade chronic emergency". In Perls, Hefferline, and Goodman, it is clearly spelt out that awareness is not an aid to solving problems, or a step on the way to action:

> But it has always seemed a mystery why 'mere' awareness, for instance recollection, should cure the neurosis. Note, however, that the awareness is not a thought about the problem but is itself a creative integration of the problem. We can see, too, why usually 'awareness' does not help, for usually it is not an aware gestalt at all, a structured content [Yes this is Perls, Hefferline, and Goodman, Wheeler please note!], but mere content, verbalizing or reminiscing, and as such it does not draw on the energy of present organic need and a present environmental help. (ibid., p. 8)

I think what is often called "awareness" is what Perls, Hefferline, and Goodman call "egotism":

> This is a slowing-down of spontaneity by further deliberate intro-spection and circumspection, to make sure that the ground possibili-ties are indeed exhausted—there is no threat of danger or surprise—before he commits himself ... Normally, egotism is indispensable in any process of elaborate complication and long maturation; otherwise

there is premature commitment and the need for discouraging undo-ing. Normal egotism is diffident, skeptical, aloof, slow, but not noncommittal.

Neurotically, egotism is a kind of confluence with the deliberate awareness and an attempted annihilation of the uncontrollable and surprising. (ibid., pp. 236–237)

There are shades here of the Zinker approach to experiments. I would say it is essentially a behavioural/RET approach, not a Gestalt one. Now, if the Gestalt approach did not work, then maybe there would be a case for rewriting the theory to include this. However, the basic theory works (in my experience) very quickly and effectively.

The other limitation of the contact cycle is that "withdrawal" does not only occur via "satisfaction" (which is not on the Zinker diagram; Parlett (personal communication) tells me that the word shown at that point on the cycle when he was training at Cleveland was "integra-tion"), but via mourning. It is not just that we go from something nice to something even nicer. Old ways of being die and are organismically mourned.

The "five layers of neurosis"

At the other pole to the attention given to the over-simplicities of the "cycle" is the lack of attention given to the model of neurosis given by Perls (1969a). This is not, and was never attempting to be, a model of human functioning. It is a model of working through neurosis, the layers that we form like a scab over authentic functioning. Each layer (apart from the last) acts as a defence against moving to the next. Thus, the layers are consecutive and discrete, and need to be worked through in order (although clients might go back to an earlier layer to move away from anxiety). It is important to make these distinctions, since there has been a great deal of controversy and misunderstand-ing in the Gestalt world about this model. It is not a global model of human functioning: that is the task of other aspects of Gestalt theory. It is a specific structural model of a particular neurotic manifestation as it is being worked through. Now Gestaltists, with our emphasis on process, rather look down on structure, although Yontef (1988b, p. 21) has accurately defined structure as "slowly changing process". The point is that neurosis in the Gestalt model is precisely a moving away from the existential anxiety involved in embracing authenticity and spontaneity, and moving to a more predictably structured activity of fitting in with the world. We limit ourselves to a structure that we experience as keeping us safe and that also manipulates the environment to act in certain ways towards us. From this perspective, neurosis is predictability, and the point of Gestalt therapy is to facilitate the client to become unpredictable.

In this model (Perls, 1969a, pp. 59–61), the client in therapy moves from meaningless clichés to role-playing, that is, identifying with a limited self-description (personality function) and a limited range of ways of being in the world. At this point, and at no other, the Gestalt experiment invites the client to move beyond the role, into the anxiety-filled impasse (Perls, Hefferline, and Goodman call this the "safe emergency"). The therapist encourages, supports, and challenges the client to stay at the impasse, and into the implosive/death layer, "the paralysis of opposing forces" (Perls, 1969a, p. 60). Perls makes clear that this is not Freud's "death instinct"; rather, it appears to the client as death, with no available energy to move in any direction. Again, supporting the client to stay with this layer allows him/her to move to an explosion of authentic functioning in the world.

For me, this describes exactly what I do in my Gestalt work, in a way that fits beautifully with an existential rather than behaviourist outlook, and also has great affinity with my experience of Zen training. It does not fit with the Zinker conception of the experiment as a behavioural tool.

The "Gestalt Prayer"

"New Gestalt" does not like the original form of this. "I am I and you are you" does not fit well with a rejection of Perls' individualism. Dublin (1977, p. 142) rewrites the Prayer to end "The truth begins with two". I want to argue here that there is nothing wrong with what is said in the Prayer: however, things are left out. To begin with, it is worth pointing out that we are back with the Mahler–Stern polarity: for Mahler, Pine, and Bergman (1975), symbiosis certainly precedes separation, and the truth does begin with two; for Stern (1985), Gestalt, and Buber, self-actualisation begins at least at birth, and the capacity for intimacy is built on this primary separation. But this self-actualisation is not an isolated "I", but an I in relation to other. So, with this in mind, let us look at the Gestalt Prayer:

I am I and you are you

For Gestalt, the beginning of selfhood is a relation with other: not just human, but the whole of the person's environment. This is the "ego" aspect of self: identification ("I") and alienation ("you"). This act of making I I and you you must be the basis for any conception of self.

I am not in this world to live up to your expectations
I do my thing, you do your thing

This is both true and incomplete. Your expectations and actions are part of the field context in which I actualise self. This has two aspects. First, there are consequences inherent in my actions relative to your expectations and actions. An interesting aspect of this is in the practice of Gestalt therapy: no therapist can live up to any client's initial expectations, as these would be coloured by the client's attempt to close the fixed Gestalt that brought her/him to therapy, which would by definition lead to the disappointment and repetition inherent in any fixed Gestalt. This would be truly "figure-bound" therapy! However, an important part of the field of my interactions with the client is what s/he expects of me. The second aspect—the one which Perls truly found difficult—is the capacity to make commitments to someone else, whether this be elderly parents, partner, children, or friends. The choosing to accept some of someone else's expectations as your own (for example, a child's for food and loving touch) is part of intimacy. Again, in therapy, I make a commitment to a client that affects my life. For example, if I want to take frequent long holidays without much notice, I would not be ethical in taking on borderline clients.

You are not in this world to live up to my expectations

This one is fascinating, and often ignored. The power of an adult saying this to parents cannot be underestimated. How many clients make their contentment dependent on a mother or father acting differently, or even having been different from how they were! By letting the parents off the hook, the adult comes off the same hook. It is the vital transition to adult maturity that I remake my relationship to these people who have—for better or worse—parented me so as to acknowledge that my survival no longer depends on them, and then make the commitments to each other appropriate to who we are now. Thus . . .

If we meet, it'll be wonderful; if not, it can't be helped

Dublin (1977, p. 142) found this part particularly despairing: he suggested that Perls change "it" to "I" in this section. However, it is the very despair that, for me, makes this so valuable. The object relations theorists have pointed out most fully that the centre of borderline and narcissistic splitting is an avoidance of despair or "abandonment depression". In Gestalt terms, all fixed Gestalten are based on false hopes: "If I go round the circle once more, things will be different." The "death layer" of the five-layer model is the abandonment depression. Thus, despair is central to Gestalt therapy, not as an end-point, as in some existentialist writing, but as the doorway to authenticity. It is also a world away from the "positive thinking" that underlies much of humanistic therapy, and much of the shallow Zinker approach: "What you have done is good, now here is something even better."

What is missing in this couplet is the idea that I can maintain a commitment even to those who do not choose to meet me. This is, of course, vital for therapy with narcissistic clients, who need my continuing commitment even while using every means to avoid contact or commitment to me. Again, I get the impression that this was outside Perls' world-view. If someone was not willing to contact him, with his own contact-hunger, he was willing to accept that, but not to maintain his openness to contact: "Get off the seat." This willingness to keep offering contact unilaterally is also important in parenting teenagers and in caring for elderly parents, as well as in maintaining a relationship with a partner during times of conflict.

Conclusion

This has been a whistle-stop tour of the current controversies in Gestalt theory and practice from a basic Perls, Hefferline, and Goodman perspective. I do not expect all who read this to agree with it in every (or any) detail; what I do hope is that I have helped an informed debate by elaborating this approach and distinguishing it from others within the Gestalt world. I also hope that I will tempt some people to read the original *Gestalt Journal* debates and make up their own minds, and that, in doing this, we can keep more of a sense of our "roots" in the development of Gestalt.

CHAPTER SIXTEEN

Awareness, the contact boundary, and the field*

This is one of my earliest Gestalt papers. I am already trying to look at the theory from a field perspective. I also like that this paper draws attention to, and continues, a period when significant theoretical discussion was taking place in the Gestalt Journal, involving many thoughtful people. In my "polemical" paper, I note that more recent ideas around interruptions to contact are going over ground covered in these discussions, but without awareness that they exist, or, at least, without referencing them.

> "... psychology studies the operation of the contact-boundary in the organism/environment field. ... The definition of an organism is the definition of an organism/environment field; and the contact-boundary is, so to speak, the specific organ of awareness of the novel situation of the field ..."
>
> (Perls, Hefferline & Goodman, 1994, pp. 5, 35)

---

*First published in 1990, in *Gestalt Journal*, XIII(2).

There has been much discussion in the Gestalt world recently about "boundary issues" (see, particularly, *The Gestalt Journal*, Fall 1988). My thesis is that if Gestalt theory bases itself radically on the operation of the contact-boundary in the field, then the theory becomes comparatively simple. If the theory is looked at from the point of view of a person encapsulated within the skin, and particularly if we speak about *my* awareness as basic, then the theory becomes utterly complex, language runs out, and we end up in the kind of multi-various expositions of boundary issues that we have seen in the literature. For example, is there meaning in the term "proflection", is it a combination of other interruptions to contact, and does that matter anyway? ("Proflection" is a term coined by Sylvia Fleming Crocker to denote interrupting contact by doing to others what you want them to do to you—the helpers' interruption!) Is the mystical "one with the Universe" experience confluence or contact? Is self-awareness awareness or retroflection?

Specific theses

The contact-boundary is a negotiation between organism and environment

> There is no single function of any animal that completes itself without objects and environment . . . The meaning of anger involves a frustrating obstacle; the meaning of reasoning involves problems of practice. (Perls, Hefferline, & Goodman, 1994, p. 4)

The reverse is also true. The meaning of the environment involves the being-ness of the organism. The meaning of a chair involves the skeletal structure of a human being (what would a chair mean to a horse?). The meaning of a tree is different to a human being, a bird, or a leaf. This is, of course, the underlying principle behind modern physics. Nothing has meaning or dimension except in relation to the present state of the unified field of observer and observed.

This negotiation with human beings as one or more of the organisms usually involves both projection and introjection. I *project* my skeletal structure and my need to rest my legs at times on to my environment to create a chair; I project the range of my senses (sight and my visible spectrum, my skin sensitivity) and my need for shelter or beauty to create the tree for myself.

At another level, the tree that I perceive will also be based on *introjects*: primarily, for me, the English language, which distinguishes trees from plants and animals and stones, but puts together under a single term the redwood and the apple tree. I can make initial contact with another human being without introjecting, but in order to satisfy any needs beyond the need for that initial contact itself, I need to introject aspects of that other person (and the other of me) so as to know what to ask for, what the likely answer will be, what the potential problems are, etc. Further, I will usually have made a quite sophisticated choice about whom to make contact with to satisfy my needs, on the basis of either assimilated skills or introjected patterns of relationship-making, which are then projected on to the other person. In choosing how to respond, the other person will go through a similar process, so that, before a word is spoken, the two people will have gone through a fairly complex non-verbal negotiation and have initial introjects of the other in place. Each will then consult the introject to determine their optimum choice of words, tone of voice, facial expression, goals of further negotiation, etc.

Most therapists will have worked with people who have not developed, or who have blocked, these relationship-making skills, or whose introjects block contact rather than facilitating it. The difficulties these people experience give strong clues to the complexities of contact-making.

The "chronic low-grade emergency" of Perls, Hefferline, and Goodman underlies our images of contact and boundaries

"Ever desireless, one can see the mystery. Ever desiring, one can see the manifestations. These two spring from the same source but differ in name" (Lao Tsu, 1972).

There are two forms of contact: "pure" contact, with an associated need just for contact; and "contact for", *in order to* satisfy another need. Pure contact does not need the projection of need fulfilment on to the other; nor the introjection of the other to consult what and how to ask for them. "Contact for" does need them, as I explained in the section above. (We are also in the realm of Buber's distinction between I–Thou and I–It, but that would be another article!)

In Perls, Hefferline, and Goodman (1994, p. 39, Goodman wrote of "Mind" (as separate from "Body" and "External World") being an "unavoidable illusion" produced by a state of "chronic low-tension disequilibrium, a continual irk of danger and frustration interspersed with occasional acute crises, and never fully relaxed". In the "chronic low-grade emergency", most contact (if not all) is "contact for".

Pure contact is contact with the environment *as part of the organism/environment field*—this is the mystical "one with the universe" feeling which is often mistaken for confluence. But it is not: the self is not lost but enhanced; clarity is not lost but gained.

Awareness is a contact-boundary function

The vital Gestalt notion of *creative awareness* cannot be understood as "a thing that I do".

"Experience occurs at the boundary between the organism and its environment, primarily the skin surface and the other organs of sensory and motor response" (Perls, Hefferline, & Goodman, 1994, p. 3).

Awareness is part of my negotiating with my environment, and, since I define my environment and my environment defines me, it is also part of my environment negotiating with me. If I am hungry, "I" will be particularly aware of an apple in my vicinity. However, the apple also gives meaning to "my" hunger: "I would like to eat that apple." In contact with another person, the situation is more complicated, but similar: in "contact for", I contact you on the basis of an imbalance (interest, wants, needs), which I believe (on the basis of knowledge, introjects, and projection) you can help me to rebalance. If my wish to make contact is to turn into real two-way contact, then my beliefs must be accurate enough that you will wish to contact me on the basis of a polar imbalance—you will wish to provide what I want and want what I provide. In this way, "my awareness of you" is an aspect of the same boundary function as "your awareness of me". In "pure contact", unmediated by desire for anything beyond contact itself, we know that awareness is greater than "my awareness", but are so unused to this situation that we can easily mistake it for a (confluent) blurring of boundaries rather than a clarification. In pure contact, I enhance my Self and, literally, lose my Mind!

Awareness looks both "outward" and "inward"

> As a boundary of interaction, its sensitivity, motor response, and feeling are turned both towards the environment-part and the organism-part . . . It is not that the self-feeling, for instance of being thirsty, serves as a signal that is noted, referred to the water-perception department, etc.; but that *in the same act* the water is given as bright–desirable–moved towards, or the absence of water is absent–irksome–problematic. (Perls, Hefferline, & Goodman, 1994, p. 36)

This follows from the principles that awareness is a function of the contact-boundary in the organism–environment field, involving the organism, the environment, and the negotiation/relationship between them. If awareness becomes either merely "self-awareness" or merely "awareness of the environment", then the field is lost to awareness, and, therefore, the parts—self and environment—are impoverished and unavailable to clear awareness.

There is a terminological problem here: what I am talking about is the "contact-withdrawal" cycle. But to speak of "withdrawal" suggests to me that awareness is seen as being "in" the person (organism). If awareness is *on* the contact-boundary, then "withdrawal" is the other side of contact within the field. Maybe terms such as "self-contact" and "environment/other-contact" would be more useful.

Having made this observation, defining confluence and isolation becomes that much easier: confluence is the process of limiting awareness to the "environment" and losing awareness of the "self"; isolation is the process of limiting awareness of the "self" and losing awareness of the "environment". The quotes around "self" and "environment" are meant to point out that both these entities are changed and impoverished by being abstracted from the field. Both involve loss of ego-boundary (= environment-boundary), but by opposite mechanisms. Confluence I would understand as an extreme form of introjection, where "environment" has been permitted to blot out both "self" and boundary; isolation as an extreme form of projection, where "self" has been permitted to blot out both "environment" and boundary. (I use the word "permitted" to emphasise that this is an activity rather than something imposed.)

Behind these permissions will be a range of other mechanisms.

- *Introjection*:
  "You are alone against the world."
  "The two of us against the world."
  "We do things this way."
  "The world is too dangerous and confusing to have anything to do with."
  "The world is too dangerous and confusing to have anything to do with; let me shelter you."

- *Projection*:
  All the above also involve projections of the introjects on to the environment.

- *Retroflection*:
  "I will not waste my energy on anyone else, but spend it on myself."

- *Proflection*:
  "I am not worthy of my needs; I will give to others instead as they are worthy." [I am aware that some people do not like the concept of proflection. I personally do. I am sure that it also involves other interruptions, but so do all the others. "Proflection" describes a common enough situation that it is useful to me to have a tag on it. Really though, there are no "pure" projections or proflections or anything else. See the section headed "From different perspectives . . .", below.]

There is a common boundary process/state of oscillation between isolation and confluence

With this sort of analysis, another aspect can become clear. I have come across many people (myself included!) who tend towards *both* confluence (fearing isolation) *and* isolation (fearing confluence). These people *oscillate* between the two poles, either with wide oscillations (as in borderline disorders) or with narrow oscillations (some schizophrenic disorders, generally people with "blocky" musculature and difficulty being "part of the world"). Underlying this oscillation is, in my experience, a particular kind of childhood learning about *individuation*. This learning has two parts:

1.   IF I GET TOO CLOSE I'LL BE SWALLOWED UP/HURT.
2.   IF I GET TOO FAR AWAY I'LL BE ABANDONED/ALONE.

One person with these introjects will relate to others by hovering at a distance between them, neither "too close" nor "too far away". When he or she forms a relationship with another person, it will be with another person with the same introjects who also oscillates between confluence and isolation. The relationship will be a curious one: neither feeling fulfilled, nor prepared to "press the right button" to make affectionate contact, nor prepared to separate unless there is another, similar relationship available. The whole shebang will be covered up with a show of contact (in front of others) and a show of withdrawal (complaining to selected people, particularly the children).

This is what I call an "oscillating relationship."

No Gestalt closure is possible: the desire for contact leads to withdrawal (by both partners); the desire for withdrawal leads to a sense of abandonment, and a rush for closeness (and back to the beginning). And we know that incomplete Gestalts will always be pushing for completion, taking energy from the here-and-now.

What of the individual in this sort of relationship? He or she will have developed a third introject: the relationship itself, particularly since it is likely to be a rerun of the relationships in the individual's family of origin. This will have a cognitive component: something like "The world's a strange and dangerous place, and we need to stay together to protect each other, but not get too close because you may swallow me up or hurt me." It will also have a somatic component: muscle flaccidity or chronic (and often severe) muscle tension, particularly in the legs, as the individual physically internalises the fight to come closer and simultaneously to withdraw. Since fear is a major part of the process, there will be either a continuous state of adrenalin arousal, or a psycho-physical dissociation process, which I suspect would involve the endorphin/encephalin system.

In clinical practice, it is instructive (not least to the couple) to ask both partners to stand "a comfortable distance apart". This will often be several yards! Then ask each partner in turn first to move closer, then further away, with a commentary by both on what they experience.

Sample comments are:

"As you came closer, I found myself shutting off, not looking at you, and my breathing got shallow."

"As you come closer, I get frightened that you are going to hurt me."

"As I went further away, I felt abandoned and alone."

Looking at these comments (which I have come across several times) it is clear that there is also a third component: the perceptual. Neither partner in the relationship is using their *eyes*, or experiencing the world as it is. Neither are they in touch with their bodies. They are living in a fantasy world, either a paranoid fantasy ("Everyone's out to get me") or a depressive fantasy ("Nobody wants to love me because I'm not worth it"). Their primary interruptions to contact are projection (they project their eyes) and deflection.

Then, suppose a couple like this have children. This will be difficult for them since they do not want to get close to each other, but they will manage intercourse of a sort by dissociating their bodies and their minds. They then either '"go through the motions", or separate out a kind of unthinking "animal sexuality" (often seen in borderline states).

The children are now going to be caught in the classic "double-bind" described by Bateson, Jackson, Haley, and Weakland (1972). They will neither receive affection, nor be allowed to individuate, nor even be seen as themselves, as their parents have abandoned seeing. The parents will discourage the child both from coming close and from keeping a distance. On top of this, the child will be given a way out of this impossible situation: dissociation—from external reality, from his/her body, from other people—and into fantasy. And within a few generations, the family culture can progress from odd to psychotic.

From different perspectives, there are one, two, many, or no interruptions to contact

There has been some disagreement about how many interruptions to contact there are. Is "proflection" a meaningful concept; is it "just" a combination of other interruptions to contact, etc.? The whole disagreement seems to me to be rather academic (in the narrow sense). Part of what I have been talking about is that the named "interruptions" (however many there are) are part of a flowing continuum, where one configuration flows into another. In this kind of situation, it is useful to name landmarks, but those landmarks are *not* the reality. Even to make contact often involves projection and introjection; projections are often of introjects; to introject is to project one's power on to the author of the introject. So, we can number the "interruptions" in different ways: we can make a sharp distinction between self and environment (which, in fact, means we are talking about "self" and "environment" in the sense of the section headed "Awareness looks both outward and inward", above) and make landmarks of the many ways they can interact (many); we can say there is only *one* interruption to contact—to interrupt contact; or we can distinguish *two* forms of interruption to contact—aware and unaware/automatic/alienated. Or we can assimilate modern theories about multi-level communication and say that what appears an interruption to contact on one level is a powerful communication to the environment on another, and that, therefore, there are *NO* interruptions to contact. For example, the following two quotations come from the same paragraph of Perls, Hefferline, and Goodman, 1994, p. 236:

> The tangible environment of the retroflector consists of only himself, and on this he wreaks the energies he has mobilised.

> This process is often shrewdly managed to give secondary results that achieve the original inhibited intention: e.g. in order not to hurt his family and friends, he turns on himself and produces illness and failure that involve his family and friends.

Or, let's put it as an exam question: Which of these is retroflection? Self-support, brushing my hair, suicide (leaving a note), suicide (not leaving a note), going to war, self-immolation (as a Buddhist monk in Vietnam), marrying a violent man? DISCUSS!

Another good example is a couple, Bill and Mary, that Swanson discusses in *The Gestalt Journal* issue I mentioned above (Swanson, 1988, pp. 10–12).

> Bill sits back in his chair, choosing his words carefully. Frequently glancing out the window, eye contact is brief and guarded. Bill expresses irritation with his wife because, "she is always needing me for something." In contrast, he expresses pride in his own ability to take care of himself without having to depend on others. A theme of

others bugging him emerges. . . . In contrast with the confluent phobic style of Bill, Mary leans forward toward me in her chair, hands clasped. Her eyes reaching out to me have a pleading quality. Her feelings pour out. Her pain and neediness pull on me. She seems to be lost and hoping I will give her direction. She expresses loneliness and hopelessness of ever getting through to her husband. "Just when we seem to be getting along, we always end up in a fight that drives us apart. And it drives me crazy when he won't sit down and talk it out."

Bill tends to isolation (is confluence phobic); Mary tends to confluence (is isolation phobic). But, on another level, what does it mean that they married each other? I would see this rather as an oscillating relationship in the sense of the section headed "There is a common boundary process/state of oscillation between isolation and confluence", above, where Bill does the isolating for both of them and Mary does the confluencing for both of them (by a process which we could call projection, or, maybe better, by the psychoanalytic term "projective identification").

Conclusions

The Tao that can be told is not the eternal Tao.
The name that can be named is not the eternal name.
The nameless is the beginning of heaven and earth.
The named is the mother of ten thousand things.

(Lao Tsu, 1972, p. 1)

CHAPTER SEVENTEEN

Introjection revisited

This is an unpublished article that I have only recently finished. It seems to me that it fits well into the themes explored in the articles in this book, looking at a core concept and trying to see it afresh.

I want to explore the meaning and use of introjection in Gestalt therapy. It was a very significant concept in the original formulation and it has often been given a significant place more recently, but I have come to the conclusion that they are different places. This is partly through a general blunting and simplifying of the founding theory, partly through Fritz Perls' own simplifying and sloganising in his California days, and partly through a more recent counter-current in Gestalt circles that questions the central organising concept of *aggression*.

The original theory

For Perls, the psychoanalytic idea of an introjected *superego* confuses two different processes, introjection and *assimilation*. His image of the difference between the two was of teeth: what the environment provides can be swallowed whole without being metabolised (intro-jected) or subjected to *dental aggression*, and only the nourishing part is absorbed to support our growth. In the situation of introjection, there is a boundary disturbance and I lose the "taste" of what I am introjecting, so that the I and the you are blurred. In the situation of assimilation, there is a differentiation from, and a contact made with, the other, and a clear sense of myself in relation to what the other offers me and does not offer me, and what I do and do not offer.

This theory was expanded in Perls, Hefferline, and Goodman to become a part of the more nuanced understanding Goodman was developing of the contacting/self-actualisation process. Goodman describes introjection to be when "the self . . . displaces its own poten-tial drive or appetite with some one else's" (Perls, Hefferline, & Good-man, 1994, p. 233). As with all the interruptions to that contacting process, a normal use and a neurotic use for introjection are distin-guished, and a theory of introjection is not a theory of neurosis. The normal use of introjection is described as an attitude towards "all the vast range of things and persons we are aware of but that do not make much difference one way or the other: conventions of speech, dress, city-plan, institutions" (ibid.). I would add to this those things we are just learning that we need to temporarily introject in order to try them out: a new way to do therapy or to swing a golf club, for example. This is important in instances where the new approach seems counterintu-itive, but I want to hold open the possibility that it will come to help me in the long run. Neurotically, the person "comes to terms with his own frustrated appetite by reversing its affect before he can recognize it" (ibid.). That is, the alienation and disgust felt towards the demands of the world, in a situation of compulsion, are turned instead towards the person's own desires. (See also my expansion of this notion as a theory of shame, in Philippson, 2004 and in Chapter Twenty of this volume.)

Parallel to this expansion of the psychoanalytic understanding of introjection is Perls' expansion of the concept of the superego. In the analytic approach, the superego battles with the id drives, while the ego develops as a referee between the demands of the inner drives and the demands of the world. For Perls, this does not happen. Instead, the superego battles with another construct, an "infra-ego" that resists the demands in the same way a child tries to get out of doing what a parent demands: wheedling, procrastinating, deflecting.

Perls renamed these "topdog" and "underdog" (Perls, 1969a, pp. 18–19), and explained that, in their battle for survival, the person's actual drives, wants, and needs get lost. The therapy is not to ally with the underdog against the superego, but to come back to a sensing of what is urgent and meaningful now.

It is not a set of words or attitudes that are alien in introjection, it is the other whose words or attitudes are taken on board wholesale who is turned from alien to identified-with, at a cost of alienating one's own impulses. Assimilation means finding our own orientation, which we might even find to be in some ways similar to the introjected orientation.

The simplified theory

In what has become a conventional approach more recently, introjection has become a matter of sets of words or attitudes the person has taken on uncritically from parents (an equivalent concept to that of the superego in psychoanalysis, or "parent ego state" or "drivers" in transactional analysis). The focus is on challenging the words rather than exploring the boundary disturbance. The truth or reliability of the words or the goodness or badness of the parents becomes the important thing and the boundary process of the client gets lost. You could say that the introject is the "bug" that the therapist helps to fix.

How did we get here? I think a major part of this is down to the simplification of Fritz Perls in his later days, reducing the concept to turning "should" into "choose to", an idea that has been introjected without much attention being paid to what is lost in such a simplification. While the sentiment involved has some meaning, and approximates the replacement of someone's own drive by someone else's, the method ties the theory to the verbal domain rather than the embodied domain of "drives and appetites"; furthermore, a person who tends towards unaware introjection is also very likely to introject this procedure. Then s/he will appear decisive as an introjected quality, but without going through the contacting process that allows real discrimination, and specifically without being able to make the vital distinction of "shoulds" as assimilated values or as content of introjection.

Such an approach allows for a version of Gestalt therapy where introjected statements act as a kind of splinter to be detected and removed. The content becomes important rather than the boundary disturbance of the original. For example:

> Look out for and explore those introjects which are deeply embedded in the self-other organisation of the individual and which give birth to interrelated resultant introjects and projections and limit the individual's options for flexible interaction with the world. (Mackewn, 1997, p. 189)

This questioning of the accuracy of the verbal aspect of introjection tends to lead towards a cognitive–behavioural way of working rather than a dialogic, embodied process between therapist and client. Furthermore, the whole simple idea of attitudes introjected from childhood has been questioned in recent years. Cynthia Cook (personal communication) has suggested that children are brought up in a limited environment, and can validly be said to have assimilated a sense of how the world is from their repeated experience in that environment. The point would then be to support a client to risk engaging with all their senses in a world they have had good reason to avoid. I have (Philippson, 1993a and this volume) discussed *pseudo-introjection*, a process that looks like introjection but is not. I reproduce part of this here.

The kind of "introject" I am talking about is: "I've got to do better, work harder, I'm not good enough." Since it is usually immediately obvious to the client which parent said these statements, this looks like a classic example of introjection. However, my experience is that if I try to work with this in ways which would normally help a client to gain his/her own perspective on these statements, something like this develops:

Therapist: Put father on this cushion. He is saying "You must work harder." What do you say to him?

Client: [Looks very anxious, avoids looking at "father", maybe makes a half-hearted attempt to protest father's assessment.]

So, what is happening here? It is important to distinguish two very different situations. In the first, a father, ambitious for his daughter, insists on her working hard academically, giving acceptance conditionally on her achieving a certain, well-defined standard which is within her capability. In this situation, the daughter is very likely to introject "I must do well", probably in some sort of balance with "underdog" attitudes.

The second situation, which is the one I am discussing here, is where the concept "doing well" is either undefined or defined in such a way as to be obviously unattainable. In this situation, what the father is really saying is, "I will never accept you, whatever you achieve, but I don't want to say this openly." However, the daughter knows! This is a devastating state of affairs for a child, and she uses the father's evasion to achieve an illusion of the possibility of acceptance. The daughter therefore joins into the deception and acts as if the situation is the first, and, if she works hard enough, becomes something other than herself enough, punishes or hurts herself enough, then she can be loved and accepted.

On drives, aggression, and the individual

The other factor that contributes to a blunting of the original Gestalt understanding of introjection is an interlocking series of revisions of the theory to remove a sense of an existentially choosing (aggressing, in Gestalt theoretical terms) individual at the heart of the theory in favour of one that is essentially social-constructivist. I am thinking of Wheeler (2000), Wollants (2008) and Staemmler (2009). The overall sense is that the Gestalt relational theory of self as field-emergent or situational does not support a sense of a choosing, wilful individual, *aggressing* on his/her environment. For example:

> Our construction of reality is always and everywhere a *co-construction* with other people, and this is as true of 'solitary reflection' as it is of public discourse and debate . . . Our feelings and values are culturally conditioned, and the experiments we conceive and make, formally and naturalistically, are those that are in some sense afforded, or offered preferentially, by the cultural field, and those whose results can be communicated meaningfully somehow to other people, within the terms of our given paradigms at the particular time and place. (Wheeler, 2000, p. 102, original italics)

Now, the curious thing here is that Wheeler uses the language of Kuhn (1970) writing about what the latter sees as "normal science", a scientific community having general agreement about its concepts, experimental methods, and expectations in a period when a particular paradigm holds hegemonic sway. However, the bit of Kuhn's thinking he leaves out is that this period is importantly self-defeating, in that it sooner or later brings that community to the limits of that paradigm, and the contradictions soon mount up. It is only then that the scientific community will listen to those individuals who have been offering an alternative perspective, and who have until then been sidelined, leading to a "scientific revolution". (I would actually imagine that this is not far from how Wheeler imagines himself in relation to the Gestalt community.)

Wheeler describes our construction of reality in terms of Kuhn's "normal science", without mentioning the role of that period in overturning its own certainties, or questioning whether the cultural community is as coherent as the scientific community, and, thus, implicitly denies the individual person's ability (in fact, I would say that anybody who has brought up a two-year-old or a teenager is led to the conclusion that this capacity is a developmental necessity) to say *at any time* "What if we said the opposite" and to follow this wherever it might lead: this is Sartre's *"negation"* (Sartre, 1978). And, to labour the point, he does this in a book whose overall form is precisely such a negation of his home culture! For Wheeler, you either have to have the perpetually isolated individual or the field relatedness. Similarly, for Wollants (2008, p. 32), "From the beginning, I am not an individuated person, over and against an outside world, as there is not an environment that is separate from me".

Within such an understanding, the concept of "introjection" loses any real meaning (as does most of what is specific about Gestalt theory, I would contend). There are no individual impulses or drives. (I have written elsewhere (Philippson, 2004 and this volume) about the unfortunate consequences of dropping the concept of drives.) If we pick up our attitudes from our undifferentiated environment, which is under no circumstances problematic on this view, it is just what is to be expected. To be able to make the individuation and say "no" on an impulse is just too "individualistic", even though we have all done it. Yet, the existential basis for Gestalt therapy provides for an understanding of a personal self that is relationally emergent, and yet real enough to make a difference to the world, as, in their various ways, Jesus, Hitler, Osama Bin Laden, and Nelson Mandela did. I can say my "no" and speak it with my body-voice, even though the "I" is not encapsulated within that body. This is not essentially different from saying that a table is emergent from a tree and a woodworker, and is given its use-characteristics by gravity, yet it will still hold a meal, or bruise you if you bump into it. The shape of the table is made to provide that ability to use gravity. If you like, you could see our predilection for four-legged tables as cultural introjects that do not most efficiently use gravity: four-legged tables have a tendency to wobble, while three-legged tables are always stable.

In the same way, we shape our self-organisation to engage with our situation, and simultaneously shape aspects of our situation through our physical motor skills and our engagement or non-engagement with others (our *aggression* on the environment, in Gestalt terms), so that we may engage gracefully with that situation. Each act of introjection, whether normal or neurotic, takes away from that grace and spontaneity. In normal introjection, that is temporary, chosen, and with an eye to a new integration, or occurs in a situation where we do not care how we do things. In neurotic introjection, it is a permanent and unaware state of affairs in areas that affect our ability to engage with the world.

The significance for Gestalt therapy

For the original theory, the important thing is to remobilise the active self–other boundary, including the self's capacity to reject some aspect of the other and to self-regulate in the widest possible range of situations. To put the theory in its simplest form, if I can mostly stay in touch with my own self-orientation in the world, those who appreciate who I am come closer and those who do not distance themselves. This might mean significant loss, but ends up with a sense of the world as homely and accepting. If I regularly abandon my orientation to some other, and adjust myself to be acceptable, I will remain surrounded by those who do not accept me for myself, and the world appears alienating as I alienate myself. There is no demand here: it is an authentic act of self to make adjustments to hold a relationship with another, whether it is parent, partner, child, friend, job, culture, so long as I can hold to a point where I will say no.

That means that the content of introjection, and its truth or falsity, are not the relevant aspects. Rather, we need to facilitate the restoration of the ability to connect and separate, to say yes and no, and to risk one's own mistakes. We do this by returning to the identifications and alienations of the immediate moment:

Client: I always think I am going to be wrong. I think you will see me as stupid and not worth bothering with.

Therapist: OK. And would that be acceptable to you if I believed that?

Client: [Looking confused] What do you mean?

Therapist: You come to me to help you and I agree to do that even though I think you are stupid and not worth bothering with. Would I be being professional?

Client: I guess not.

Therapist: Try saying "I will only accept you as my therapist if you have respect for me". See how that is for you, if it is true for you.

Client: I don't want to say that.

Therapist: You could also try the opposite: saying "I will accept you however you treat me, because you are right and I am wrong".

Client: [With more feeling] I *don't* want to say that!

Therapist: What did you experience in your body just then?

In this way, I am not in the bind that any reassurance I give tells the client "You think you are wrong, but you're wrong". The saying of what they see in the therapist provides an immediate here-and-now laboratory of the issues at hand. Notice that the more currently conventional way of working with introjection seems to follow a similar path, encouraging the client to put down a boundary with a parent or a partner. But, since it is only done in fantasy, there is no real encounter, and there is no more evidence that the partner, for example, despises the client than that I do. Furthermore, the aim of setting a boundary is the re-establishment of a new relationship, not just a making of the other wrong instead of oneself. This can only be done with a real person, not a projective fantasy figure. I am reminded of Perls' critique of Encounter groups, that people are only encountering their own projections in them.

Usually, the parents, partners, bosses of the clients are "advanced work", people in relation to which it might be a meaningful life choice not to set the boundary too starkly. If the client can make a more contactful engagement with the therapist, and then with other people in their lives, they are in a good position to make those choices with the difficult people, those they do not want to move out of their lives even if there is some cost to themselves.

Conclusion

I have tried here to clarify the concept of introjection in Gestalt therapy, the ways the meaning has changed and the pressures under which this has happened.

I have pointed to the significance of the differences in outlook in the therapeutic approach, and some of the reasons why I strongly recommend a return to the original theory.

CHAPTER EIGHTEEN

Pseudo-introjection*

Already, in 1993, I was concerned about the emphasis on introjection as a simple process of "taking in" something alien. Often, with real clients it seemed far more complex than that. See also my chapter "Introjection revisited" in this volume (pp. 145–153).

In this chapter, I am going to look at a common stance that clients take, which looks like introjection, but which actually involves a quite different process: deflection. Attempts to work with this process in ways appropriate for introjection meet with resistance and anxiety.

In terms of the *DSM-III-R* classification, this process would manifest as obsessive compulsive personality disorder, and possibly in the proposed category of self-defeating personality disorder.

The kind of "introject" I am talking about is: "I've got to do better, work harder, I'm not good enough." Since it is usually immediately obvious to the client which parent said these statements, this looks like a classic example of introjection. However, my experience is that

---

*First published in 1993, in *Topics in Gestalt Therapy*, 1(2).

if I try to work with this in ways which would normally help a client to gain his/her own perspective on these statements, something like this develops:

> *Therapist*: Put father on this cushion. He is saying "You must work harder." What do you say to him?
>
> *Client*: Looks very anxious, avoids looking at "father", maybe makes a half-hearted attempt to protest father's assessment.

So, what is happening here? It is important to distinguish two very different situations. In the first, a father, ambitious for his daughter, insists on her working hard academically, giving acceptance conditionally on her achieving a certain, well-defined standard which is within her capability. In this situation, the daughter is very likely to introject "I must do well", probably in some sort of balance with "underdog" attitudes.

The second situation, which is the one I am discussing here, is where the concept "doing well" is either undefined or defined in such a way as to be obviously unattainable. In this situation, what the father is really saying is, "I will never accept you, whatever you achieve, but I don't want to say this openly." However, the daughter knows! This is a devastating state of affairs for a child, and she uses the father's evasion to achieve an illusion of the possibility of acceptance. The daughter therefore joins in the deception and acts as if the situation is the first, and, if she works hard enough, becomes something other than herself enough, punishes or hurts herself enough, then she can be loved and accepted.

This explains the client's reluctance to give up the "introject". The magical, obsessive sentence "I must do better" (which she does not really even believe) is all that stands between her and the pain of despairing of being accepted by father. In a sense, the task of the client is not to abandon the sentence, but to abandon hope. And this abandonment of hope is only survivable after the client has allowed herself to be aware that acceptance is available elsewhere, and specifically from the therapist.

Working with pseudo-introjection

When I take on a client whose process is a pseudo-introjective deflection from the despair of abandonment, I am aware that the client is embarking on a project of an emotional difficulty on a par with climbing a mountain! And, like climbing a mountain, there is a danger of the client falling to her death. There is a real danger of suicide, either overt, or—continuing the theme of self-deception—"accidental". Therefore, I take a lot of time contracting with the potential client. The points I make are: the therapy will be hard work and painful, and probably long in duration. (Fortunately, this will appeal to the client, although, in keeping with her process, she will also believe that she will ultimately fail.)

My guess is that at some time(s) in the therapy, she will experience strong suicidal fantasies and urges, and that these will mark an important turning point in her therapy. What she will be saying in these fantasies is, "I am not going to be like this any more." If she commits to staying alive, this is the point at which her patterns of contacting will fundamentally change. In Gestalt terms, this can be seen as the killing of one (relational) self and the formation of another. (I want to note here that I have received criticism for raising the issue of suicide so early. I believe that there is much more danger in not doing so. My intervention actually positively values the suicidal fantasy, not as a precursor to death, but as a precursor to coming alive. This has the added benefit of reducing the client's fear of these urges.)

My treatment plan as the therapy develops is to affirm the client non-verbally, while, at the start of therapy, to hold back from verbal affirmations as being too frightening. I want to hold for myself a warm sense of the frightened, hurt person who both wants and fears to emerge, and I can often see that person in the client's hungry gaze or flickering peep when she thinks I am not noticing. In my eye-to-eye contact, it is to this persona that I am making a connection.

As therapy progresses, I start making more overt, graded, verbal affirmations. These always provoke a frightened and/or hostile response. It is important that I do not make these verbal affirmations as a technique, as the client will be expecting every affirmation to be false, and will usually pick up deceit if it is there (and often when it is not!). It is also important to be able to hear the client's hostility without defensiveness, and also without giving ground on what I believe. Of course, if the client disagrees with me, it is open to me to accept that I agree with the challenge, and to tell the client so. In this way, I am also modelling a way of being challenged without losing my sense of myself.

This process can take a long time, and the aim is that the client develops sufficient self- and environmental support to be able to face the despair involved in acknowledging: "There was nothing I could do to get my father/mother's love or acceptance." As this becomes a perceived possibility, the suicidal fantasies often start. This is the beginning of the process of mourning the loss of an illusory parental figure, and of an illusory life, geared towards pleasing the implacable.

At this stage, my contact with the client is usually a lifeline for her, and I need to be aware of the implications of my importance for her therapy and, sometimes, for her survival. I would offer my home telephone number (without necessarily being asked). This is often enough for clients to feel supported without having to ring me often. I have not had my offer of phone time abused, whereas I have frequently come across situations where a therapist who does not give out his or her phone number is constantly rung by clients who have ferreted it out (James Masterson makes the same point about work with border-line clients). If I go away on holiday, or to a conference, I tell the client in advance and let them work out how to get through the time I am away. I might let them have something of mine to remind them of my continuing interest and involvement in their lives. Some clients ring my answerphone to hear my voice. If possible, I arrange for a colleague to be available, at least to be rung, during my absence.

I also need to be able to manage my own countertransference. I might, out of my own anxiety, try to steer the client away from the despair that she needs to experience in order to get beyond this impasse. The client would be used to fitting in with a shared illusion that things are not as bad as all that, and would in some ways be inviting this, for example, "I'm just making a fuss about nothing." I might also react against this countertransference by confronting the deflection too quickly and roughly (some Gestaltists are noted for doing this). I need to be well in contact with myself and with the client, monitoring both my own and the client's anxiety levels. Too much anxiety on either of our parts and we will lose the contact which is so vital to this work.

If these conditions are met, the client can be supported to face and work through the despair and drop the illusion. She can then take in the nourishment that the real world offers to her as a human being no better or worse than anyone else, rather than as a uniquely deficient aberration.

CHAPTER NINETEEN

The paradoxical theory of change: strategic, naïve, and Gestalt*

One of my ongoing themes is that the basic theory of Gestalt therapy is complex, and, rather than attending to the complexity, trainers have taught various simplifications, such as the Cleveland cycle of experience. While some of these actually change the theory into something quite other than the original, others, such as the paradoxical theory of change, are nice statements of the theory, so long as the limitations of the simplification are understood; that is, if there is enough awareness of the theory from which it emerged. Because this is often not done, even a useful and beautiful simplification like this one become problematic.

"The paradoxical theory of change" is the title and theme of a very important and beautiful paper in Gestalt therapy by Abraham Levitsky (Beisser, 1970).

In his paper, Levitsky questions the role of the Gestalt therapist as a change agent. Rather, ". . . change occurs when one becomes what he is, not when he tries to become what he is not" (Beisser, 1970, p. 88).

---

*First published in 2005, in *International Gestalt Journal*, 28(2).

According to Beisser's analysis, the client experiences some area of her functioning as not hers and, therefore, outside her boundary of control, the situation Perls, Hefferline, and Goodman (1994) call "loss of ego functions", and the client is likely to call "symptoms". If the therapist tries to help the client to change these "symptoms", s/he is accepting the client's configuration of these areas as some alien problem, rather than an alienated action. This ends up with the therapist playing topdog, and the client playing underdog, rather than a relationship that transcends this polarity. However, if the therapist helps the client towards experiencing and owning her own activity and position in the world, however unacceptable to the client, she can then decide to act in new ways, or even make her own choice to stay with the old ways of acting, but from a position of ownership of her own actions.

As Miriam Polster (personal communication) puts it, "What is, is; and one thing follows another".

Since this idea is much loved in the Gestalt world (and also much loved by me!), and yet is a simplified statement of the theory of Gestalt therapy, it is important to look at it in relation to the wider theory, and to see how it can be understood and misunderstood. For, as I can see from supervisees and trainees, the theory can be, and is, used in three quite different ways, which I call the strategic, the naïve, and the Gestalt. I shall, in this chapter, describe and differentiate between these understandings.

Strategic paradox

There is an approach to strategic family therapy, made famous by the "Milan School" of Selvini Palazzoli and her colleagues (Selvini Palazzoli, Boscolo, Cecchin, & Prata, 1978), which is based on paradox, and, in fact, their most famous work is entitled *Paradox and Counter-Paradox*. Their use of paradoxical intervention is called "prescribing the symptom", and consists of positively connoting what they bring as a symptom of a problem in the family or, more often, a problem with a family member. The therapists get a sense of how the "symptom" is a way for the family to deal with what seems an otherwise impossible situation. In their own words, ". . . what we are connoting positively is the homoeostatic tendency of the system, and not its members" (ibid., p. 58). They then earnestly encourage the family to continue this way of acting, pointing out to everyone the terrible consequences that would ensue if they stopped.

The family here is presenting the therapists (who work as a team) with a paradox: to help them to change, while insisting that they are not involved in the problem in the first place. The therapists are returning the opposite paradox: we will help you to change by making very powerfully prescriptive interventions that tell you to keep doing what you are already doing. The family is caught by the therapists' certainty, and by their agreement with the family's own assessment of the situation. Therefore, they follow the prescription, and end up, similar to the Gestalt paradox, taking new ownership of what they are all doing (assuming the therapists are right in their analysis).

However, it is important to note that the therapists do not actually want the family to end up acting the way they insist they want them to act, and do not believe, though they say they do, that this is the only thing the family can do. They are manipulating the family into owning and then dropping a fixed behaviour. There is no meeting between the family members and the therapists. In fact, some of the therapists are behind a one-way screen, communicating with the therapists who sit with the family by telephone, so that they avoid as much as possible being part of the process in the therapy room. There is no dialogue, because, of course, the therapists do not want the family to question their judgement. The approach is a child of psychoanalytic psychotherapy mated with the systemic thinking of Bateson and Haley (see, for example, Bateson, Jackson, Haley, & Weakland, 1972).

The other similar approach is in neuro-linguistic programming (NLP), and its approach to "pacing and leading". The NLP therapist takes careful note of the client's method of communicating—voice, metaphor, rhythm, breathing, etc.—and copies it to encourage a confluence between therapist and client. The therapist can then alter these slowly to lead the client into a new way of acting. Again, the therapist is acting in agreement with the client in order to achieve compliance with a process that the client is not aware of, and not out of any interest in the truth of the therapist's intervention.

A superficially similar approach appears in the Gestalt world in Enright's (1980) technique of "the velvet steamroller". Enright, who sees Gestalt therapy as being at best an approach to enlightenment, not to therapy, has made a particular study of *comparison* as a major aspect of awareness. When we describe our activity, we judge it in comparison with other things we could have done. For Enright, when we think we have a problem it is because of the comparisons we are making between what we do and what we assume others are doing. The problem is an illusion. Enright pointed out that Perls usually compared the client's activity negatively with more self-supporting, more aware, or more owned ways of acting. He then described a way of responding to the client with the opposite comparison: comparing it with other *less* self-supporting, less aware, less owned ways of acting. For example, with a client who drinks heavily:

> Therapist: I respect that you are aware of this as a problem. Many people are not.
>
> Client: But I don't change it.
>
> Therapist: You realise that just being aware of it doesn't change the situation, and have come to look for help to change, knowing that just thinking about it isn't enough.

The technique is still a technique, not a dialogue. Yet, there is a difference from the Milan or NLP approaches. The therapist is not telling the client to keep doing what he is doing, or that it is right, just that the client is making choices, and there are plenty of worse choices than the one he is making, as well as better ones. The therapist is also not going outside what is true, merely embracing the unattended opposite polarity. The client often ends up desperately trying to convince the therapist how bad he is!

However, it is important to notice that Enright's method is not paradoxical in any sense. Once one can see the significance of Enright's focus on comparison, his methodology becomes clearly logical and linear.

I now turn to the actual Gestalt version of the paradoxical theory of change, and start by pointing out the problems inherent in a naïve reading of the theory.

Naïve paradox

> Client: I feel as if people can see what a terrible person I am, or, at least, if they did see, they would reject me.
>
> Therapist: [In a muddle. Does not see anything terrible, yet is hesitant to act from her belief that the client is misjudging the situation, because (a) this would deny the paradoxical

theory of change, and (b) it would deny the client's phenomenology. So the therapist is caught between two unsatisfactory responses:]

Therapist 1: [Being honest.] I don't understand when you say that. I don't see anything terrible.

Client: [Ignores this.]

or

Therapist 2: [Being "paradoxical" or "phenomenological"] I understand that you feel this. Tell me more.

Client: [Recounts situations that she has interpreted as total rejection, which the therapist is aware could have been quite insignificant to the other person concerned.]

In either case, the client is likely to be completely within his familiar responses. We need something much more subtle than this!

Let us deal with the misunderstanding of phenomenological method first. For both Husserl and Heidegger, the aim of phenomenologically bracketing my everyday assumptions about the situation is not so as to see more clearly the other person's assumptions. That is Rogerian "reflecting back", not phenomenology. The aim of phenomenology (where there is not assumed to be a therapist involved at all) is to bracket everyday assumptions, full stop. In the therapy situation, this would mean bracketing both the therapist's *and* the client's assumptions, to try to get as close as possible to a description of the present moment in its uniqueness. In Gestalt terms, the aim is to deconstruct fixed Gestalten, and face the assimilable novelty.

So, a phenomenological approach to the client above would be something like an enquiry into the client's physical experience, his experience of me, my physical experience (sad and confused), the fact that the client is in the room and wanting something from me, and that I do not know what it is, and that his words do not communicate anything meaningful to me, yet I am willing to sit with the client and see what we can manage together.

Gestalt paradox

There are some major limitations to a simple interpretation of the paradoxical theory of change in Gestalt therapy. To start off with, if the theory requires that the client accepts who she is and where she is, there is an immediate complication in a Gestalt context. For "who I am" in Gestalt theory is relational, not a given. In a therapy session, who the client is involves who the therapist is (and vice versa), and the contact between the two.

Compare the paradoxical theory with the following from Perls, Hefferline, and Goodman (1994):

> If a man identifies with his forming self, does not inhibit his own creative excitement and reaching toward the coming solution; and conversely, if he alienates what is not organically his own and therefore cannot be vitally interesting, but rather disrupts the figure/background, then he is psychologically healthy, for he is exercising his best power and will do the best he can in the difficult circumstances of the world. (p. 11)

This is clearly the same territory, yet stated in a way that is consistent with Gestalt therapy's field–relational theory of self.

So, the self-critical client above does the opposite of this: ". . . if he alienates himself and because of false identifications tries to conquer his own spontaneity, then he creates his life dull, confused, and painful" (ibid.). In order to become who she is becoming (rather than who she "is"), we need to find some area of creative excitement and solution finding. Usually, this is done by the therapy offering a problem that the client cannot solve in her habitual way. This is very similar to the use of the *koan* in Zen Buddhism, which influenced both Fritz Perls and Paul Weisz from the original New York group.

Now we can see a possible next step for the therapist with this client:

Client: I feel as if people can see what a terrible person I am, or, at least, if they did see, they would reject me.

Therapist: I understand that you want something from me, yet I do not know how to engage with you at this moment. Is there something you want me to do with what you have just said?

And I could keep on saying this in different ways for as long as the client is engaging with her personality function rather than with me.

Looking more closely at the requirements of the phenomenologi-cal method also points out the problem that the paradoxical theory cannot simply be applied to situations where the client is sensorially out of contact with the "where", and taking her experience of the "who" from some fantasy world, maybe a replay of childhood, maybe a world where she can follow her whims because she is evil, or has no responsibility because she is so weak.

Yet, even here, the paradoxical theory holds, if viewed in a reason-ably sophisticated way. It points out that I cannot change the client's mind by pointing out that I see him positively: that would only be saying to the client once again "I am right, you are wrong". I can maybe encourage the client to look and say what he sees with as little interpretation as possible. I can maybe encourage the client to risk saying what he likes and dislikes in the room, thus turning outward retroflected self-criticism into critiquing the environment. I can maybe encourage the client to notice and tell me his physical experience moment by moment, once again with as little interpretation as possi-ble. All these can allow for more of the basic elements of the para-doxical theory, and all will be likely to bring to awareness feelings of shame. This is not because I am "shaming" the client: it would be more true to say that I would be acting in a shaming way if I tried to change the client's experience by arguing that she is seeing it all wrong; rather, it is because the shame is already inherent in the client's disconnection from the world, self-disgust and projection of the disgust on to the world around him.

So, in accordance with the paradoxical theory of change, I stay with and accept what is: our disconnection from each other, my wish to connect, my lack of understanding of what the client wants from me, my seeing the client not looking at me. I then do not try to move on. We have to stay with this until a new figure can emerge between us.

Neurological considerations

The other assumption behind the theories of self-regulation and para-doxical theory of change is that the client's neurological development can support the self-regulating and growthful responses. We now know, since the work of Schore (1994), Damasio (1999), and others that this is not so. Human infants are born with extremely immature levels of brain development, compared with other animals. In the first eighteen months of life, there is massive overproduction of neural connections, which are then whittled down to what helps in the infant's environment. Thus, if the environment is mostly painful and isolating, the neural connections that support the infant in that environment remain, and those that would respond to love and pleasure are sacrificed. The brain that remains is neurologically incapable of seeking pleasure in intimacy.

Further, in the absence of the hormones released by touch, particularly oxytocin, connections between the midbrain and the frontal lobes, involved in impulse control and delayed gratification, do not develop properly.

These factors are usually present in severe personality disorder, which are, thus, as much neurological as psychological, in the sense that the person's brain cannot support different ways of being. Fortunately, we know that, except in very extreme cases of deprivation, such as the babies in Romanian orphanages, a great deal of development is possible in later life, but that the important therapeutic factor in promoting this change is a committed and clear relationship with the therapist, open to both intimacy and touch.

Even here, the paradoxical theory has things to say. If the relationship is an attempt to create change by mimicking some idealised parental relationship, it is less effective than if a real intimacy develops organically (and with great difficulty at first) between therapist and client.

Conclusion

In this chapter, I have attempted to bring some consistency to Beisser's "Paradoxical theory of change". I have shown how "becoming who he is" cannot have its everyday meaning in a therapy with a field–relational understanding of self. I have distinguished between Gestalt paradox and strategic uses of paradox, and indicated some situations where the paradoxical theory either does not apply, or needs to be applied with some care.

CHAPTER TWENTY

The experience of shame*

Writing and presenting on shame has been appearing very often in the recent Gestalt world, mostly with a subtext that dismisses all previous ways of working as shame-inducing. The emphasis then comes on to support and away from challenge. The client is seen as inherently fragile and needing protection, and the original Gestalt emphasis on therapy as an act of courage is lost, or seen as inherently shaming. Yet, there is a real issue: I have seen ways of doing Gestalt therapy that is oppressive, leading to many clients and trainees hiding their fear and anger and becoming what the therapist or trainer wants them to be, often loud and challenging from an uncontactful place. I thought that if I was going to criticise the writing on shame, I should also put forward my own view.

There has been much writing on the theme of "shame" recently (see, in particular, *British Gestalt Journal*, 4(2), 1995, and the *Gestalt Review*, 1(3), 1997). This chapter is an attempt to put a slightly different emphasis on the topic.

*First published in 2004, in *International Gestalt Journal*, 27(2).

Most of the writing on shame in the Gestalt literature emphasises the activity of the person who "shames" the other (I would exclude Wheeler and Resnick here). The image that comes across to me of the person "shamed" is of an injured innocent, who is not response-able for her/his experience, which is induced from outside. Now this, for me, is not in line with a Gestalt relational approach, where each person configures his/her own experience, and, in doing so, is part of the other's self-configuration. There are no "innocents" in this approach!

To take this a stage further, I believe there is often a kind of not-so-subtle blaming in talking about "shaming" as something one person does to another. At its best, the response-ability approach of Gestalt therapy gets away from a paradigm where the "guilty party" is the generation before the client. This client then comes to a therapist whose views on child-rearing are more humane and right than that of the client's family or culture (and whose children, of course, have a better time in the world than those of less enlightened ones). In the 1970s, we called this sort of thing "cultural imperialism". Gestalt therapy is distinguished by not having a normative theory of how people should be or act, rather saying that such introjects *in themselves* take away from the contactfulness of relationships. (Lasch (1979) makes the same point from a more psychoanalytically informed perspective.)

To quote Mathys (1995, pp. 105–106), working with a father ashamed of his (African) culture:

> And yet there I was, a white European woman, the professional representative of the educational system that was engaging (and judging) this man's son . . . Anthony's life was unfolding in a bicultural world – and not simply a bipolar one but one in which one pole, the white European, was often privileged and valued, while the other, the black African, was often held to be inferior or outmoded or otherwise devalued.

It is vital and ethical to be wary of assuming our values are better than that of the client's family and culture. To do so can *in itself* encourage the client to feel belittled even while ostensibly being supported. Then, in order to keep this support, the client will experience pressure to adopt the therapist's cultural bias and distance her/himself from the family and culture from which s/he comes.

Thus, I want to focus here on the experience of shame *for the person who experiences it*, and on that person's response-ability for that experience. In doing so, I do not want to detract from the response-ability of the other in the situation. One of the beautiful advantages of looking at responsibility in this way is that it is not a matter of working out percentages of responsibility: each partner in the interaction is 100% response-able. I want to start with one of the most perceptive of the recent Gestalt writers on shame, and chart the development of my thinking. Wheeler (1995, p. 83) focuses on shame as a "break in the field of self-experience", a rupture in the field as the environment "refuses to receive me as I know/fear myself to be" (p. 82). It is, thus, an interruption to contact at the contact-boundary. But which interruption?

I go back to *Ego, Hunger and Aggression* (Perls, 1947), and to Perls' discussion of *disgust*. Developmentally, Perls understands disgust as a response to being fed (literally or psychologically) something alien and unassimilable. The physiological response is to spit or vomit out the other: it "belongs to the class of annihilation" (Perls, 1947, p. 113). However, in some circumstances it might be seen by the infant (or adult) as too dangerous to spit out the "food", and s/he therefore inhibits the disgust reflex. I believe that this is the experience towards which Wheeler (1995) is pointing. Not only is the person being offered something "disgusting", but is afraid of the consequences of ejecting it back to the environment: fear of abandonment or pain, or of damaging a loved other.

An energetic, emotional expression of a vital boundary function does not merely disappear, however: it is retroflected. To be more precise, the boundary identifications and alienations of the ego are altered, so that the child identifies with the force-feeder and alienates her/his disgust response as an "other", whose disgust is then aimed at the "self" that is the source of the poisoned food (see Figure 1). (I emphasise these boundary shifts because I believe it is vital that Gestalt therapy stays clear of a simplified cathartic model of "stored emotional energy" which needs to be "discharged".)

In the retroflection, disgust becomes self-disgust; annihilation becomes self-annihilation; physically, the posture would be one which inhibits vomiting: head down, shallow breathing, taut abdomen. The person would experience nausea. Little energy is available for contacting the real-life other. This *retroflected disgust reflex* would be how I

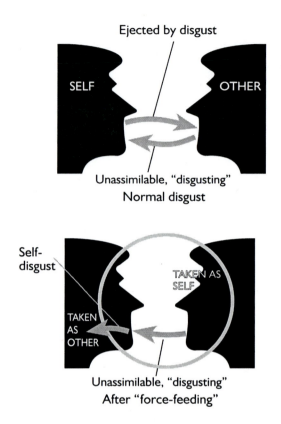

Figure 1.

understand the shame experience from the perspective of the person experiencing it. It fits with my own experience of shame, and with that of my clients, both psychologically and physiologically. Later, I will show how clinically useful this definition is.

What is more, the white circle in the second picture shows how part of the boundary reconfiguration is to bind oneself to the image of the force-feeding care-giver (for example, a parent). This tie will usually be clung to, since it may be the only link available to a narcissistically unavailable parent. Thus, the self-criticism will usually be in the voice of this other person, who has now become part of my self-identification.

The next question is: what form of retroflection is this? Recall that there are essentially two types of retroflection: retroflection of a forbidden impulse, and narcissistic retroflection, doing for myself what I want the environment to do for me, but I am too scared to ask for. I have described this disgust-retroflection as originating in the turning inwards of a forbidden impulse. However, having made the required boundary shifts, consider the way the shame-experiencing person will perceive the world. For the alienated, disgust is projected on to the "other", and, therefore, on to the person's world, which would then be perceived as very dangerous and rejecting. Or, to put it in terms of my diagram (Figure 1), I can easily flip into identifying with the part-self that is the object of disgust (on the left of the diagram), and alienating the rejecting part-self as other.

Furthermore, behind the fear of seeing the world as rejecting is *always* (in my experience) the fear of seeing acceptance. To see rejection, while uncomfortable, does not demand a reconfiguration of my self/other experience, and to see acceptance does. If *confronted* (I use the word advisedly—see below) with acceptance, I need to own my own disgust. I will also be letting go of the fantasy boundary that ties me to the original force-feeding care-giver. Rather than face my self-responsibility and the loss of the (fantasy) parental link, I might try to reinstate the rejecting–rejected dyad, and attempt to undermine the accepting person by instilling self-doubt and self-criticism (very common with narcissistic clients and their therapists). In general, though, I will avoid taking such self-authority. I am then caught up in the world of narcissistic retroflection, doing things for myself since I take the world as hostile and rejecting.

Working with shame

If shame is, as I am proposing, a retroflection of the disgust reflex, then the work of therapy is a reopening of connection to the real other (in this case the therapist), leading to a re-placing of the self–other boundary and a reinstatement of emotion as a connection to the environment. Specifically, the client is given a relationship where s/he can risk reowning his/her capacity for disgust and rejection. The therapist must be available in a way that does not fit into the rejecting–rejected dyad, as I have said above. As therapist, therefore, I must hold the following characteristics.

1. *I must be accepting of the client*

    It is important to understand this "acceptance" properly. It does not mean "attunement" to the client (Erskine, 1995; Philippson, 1996), or requiring the therapist to feel warmth or liking for the client. What I mean is that I show myself to be willing to stay with the client, even when the going is difficult for both of us. For a client who retroflects as a way of avoiding both (projected) rejection and the unknown of acceptance, I would understand such a stance to be at least as much a challenge as a support. I am supported cognitively in such acceptance by understanding it as a challenge, and, thus, not expecting the client to welcome my demonstration of acceptance, but, rather, to treat it as a threat to be neutralised by demonising or idealising the therapist. Furthermore, behind the rejecting behaviour lies the remobilisation of the client's capacity to reject the unassimilable: expression rather than retroflection of the disgust reflex.

    If I can understand the confrontation involved in accepting the shame-experiencing client, I can understand the client's response enough not to be unbalanced by his/her rejection or idealising, and to be sensitive to how difficult this radical acceptance is for the client to assimilate.

2. *I must be accepting of myself*

    To work properly with shame, I need to have enough self-support to stay grounded when faced with the client's rejecting polarity. I need the sheer bloody-mindedness to be there at the end of the attack, and enough sensitivity to the process that I do not then launch a counter-attack (which, historically, is what the client's expression of disgust would be likely to have resulted in). The client might actually prefer to be rejected or punished after expressing disgust, as a reaffirmation of her/his expectations from the world. However, if I counter-attack, either the client will leave, or become compliant. As one client said about a previous therapist: "I only told her what she would be willing to hear." (Of course, I need to be aware that the client might have been telling me what she thought I wanted to hear!)

3. *I must not force-feed the client*

    While remaining available and accepting of the client, I must not hurry the process of the client agreeing to drop the retroflection and contact me. I will need to keep a clear sense of the boundary

between us, and stay just on my side of it. What is on my side is
that I do not get pushed away, and that I offer contact; what is on
the client's side is whether and when to take up my offer. I must
not override the client's disgust reflex and force-feed him/her
with my own agenda.

On blundering around

From the very beginning of a therapeutic relationship with shame-
experiencing clients, I avoid painting myself into a corner where the
client expects me to show hypersensitivity to her/his needs, and in
turn becomes hypersensitive to the times when I misunderstand
her/him. If I let myself be more blundering at the start of therapy, so
that it becomes an accepted part of our relationship that I am the kind
of dancer that will sometimes step on his partner's toes, my inevitable
toe-stepping will be a source of annoyance for the client rather than a
sudden revelation of my fallibility.

The major obstacle in the way of this willingness to blunder is if
my own grandiosity leads me to try to fit in with my client's wish for
perfection from me. Then it is not my client's disapproval that is
destructive, but my self-disapproval at falling short of my own
idealised image, which is supported by the client.

Working through retroflected disgust

By providing such a relationship (committed, bumbling, accepting
and self-accepting, bloody-minded), I create a framework where the
client (should s/he so wish, and when s/he feels ready) can undo the
retroflection of disgust. Often, the client's reported experience is feelings of nausea, painful feelings of shame and fear coupled with specific memories arising spontaneously. Physically, I encourage the client
to breathe into the feelings of nausea, and to straighten his/her back
and hold up his/her head (supporting this with my hand on the
client's back if physical contact is appropriate). Sometimes, rarely, the
client will physically vomit, and I keep a bucket available for eventu-
alities where this looks as if it is going to happen. Most times, what is
"brought up" is powerful grief at the ending of an idealised confluent
relationship, usually with a parent.

While this phase is painful for the client, it is actually not in the therapy room that it is problematic. The major difficulties arise in the client's life and relationships, for the client will be exercising her/his newfound ability for alienation in her/his everyday life. At this time, I encourage the client to become aware of what is "to his/her taste". However, I also discourage over-impulsive ending of important relationships. Some relationships are too important to use as a proving ground for newly recovered abilities. Nevertheless, most clients will start making their own decisions about their preferred relationships at this time, and start learning to negotiate for what they want, and setting limits around what they are not prepared to accept. Often they will make or deepen new relationships and end some old ones.

Often, shame-experiencing people will take on the interests of those who offer a relationship to them. In this phase, they might need to learn how to develop their own interests (develop their identification ego-function), and to find the places where they can share these interests, and meet people whose interests they share. This can provide new possibilities for relating, based on something more substantial than immediate sexual interest or idealisation.

Shame and communality

Polster (1993) has written about the need to reincorporate a more community-based perspective into Gestalt therapy. Writers outside Gestalt, in particular Lasch (1979) and Hillman and Ventura (1992) have echoed Polster's concern about the individualising effects of psychotherapy. I would want here to put this particularly in the context of work with shame issues. In this, I want to echo Wheeler (1997, p. 234), who argues cogently that the individualist paradigm is not adequate to describe shame. He continues:

> That is, in this model we understand shame as the affect of that disconnect in the field, that sense of the field pulling away from me, not receiving me, with all the judgment and associated feeling that are carried by that field structure.

What I would want to do here, given the orientation of this chapter, is to try and bridge the gap between the individualistic and the communal approach by asking what the individual *does* in relation to a rejecting field. The answer I have given is essentially that the individual *gives up* on field connectedness, first by impulse retroflection (of the disgust reflex), then by narcissistic retroflection. Having done this, it actually becomes very difficult for the field to make a connection with that individual. Support, like all other psychological entities in Gestalt theory, is relational. That is, the Gestalt concept of *self-support* is primarily about orientating oneself in the field so that the field can support one, whether it be by standing so as to be supported by gravity, or opening oneself to receive support, and being in the physical location where that support might be available. This requires the individual to be in contact in the field.

I want to point out that the therapist can short-circuit this process. If I see myself as providing the support for the client, and do not encourage her/him to find her/his own support in the community, it can actually be my relationship with the client that acts to disconnect him/her from the community, from the wider field. I can be the bought intimacy, with no agenda of my own, with a code of acceptable behaviour. Even my agreement on confidentiality has its problem, since, by not talking to others about what the client has told me, I draw a fence round the client, removing him/her from the buzz of community talk.

In saying the above, I am aware that some clients will start by confiding in the therapist (or in a group), and then take the risk of opening more widely in their everyday world. This is fine, so long as the therapist is aware of this as a staging post, and with two specific personal provisos: that the therapist does not rely on clients' dependency for her/his own personal reasons, and that the therapist is also able to connect to the community. I would question how far a client will be able to go with a therapist who is not able to connect with her/his own community, or connects only on a professional level. I appreciate Erickson's integration of his solid local knowledge with his therapy (see Erickson, 1980).

Reorganising the self–other boundary

I want to return here to the theoretical map, and emphasise that the aim here is for the client to reinstate a self–other boundary that is reasonably consistent with the contact boundary (inside–outside the skin). That is, in the words of the "Gestalt Prayer" (Perls, 1969a): "I am I and you are you". Recall that the self–other boundary in shame is as in the lower part of Figure 1, where the force-feeding other is incorporated as part of the self, and part of the self is split off and made rejected other. Another way of saying the same thing is that the ego functions of identification and alienation return to their proper function, and allow contact.

This also shows how the notion of the "false self" (see, for example, Masterson, 1981) has its place in Gestalt theory. The self in the lower part of Figure 1 can be seen as an example of false self, with the ego function of alienation used to disown and reject vital aspects of my own functioning.

To move from the lower half of Figure 1 to the upper image is difficult and frightening, as it requires what is quite literally a death and rebirth of self. This will often appear during the therapy as suicidal or death images. I would work with the client to normalise and explain this, and, in fact, see the suicidal fantasies as evidence of movement towards the change they are in therapy for.

The work is challenging for the therapist, who must be able and willing to maintain selfhood and contact (without crossing the boundary into force-feeding) in the face of a client who alternates between idealisation and rejection. There will often be strong hints that the therapy will be more successful if the therapist's responses and feelings are other than what they are. If I have a desire to "attune", I can end up role-playing the therapist wanted by the client, while also wanting to be myself. I can then easily misplace my own self–other boundary. It becomes clearer how inaccurate the client's self-assessment of needs is when we focus on the "self" that is making the assessment. At the same time, I need to acknowledge how difficult it is for the client to face who I am, and, thus, who s/he is).

Conclusion

I am aware that this statement of theory and clinical practice takes place in relation to a background of debate (within both Gestalt therapy and object relations theory) of the best way to act with self/personality-disordered clients. It is, for example, much more consistent with the approach of Masterson (1981) than that of Kohut (1977). My hope here is that I have moved forward the task, ably begun by Wheeler (1995), of grounding our understanding of shame in the relational theory of Gestalt therapy, and in a way that is consistent with the Gestalt approach to self-responsibility.

This is not just an intellectual exercise for me, though. This is the theory on which I base my work with self-disordered clients, and it works very well for both me and them. It also has the advantage for me that I do not have to move conceptually outside my own Gestalt therapeutic paradigm. That is, I do not have to say "This client shows narcissistic process, so I have to drop a Gestalt relational approach and act as a (relatively untrained) object relations or self psychology therapist". While some psychodynamic therapists will recognise similarities with my way of working, and there will be some crossover in our theoretical formulations, I can remain grounded throughout in my Gestalt approach.

A further advantage to maintaining the same conceptual basis across the range of clients is that there are few "pure" narcissistic or borderline clients. It seems to me far better to be able to work with whatever boundary considerations apply to a particular client at a particular time, than to "flip" into a different way of working and conceptualising at a somewhat artificial boundary.

Finally, we need to be taking our own theory seriously. This means not only knowing the theory well and relating it to practice, but being willing to develop it in areas which are underdeveloped. This development should lead to an integrated, internally consistent theory. I have argued elsewhere (Philippson, 2001) that there is a potential problem in teaching Gestalt therapy if it is taught as a series of isolated clusters (dialogue, experiment, awareness, polarities, paradoxical theory, existentialism and phenomenology, interruptions to contact, contact cycle, five layers) with no integrated 'map' to join them. The map implicit in this paper is not the only possible one, but I hope it can show an example of the kind of integration I am suggesting we need.

CHAPTER TWENTY-ONE

Field theory: mirrors and reflections*

This was originally a lecture given at a day conference honouring Malcolm Parlett on his retirement as editor of the British Gestalt Journal *(BGJ), and then published in the BGJ in a Festschrift edition. It encompasses the development of my understanding of how recent discoveries in neuroscience support the Gestalt field approach. It also confronts what I see as a kind of anti-materialism, or anti-science, in the name of avoiding reductionism, which, at its limit, would turn what was grounded in research into a kind of religious faith, a creed to be followed with no external criteria on which to evaluate it.*

Introduction

While the emphasis of Gestalt therapy as a field theory was present in the earliest days, for most present-day Gestaltists, the primary source of discussion on the theme is in the writings of Parlett (1991, 1997). Since these were published, there have

*First published in 2006, in *British Gestalt Journal*, 15(2).

been startling advances in our understanding of the neurological underpinning of human behaviour, which have both confirmed and added to our understanding of the field nature of human consciousness and selfhood. In this chapter, I explore some of these advances and their implications for the development of a Gestalt field theory that is true to our tradition, and also in line with what we are currently discovering.

*   *   *

This is an exciting and also a worrying time for psychotherapy theorists of all persuasions. We are in a period of new experimental methods, able to test some of our assumptions about how the brain contributes to human functioning, and, in particular, to how human beings are conscious and aware. We have the potential to develop new and more sophisticated understandings, but also to find out that what we have considered axiomatic is contradicted by the evidence.

There have been various responses to this situation. For some, it is irrelevant, since "reductionist" studies cannot capture the functioning of a human being (see, for example, Kennedy, 2003). For others, including myself, it is fertile ground to be embraced. For Gestaltists, as I will argue, these new discoveries support and underpin much of what we have been saying for the past half-century. In particular, our field approach is both affirmed and even extended. In fact, given Fritz Perls' work with Goldstein at the Institute for Brain-Damaged Soldiers, I would argue that the origins of Gestalt therapy were influenced by the cutting-edge brain research of the day.

I want to be clear that this is not about reductionism. In the attempt to separate the "phenomenological field" from the scientifically explorable physical field, I would see a reintroduction of dualism, separation of mind and body, as two fundamentally different realms that interact. The new discoveries, on the other hand, show that any person's consciousness cannot be reduced to the activity of that person, let alone to that person's brain.

The image I want to present here is "reflections", different levels of existence reflecting, subtly altering, and adding to each other. Thus we come to . . .

Field theory

> The essence of field theory is that a holistic perspective towards the person extends to include environment, the social world, organizations, culture . . .

> What happens to something placed in this [electrical or magnetic] force field is a function of the overall properties of the field taken as an interactive dynamic whole. The field as a whole is also changed as a result of the inclusion of something new. (Parlett, 1991, p. 70)

In the fifteen years since Parlett wrote this, his writings on field theory (Parlett, 1991, 1997) have become standard texts on the subject in the Gestalt world, and have also been triumphantly vindicated by neurological and developmental research. For example, in 1991, many of us were already excited by the developmental ideas of Stern (1985). Who would have guessed then that Stern would be collaborating with Gestaltists (specifically Margherita Spagnuolo Lobb in Italy), based on a convergence of our field approaches to self, and that his next major book would be called *The Present Moment* (Stern, 2004).

These researches have also helped us become more specific in our knowledge. A very significant development has been the discovery of "mirror neurons" (Rizzalatti & Craighero, 2004) in the pre-motor area of the brain. These neurons, first discovered in monkeys, fire when we observe others carrying out an action. They allow us to have an empathic sense of what the other is doing: not only their actions, but also their intentions. Thus, one particular "flavour" of Gestalt therapy, insisting that we can only guess or project what is going on for another person, is not accurate, whereas the orthodox Gestalt theory of self as not inherently separate from other selves is supported. As Stern (2004, pp. 77–78) puts it,

> The idea of a one-person psychology or of purely intrapsychic phenomena are no longer tenable in this light . . . We used to think of intersubjectivity as a sort of epiphenomenon that arises occasionally when two separate and independent minds interact. Now we view the intersubjective matrix . . . as the overriding crucible in which interacting minds take on their current form.

> Two minds create intersubjectivity. But equally, intersubjectivity shapes the two minds.

Compare Perls (1978, p. 55): "Now the 'self' cannot be understood other than through the field, just like day cannot be understood other than by contrast with night".

Our understanding of field theory has, thus, moved from the image of human beings like iron filings in a magnetic force field: we are emergent aspects *of* the field, rather than *in* the field. The question becomes not how we connect with others, but how we can achieve any differentiation, what Sartre (1978) calls "negation". As Sartre's translator puts it in her Introduction (Sartre, 1978, p. xxvii), "And it is by means of knowing what it is not that consciousness makes known to itself what it is". Parlett (1991, p. 74) states that "The field theory outlook re-introduces the sense of a unified whole in which subject and object cease to be in opposition". We now know that the world of a human-of-the-field is *so* unified that it is only to the extent that there is some opposition that "subject" and "object" can even be meaningfully differentiated. Something must arise that the mirrors can reflect. I am reminded of how the early electronic engineers designed the original title sequence for *Dr Who*: they discovered that the swirling effect was produced if a camera was pointed at its own monitor. Something new emerged from the repeated looping of reflections.

But Stern is saying even more than this. He reminds us that the neurological explanation for consciousness is in terms of "re-entry", where a stimulus activates one group of neurons, which then activate a different set of neurons, which then, in turn, act on the first set, creating feedback loops round the original stimulus which we experience as consciousness. The normal theory of re-entry is understood to operate within a single person's neural system. However, given the existence of mirror neurons, a more startling possibility emerges: that consciousness can arise through a looping backwards and forwards between two or more people:

> . . . intersubjective consciousness is viewed as an interpsychic event requiring two minds. An experience is had by one individual. This is felt directly. It activates almost the same experience in another individual, via intersubjective sharing. This is then reflected back to the first individual in the regard and behavior of the second individual. As they encounter each other in this shared present moment, a reentry loop is created between the two minds. (Stern, 2004, p. 126).

My consciousness does not just have to be "in me", if this is right. It arises, rather, out of my contacts, those that are present and those that have been internalised. This is, of course, precisely what Gestalt self theory has been saying (in less informed and precise ways) for fifty years, and Buber before that in his writings on the "Between".

Thus, we can move out of the linear cause-and-effect world that psychotherapy has often been caught in, where often trauma or specific pieces of bad parenting have taken the place of germs; the Alice Miller world where the child is innocent and the parent is guilty. Or theories of "attunement", where the paradigm is of an influence that only passes one way, a therapist attuning to the separate selfhood of the client, rather than understanding the therapeutic relationship as an inevitable co-creation of therapist and client in the therapeutic relationship.

> Researchers have learned that much of child development is reciprocal, with characteristics of a child influencing the way that child is parented in addition to parenting influencing characteristics of a child ... it may be that exhausted parents of very active and inattentive children resort to using the television as a 'babysitter' more commonly than do parents of less active and more attentive children. (Stevens & Mulsow, 2006, p. 666)

The same considerations show that the experience of the therapist is as much a window on the client (as actualising in the therapy situation) as the experience of the client.

Complexity

A major area of research and theory in the past thirty years is in the complex systems that occur throughout nature, economics, weather, etc. The important point is that these systems are *non-linear*, that is, they have feedback loops. The startling discovery is that such systems quickly become *self-organising* (Prigogine & Stengers, 1984)—work for which Prigogine received the Nobel Prize in 1977.

> Such self-organizing structures are ubiquitous in nature, said Prigogine. A laser is a self-organizing system in which particles of light, photons, can spontaneously group themselves into a single

powerful beam that has every photon moving in lockstep. A hurricane is a self-organizing system powered by the steady stream of energy coming in from the sun, which drives the winds and draws rainwater from the oceans. A living cell – although much too complicated to analyze mathematically – is a self-organizing system that survives by taking in energy in the form of food and excreting energy in the form of heat and waste. (Waldrop, 1993, pp. 33–34)

Kauffman (quoted in Waldrop, 1993, p. 108) coined the term "order for free" to describe such self-organising systems. The rules for the emergent, complex system are not reducible to those of the less complex system from which they emerged, but must be compatible with them. So, living cells have their own rules for functioning, but none of their behaviour can contradict the laws of chemistry or physics. And human consciousness has its own emergent rules, not reducible to the rules for cells or the rules of chemistry, but never contradicting them (I cannot choose to walk through a wall, and I cannot "fly because I think I can", as some drug users in the 1960s tragically discovered).

I believe it is difficult to overestimate the philosophical and therapeutic significance of this. Philosophically, it provides a way of looking at life and consciousness that is neither reductionist nor dualist. Therapeutically, it says that the very act of there being another person (therapist or group member) open to aware contact and response opens up a field of new and complex possibilities. And this is what Gestalt therapy has been saying now for fifty years. The discovery of mirror neurons adds to this by telling us that the response loops between people are not only to do with sensory awareness (sight, hearing, etc.), but with our direct apperception of other people and them of us. If I am stuck neurotically in a way of perceiving and acting, the presence of another person open to different possibilities provides me with a direct non-verbal perception of a wider world.

This is particularly important when we come to my final foray into new discoveries . . .

Attachment

Many researchers are looking into the early development of an infant's brain. Uniquely among animals, human brains are not by any means fully developed at birth. The developmental stages a child goes through in his/her early years are signs of maturation in the neurological connectedness of the brain as well as of developing social interactions in the world. And what has become clear is that these two are not separate, but profoundly and mutually affect each other.

> Human development cannot be understood apart from this affect-transacting relationship [with the primary care-giver]. Furthermore, these early social events are imprinted into the biological structures that are maturing during the brain growth spurt that occurs in the first two years of human life, and therefore have far-reaching and long-enduring effects. (Schore, 2003, p. 4)

During these first eighteen months to two years, the infant brain over-produces neural connections, which are then whittled down on the basis of use. That is, if a baby is brought up in an environment where there is plentiful love, holding, and pleasure, and a little pain and frustration, s/he will come out of this period with rich connections for pleasure and love, and comparatively sparse connections for pain and frustration. Pleasurable experiences will be felt more acutely than painful ones, not because of immediate figure–ground formation, but because there is more "wiring" to process it. Conversely, if there is a lot of pain, rejection, and frustration, and little pleasure or love, the brain develops so the painful experiences are more acute than the pleasurable ones. That is, we have another reflection: the infant's brain develops a biological image of his/her caring environment. And not just the brain: Frank (2001) has written about how the whole body development of a child encodes that child's history.

In the years following this initial developmental spurt, the brain develops connections more slowly right through adolescence. In adult life, the development of new neural connections is slow and difficult, made more so by the fact that for an adult to take the actions that might help them to develop connections that are lacking would seem unnatural and false. I have argued elsewhere (Philippson, 2005) that the paradoxical theory of change (Beisser, 1970) does not apply in these circumstances of profound early neglect and/or trauma, and the therapist must be willing to be a change agent in encouraging the client to make more intimate relationships and hold the discomfort and sense of falseness involved. It is only when there is a reasonably well functioning neurological development (either in infancy or as a result of later experience slowly integrated) that the person can self-regulate effectively and contactfully.

This answers a question in our Gestalt history, put most clearly in Marcus (1979). Marcus recounts a piece of work where he plays an "ideal father". John Stevens, the publisher, adds a critique: "I just disagree totally with the new nurturing parent. It is putting the responsibility on someone else and it is not staying with the bad situation until she deals with it fully" (p. 87).

Marcus replies: "An eight-year old *cannot* get past such an impasse" (p. 88, original italics).

With the analysis we can now bring to the situation, we can move beyond this dichotomy. If the parenting was "good enough", and the self-regulation functions of the brain are well enough connected, the client will be able, as Stevens says, to "stay with the bad situation" and "deal with it fully". If not, then there is a need for the therapist to take more responsibility to lead the client into more contactful relating and the slow development of new neural connections. I would still say that the need is for a "contactful-enough" other, not for someone playing an "ideal father".

However, once again mirror neurons change what is seen as possible. For if, as Stern argues, consciousness is not a purely intrapsychic event, but can involve "re-entry" through connection with another person, it explains how the developing relationship between therapist and client can *by itself* lead to the client experiencing new possibilities for living, even if they are, in the moment, outside the client's range.

Conclusion

What then do we now know about field theory that was not so clear in 1991 when Parlett wrote his original paper? I have argued here that the twin discoveries of mirror neurons and of the profound way the infant's developmental environment affects neural development have shown us a level of field-relatedness of human beings which is far closer than we then knew. Our conscious selves, as Perls and Goodman knew, emerge *from* the field rather than existing and interacting *in* the field. Paradoxically, this level of relatedness means that more attention has to be paid to the emergence of the choosing individual from what Stern (2004) calls the "intersubjective matrix". The question has become "How can I act autonomously and make choices?"

We also know that the very presence of others (a therapist or a group) open for contact can provide a matrix for change even without "doing" anything. I would, in fact, argue from both theory and experience that group psychotherapy fits with the newly developing understanding much better than individual therapy, having a greater ability to promote change on the level of the intersubjective matrix by the richness of the environment, the number of mirror neurons active. Conversely, we know that, for some clients coming from severely deprived or abusive backgrounds, we need to be willing to provide and encourage specific experiences which then promote the possibility of the client developing an ability to self-regulate. This is because, in these cases, the significant reflection is of the early environment mirrored in the client's neural functioning.

In each of these situations we are responding to order emergent from the reflections and subtle transformations that occur when the field contains feedback loops, mirroring aspects of the field at new levels of complexity.

CHAPTER TWENTY-TWO

Two theories of five layers*

This is a paper based on theoretical work as directly developed by Fritz Perls, rather than through the rewriting and reinterpretation by Paul Goodman. As such, it is very little known in the Gestalt community, yet it seems to me very important. It is also fascinating to me that Perls, in 1957, described a developmental theory so close to the one later developed by Stern in his book nearly thirty years later.

I want to introduce two pieces of theory produced by Fritz Perls, the first of which is virtually unknown in Gestalt circles; the second is known, but rather out of fashion. For me, they are quite central to an understanding of the formation of relational self, and of the nature of neurosis and the process of reintegration.

---

*First published in 1995, in *Topics in Gestalt Therapy*, 3(1).

Five developmental layers

I can only find one reference to this: a lecture Perls gave in 1957, reprinted in Perls (1978). It seems likely to me that it was a stepping-stone on the way to the second set of five layers. However, it is quite distinct from the latter, and comes close to being a distinctive Gestalt developmental perspective with interesting similarities to the work of Stern (1985). Suffice it to say now that this present theory shares with Stern the perspective of a number of phases of being and relating which build up sequentially, but which are never completed (cf. the theories of Mahler, Pine, and Bergman (1975) and others, where each phase starts on the completion of the previous one). Rather, the phases interact with each other, and we move between them. I shall say more about this integration later.

Layer 1: "Animal self"

This is the layer of "little children, merely organic beings with their needs, their primitive functions, though often very differentiated functions, and their feelings" (Perls 1978, p. 64). Nothing more is said in the lecture about this layer, but we can see its similarity to the "id" in psychoanalysis, the "emergent self" of Daniel Stern, or the "child ego state" in transactional analysis. The work of Stern has shown that this way of experiencing self is joined by other modes very early on in an infant's development. However, remember that this layer does not end with the formation of successive layers: we are limited unless we can still operate from our basic needs, wants, and feelings—although some people try to suppress these as "infantile" or "primitive".

Layer 2: The "as-if" or "social" layer

Here "the loss of nature is replaced by the rules of games" (Perls 1978, p. 64). We learn to fit in with the rules of the society in which we live. Perls points out that we immediately invest less energy in our action if we are playing a role or obeying a rule than if our action arises out of an organismic "animal" need. Harris (1990) writes about three sub-stages here: simple behavioural learning, where

> the child exists in the midst of innumerable routines and social struc-
> tures, the practices, norms and rules of the family neighbourhood,

society and wider culture. From the first the child is encouraged and trained to behave in certain ways and not others – 'potty' training being a classic example. (ibid.)

Internalisation of "social structures" follows, so that

the rules and norms of the family and the wider society begin to be internalized as the child learns how to behave. They are internalized as messages, injunctions and exhortations . . . usually reinforced by the threat (explicit or implicit) of punishment, so that a fear of breaking them is powerfully instilled. (ibid.)

The third step is externalisation of internal structure, where "we begin to use the 'social structures' we have internalized in order to influence our environment" (ibid.). Again, what Perls is talking about shows similarities to the psychoanalytic "superego" or the transactional analysis "parent ego state". Its relationship to Stern is more obscure this time, since Stern does not particularly look at the infant in relation to society. However, the demands of society are there, if only in reflection in the socialisation of the parents, which impinges on the kind of birth the infant has, the physical, sensory, and emotional contact they have with the infant, the patterns of feeding, and the patterns of contact with the wider community (including patterns of habitation: as a nuclear family, an extended family, or some more varied communal living style). All these will then affect how the infant relates to the world and to him/herself. Furthermore, Stern's category of "core self" is in here somewhere, since, in the domain of "core relatedness", a major new factor is precisely this awareness of how we are seen by others.

The other aspect of this layer, which Perls does not speak about, is the inevitable clash between what the infant wants and what the world, especially parents, are willing or able to give (and vice versa: between what parents want and the baby is willing or able to give). The baby experiences disappointments and frustrations as well as experiences of gratification of their needs and wants. Writers in object relations theory and self psychology (e.g., Kohut, 1977) have written about the importance of these frustrations in the infant's development. Children, at a very early age, learn how to avoid the worst of the hurts and frustrations from their environment: this is the beginning of socialisation. For example, Lakota Sioux babies in previous centuries had to learn quickly not to cry, as this might give away the tribe's position to an enemy (Beebe Hill, 1979).

Layer 3: The "fantasy layer" or "mind"

Perls pointed to Freud's formulation of the realm of thought and fantasy as a "trial act". I visualise my potential actions as a rehearsal for some complex action, or one where the consequences of some possible actions are significantly painful or desirable. For example, I would want to think about what I am going to say in an interview for a job I want, or as a defendant in court.

Perls, Hefferline, and Goodman (1974) have more to say about "mind", in a fascinating section. The authors write about "mind" as an unavoidable illusion in a complex society where "there exists a chronic low-tension disequilibrium, a continual irk of danger and frustration, interspersed with occasional acute crises, and never fully relaxed" (ibid., p. 39), which keeps us in a continuous state of "chronic low grade emergency". In such a society, whenever we introspect, we become aware of ourselves thinking, and, thus, inevitably interpret this thinking as coming from a separate "part" of ourselves. In a simpler society, much of our action would not need to be prefaced by thinking, and, thus, thinking would be merely one of the things we do. (Incidentally, given that this is how Perls understands "mind", his dictum "Lose your mind and come to your senses" becomes a much more interesting and complex idea than it is usually taken for.)

Of course, in any society, our fantasy life also develops as an end in itself, especially in our dreams. So, in Australian aboriginal society, the split is not between mind and body, but between the material world and the "dreamtime". Both of these are experienced as important, and as informing each other.

Layer 4: The "objectivation layer"

"Here you tear sounds and tools out of their context and make them ready for a new organisation" (Perls, 1978, p. 65). Raw materials are made into tools, art, or artefacts, which are then kept in their made-up form. Metal and wood are made into a hammer, for example, and the object "the hammer" is seen rather than the metal and wood. So, the hammer stays as a hammer, and it is a rare person who will be able also to see wood for burning and a metal doorstop as further possibilities of the same matter. What de Bono (1973) calls "lateral thinking" is, essentially, an ability to put aside this "objectivation", and see things from a number of different, even contradictory, perspectives simultaneously.

Similarly, we "objectify" sounds, and create words and tunes and doorbells. What all this amounts to is that we inhabit our world with complex, created objects, not just simple, naturally occurring ones. Part of the Gestalt of the complex object is its use, its meaning. Perls suggests to his listeners that they read Wittgenstein for more on the subject.

This "objectivation" also underlies what Stern (1985) calls "inter-subjective relatedness", where we come to know other people as being subjectivities like ourselves by objectifying our experiences as human beings, and recognising these experiences in other people.

Layer 5: Organisation of symbols and tools

Now we learn to take the complexity even further, and go beyond tools to machines, beyond words to language, beyond tunes to musical form, beyond immediate community to "society". We have formed our symbols into a symbolic world, whose contours we have named. This is the world of what Stern (1985) calls "verbal relatedness".

The coexistence of the layers

For Perls (1978, p. 66), "The essence of a healthy person is that there is a unity, an integration of all the layers; he does not live merely in one level . . . by integrating all these five layers we become truly ourselves, which means, we can discover the other, the world".

So, the vision underlying this model is a grand and creative one, of each level interacting with the others, with each needing to be available for full human functioning. In therapy, we can explore this interaction. Which level of the client's experience is relied on to the exclusion of which other? What are the implications for this in the client's life and contacting?

I shall now move on to Perls' other five-layer model. This one, from Perls (1969a), has a completely different form and status. It is a model of working through neurosis, the layers that we form like a scab over authentic functioning. Each layer (apart from the last) acts as a defence against moving to the next. Thus, the layers are consecutive and discrete, and need to be worked through in order (although clients might go back to an earlier layer to move away from anxiety). It is important to make these distinctions, since there has been a great deal of controversy and misunderstanding in the Gestalt world about this model. It is not a global model of human functioning: that is the task of the model above, and other aspects of Gestalt theory. It is a specific structural model of a particular neurotic manifestation as it is being worked through. Now Gestaltists, with our emphasis on process, rather look down on structure, although Yontef (1988b, p. 21) has accurately defined structure as "slowly changing process". The point is that neurosis in the Gestalt model is precisely a moving away from the existential anxiety involved in embracing authenticity and spontaneity, and moving to a more predictably structured activity of fitting in with the world. We limit ourselves to a structure that we experience as keeping us safe and that also manipulates the environment to act in certain ways towards us. From this perspective, the point of Gestalt therapy is to facilitate the client to become unpredictable.

Layer 1: "Cliché" layer

This is the first and outermost level of relating: small talk, words to make some shallow contact, but not to communicate anything beyond the intention to make that level of contact. Actually, I rather approve of this kind of contact. I quote from an article I wrote on the subject in a previous *Topics* (Philippson, 1993a, and Chapter Two, this volume):

> We can be an intense lot, we psychotherapists. Close relationships are important to us, and we gravitate to, and attract, other people who are also quite intense. We enjoy the intense, significant relationships we have with our clients. We analyse our relationships, aiming for the ultimate 'I–thou'. And we're often not very good at casual friendships, especially with people who are also good at casual friendships: often we scare them.

> My early experience, and, I suspect, that of many psychotherapists, was of difficulty in making shallow, simple relationships, making small talk. My relationships were all-or-nothing, my boundary tendencies towards confluence or isolation.

And yet, there is a problem here. As therapists, we live in a subculture where this works, after a fashion. Our relationships can be stormy, but we rather enjoy the storms, the drama, the sorting out of the crisis even at the brink of separation. Our clients do not necessarily live in such a subculture. They could come from a more common subculture, where the usual path to friendship is via casual encounters: in pub, club, leisure activities, or in bed. The pattern of relationship making in this subculture is in many ways more organic than ours, moving from casual contact, to fuller contact, to intimacy. However, some people, like the stereotype psychotherapist, find such casual contact difficult. They have not learnt to "fit in", or, rather, they have learnt to walk around with a mind-set that they do not fit into whatever environment they encounter. I remember a Groucho Marx quote, "I wouldn't join any club which would have me as a member". In such a situation, the therapeutic method is often not modelling the kind of relationship the client needs to experiment with. Not only do we go for the deep significant relationship fairly quickly and value it very highly in comparison with casual encounters, we are doing it in a context where the therapist–client relationship says to the client, "You don't fit into my world."

With such clients, I encourage small talk, development of interest in the minutiae of the therapy room, even of my life. We talk about possible contexts where the client can meet people on a casual basis, for example, evening classes, sports activities, social clubs of various sorts, and the importance of deeper contact developing from casual "shallow" contact. However, especially in these days of AIDS, I do not encourage casual sex (and will often discuss the health dangers, and the problems associated with the trivialisation of sexuality). In the therapeutic process, our engagement in more profound work must similarly be based on an ability just to be interested in each other (and certainly not just interest in each other's problems and issues!). The Gestalt approach, emphasising the "surface", phenomenological way that the client presents in the here-and-now encounter of therapy, is very useful here.

Having said all this, the problem with the clichés in the therapy setting is when this is a deflection of the anxiety associated with a particular unfinished Gestalt/neurosis, or (putting the same thing a different way) an avoidance of contact in which they will feel in a way which is unfamiliar or painful. The therapy session then can be reconfigured as a chat, or a discussion of items of mutual interest, or "tell me what to do, doctor".

Layer 2: The "role-playing" or "as-if" layer

In this layer, we show part of how we can be, but act as if this is us. The concept of "self" is reduced to parity with "self-concept". For example, I can show you myself as if all I am is a therapist, or a trainer, or a writer, or a kind, sensitive person, or a victim of unfortunate circumstances, or a criminal, or a bureaucrat. In the language of previous sections, I am splitting, or putting up a ring-fence, identifying with some of my possibilities, and alienating their polar opposites. This concept has similarities with the Freudian "ego" or the Jungian "persona". This layer, like the previous one, avoids the rawness of spontaneous contact, and its consequent anxiety.

Often, therapists stick at this layer, and help clients to play a new, expanded role that is more useful in their particular situation. This is particularly the case with behaviourist (including assertiveness training) or constructivist therapies (including much of NLP and hypnotherapy). As a generalisation, this is as far as one can go with a therapy that avoids anxiety. It is even possible to adapt Gestalt techniques to this end: for example, using the "empty chair" to help someone to find new "strategies" for dealing with a difficult person or situation.

However, Gestalt is about self, not self-concept, so we need to find a way to move beyond this identification. This is the place of experiment in Gestalt therapy. The experiment is a recognition that the self of the client is more than her/his self-concept. Further, since the experiment grows from what the client has presented, it shows that the client reveals these further possibilities at the edges of their awareness. Perls (1973) presents shuttling experiments as an adjunct to awareness work, which would eventually achieve the same results, but take much longer.

Layer 3: The "impasse" or "phobic layer"

Now the client is beyond the everyday layers that replace rather than facilitate spontaneity and organismic self-regulation. The vista of free functioning opens up: anything can happen here! However, rather than welcoming this, the client feels anxious, projecting on to this vista his/her own catastrophic assumptions, and pulls away from embracing the fullness of her/his possibilities. What if I die (sometime you will!); what if I kill (is that what you want to do?); what if people are angry with me (and they might be)? What the client experiences is stuckness.

A person does not need therapy to be brought to this impasse: the world regularly provides situations where our clichés and self-concept are not adequate. Many people live much of their lives in this place. Many forms of helping are geared to making the impasse more comfortable: relaxation, drugs, various "supportive therapies". And there is always tobacco and alcohol and sex and loud music.

Where therapy, or at least some sort of unflinching contact, is vital is in moving through this impasse to the next layer. At this point, anything that helps a client to "feel better" is a hindrance. What the client needs is contact, knowledge that the therapist is there, and knows this place from personal experience.

Layer 4: The "implosion" or "death layer"

Now the client is willing to move forward and mobilises energy for that move: but where to? All the signposts are gone! Nothing is familiar. There is no "right thing" or "what" to do. The energy of anxiety rises as well. Perls (1969a, p. 60) writes, "This fourth layer appears either as death or as fear of death. The death layer has nothing to do with Freud's death instinct. It only appears as death because of the paralysis of opposing forces".

This is the realm of "the void" or "no-thingness" that is central to much Eastern thinking and practice. It can be profoundly frightening: one can identify it with the "dark night of the soul" of St John of the Cross. I believe it is also the place where suicide can become an option, as the "death" of paralysis is identified with bodily death. In fact, there is a death here: the death of a way of being that is assimilated into our much wider range of possibilities. There is also a decision: "I'm not going to be like this any more", which also can appear as a decision to die. The client once again needs contact from a therapist who knows this place.

Layer 5: The "explosion"

At the bottom of all this is the "unfinished business", the interrupted activity in the world whose consequences seem so dangerous that it is preferable to become only partially me than to risk this kind of action.

This "layer" is not really a layer, but an opening out into authentic emotional functioning. The trackless waste of the "death layer" becomes fertile as the client discovers his/her authentic needs and interests in the environment. Perls (1969a, p. 60) identifies four different kinds of explosion: the grief of beginning to accept and work through a loss or a death; orgasm (and, I would add, strong sexual and sensual feelings) as the client begins to accept his/her sexuality; anger, often in my experience connected with the client asserting her/his own significance; and joy/laughter/*joi de vivre*. I would add to this list love: an opening of the heart to another person or to the world; and (I can hear Fritz rolling in his grave) dependency: an opening out to receiving love and affection.

In a vital word of caution, Perls (1969a, p. 61) insists that the therapy does not stop at this point: ". . . a single explosion doesn't mean a thing. The so-called breakthroughs of Reichian therapy, and all that, are as little useful as the insight in psychoanalysis. Things still have to work through". The working through is precisely the meeting of the client's newfound energy and possibilities with that client's environment with its energy and possibilities. The most beautiful example of this that I have come across is Jim Simkin working with Mary, "a passive patient", in Fagan and Shepherd (1970, p. 191):

> M: And the ropes are getting looser, and I can take the hands and . . . (sigh). I'm beginning to breathe. (Voice gets firmer.) I have some space there to take in. (Pause.) My feet are untied. I can move. (Gets up slowly, stretches.) Support myself way up to the ceiling and back. I can move around.
>
> J: Now I recognize you.
>
> M: I can see! I can feel!
>
> J: Yeah. I'm very interested in what you do next.
>
> M: (Laughs.) You son of a bitch! (General laughter.) No, I'm not going to do anything.
>
> J: Yes, you are. (Mary continues to laugh.) You're laughing.

Jim Simkin continues to track what Mary does with her newly found energy, allowing her the opportunity to lapse back into passivity or, from herself, to choose vitality in the world.

Thus, in the working through from the "explosion", which seems to me to connect with the "Animal self" layer, the client moves between the other developmental layers, exploring the ways their energy can interact with their environment. The explosive wave meets, transforms, and is transformed by the client's culture, thoughts, and fantasies, objects and systems. This is a very different emphasis from approaches that present a picture of a predictable developmental process in a static society to which people must adjust themselves.

CHAPTER TWENTY-THREE

Body and character as a field event

In 2001, I became involved in an advanced summer training programme with an international group of Gestaltists, where we looked at Gestalt theory and its practical application from our different theoretical and cultural perspectives. I gave a lecture in the first programme on self-formation as an ongoing process. In the second programme in 2002, I gave this lecture at the Gestalt Therapy International Network summer programme in Mexico, which was to look more at how self stabilises.

The idea I want to put across is that the "somebody" that I am being is a field event. It is not just my event. There are things that I do to stabilise myself, there are things that the field does that keeps self stable, there are things that my environment does that stabilise self, and I want to maybe point out some ways that each of these happen. I am going to do this at two levels, so I shall talk about the first level, and then I shall say something of the opposite in the second level. So, I hope that somewhere between these two levels, you can gain some kind of a sense of the way I am talking about it. To put this in context, last year in our workshop we talked about self as created at the contact boundary: the immediacy of self. Our theme this year is more about stability of self, so it is a kind of balancing up, and that is what I want to talk about. To give you some kind of idea of what I mean about the field dependency of body and character, I would like you to try an experiment: I would like you to pair up with somebody and stand at a distance from the other person and notice your experience of your body and yourself, and then move slowly towards each other and notice with each step how that experience changes. Philip's has already changed massively—and then move away and notice how your experience of your body changes just as you do that. So, could you try that just for a few minutes . . .

Three boundaries revisited

Basic Gestalt theory of self gives the function of assimilating a unified experience of self to the personality aspect, which is described in Perls, Hefferline, and Goodman (1994) as "essentially a verbal replica of self". I would like to focus on and expand the concept of personality, because there is a lot more than that going on. If it were merely my verbalisable representation of myself, then it would not be a field event but an intrapsychic one. What I want to do, with some apologies to the people who were here last year or who read the book of lectures, is to restate the theory of three boundaries that I presented last year, but to take it a bit further while doing that. I described three boundaries based on Perls, Hefferline, and Goodman's senses of self or aspects of self that between them describe how we experience ourselves. I would like to add to these some kind of understanding of body and how body relates to each of these boundaries and to bring in some thoughts from somebody whom I am reading at the moment, Damasio. Have you read Damasio's work? He is a neurologist and I would like to read something from Damasio now just to show how compatible he is with Gestalt theory. He starts off talking about non-human organisms:

> True enough, organisms had a body and a brain, and brains had some representation of the body. Life was there, and the representation of life was there too, but the potential and rightful owner of each individual life had no knowledge that life existed because nature had not invented an owner yet. There was being but not knowing.

Consciousness had not begun. Consciousness begins when brains acquire the power, the simple power I must add, of telling a story without words [without words I think is particularly important here], the story that there is life ticking away in an organism, and that the states of the living organism, within body bounds, are continuously being altered by encounters with objects or events in its environment [so, field related], or for that matter, by thoughts and by internal adjustments of the life process. Consciousness emerges when this primordial story—the story of an object causally changing the state of the body—can be told using the universal nonverbal vocabulary of body signals. The apparent self emerges as the feeling of a feeling. (Damasio, 1999, p. 30)

I think it is beautifully written, and it is totally compatible with the field aspects of Gestalt theory.

He then goes on to talk about what use there is of this, the merits of consciousness. "Consciousness is valuable because it introduces a new means of achieving homoeostasis" (ibid., p. 303), so what he is talking about is creative adjustment, the central and, I think, one of the most beautiful themes in Perls, Hefferline, and Goodman, that creativity and homoeostasis are not enemies, and that creativity is vital to achieve homoeostasis in an ever-changing field.

Organism–environment

The three boundaries are also talked about, precisely I think, in Damasio. The first one is a very physical boundary: organism–environment, it/not-it. We are talking about meat here, we are talking about something which develops out of the field at a boundary, and a thing about the boundary is that it is not a third event, but it is an area where the processes on one side and the processes on the other side are different. There are, of course, links, because they co-create each other, but they have enough difference that they can rub up against each other, if you like. So, what happens at this boundary, the function of this boundary in our terms, is experience, which is the first word that Perls, Hefferline, and Goodman give us: that experience happens at this boundary. I take a quite rigorous position that this is, at this stage, not "my experience": that story has not yet been told. This is, if you like, a play of the field, an experiencing of the field. The aspect of self that it connects with is id, which is "passive, scattered, irrational . . . the body looms large . . . proprioceptions usurp the field" (Perls, Hefferline, & Goodman, 1994, pp. 159–160). So, it is a very bodily thing, but it is not yet in the terms that Damasio was using when talking about "my body". Damasio calls this "proto-self" and Stern calls it "emergent self". It is not a place at which I speak of ownership. This "passive, scattered, and irrational" process now sets the scene for the second boundary.

Self–other

Based on the experience at this boundary (which is not *my* experience, it is experience) there is a second boundary, which is the self–other boundary. For me, organism–environment and self–other are two very different things. Now the story is being told in a non-verbal way. It is I/not-I. What this is saying is that there are two kinds of words: there are words that define a table; a table is a thing. Yes, there are comparisons going on, but essentially there is a table that I can put my books on. The second kind of word is a comparison word: big, small; high, low; beautiful, ugly, and each of those words has absolutely no meaning except in relation to its opposite. And essentially, what the Gestalt theory of self is saying is that self is the second kind of word, that self and other co-define each other. There is a creation that goes on between self and other, and if there were no other there would be no self. If there were no self there would be no other. So, at this stage, I am asserting, but also in some ways the whole way the field operates is asserting, that it is my self, my body. I can be active, I can be deliberate, it is me doing this. Notice that this is a non-verbal story: we are not talking about words here.

The body

This is, for me, why bringing body process into Gestalt therapy is so important, because change does not happen through words. Words can point us, between me and my client or my therapist and me, in the direction of change, but the change does not happen at a verbal level. This is not rational–emotive therapy.

The second reason I think body is important is because we can only really know things through the body. So, body is quite central to my way of thinking about things.

The aspect of self here is ego: ego functions of identification (me, mine, self) and alienation (you, yours, other). It is not just about figure / ground, but it is at a much bigger level of identification as self and alienation as other. And the experience of body is active and deliberate, the functions of body are orientating, moving so that you can see me, I move so that I can see you, see whether there are any faces which are too blank here. Manipulating: turning the pages of the book, touching, shaping, active, so that it is a very different body from the passive, scattered, looming body of the first boundary.

Personality

The third boundary: personality, me / not-me, and now I am using my ego functions retroflectively, if you like, to say that this aspect of my possible relating I identify with me. I am somebody who stands up here and gives lectures; if I did not have a sense of that as being part of me, I would be in a much more anxious state than I actually am. So, people would have a sense of themselves as generous or not generous, or happy or not happy, all sorts of different things, which would be the verbalisable, autobiographical aspects of ourselves, the verbal story. Notice this is a different story. Damasio talks about autobiographical self, Stern talks about verbal and narrative self, but I want to expand the idea of personality. Do you know the idea in chaos theory of an attractor? An example of a chaos-type set-up is cloud formation. Every cloud is different, but there are particular shapes of clouds that occur. There are attractors towards particular kinds of ways of being a cloud, depending on atmospheric conditions, depending on the state of winds, sun, moisture in the air, sea underneath or land underneath, you will have different cloud formations, and there are recognisable types of clouds—does that make sense? So, I would like us to see personality expanded beyond the verbal autobiographical, in line with what Damasio is saying, to the non-verbal autobiographical way of seeing things, which is "this is the sort of shape we are, this is how we in our field forces will sort-of look". It does not mean we will always be like that, we have a vast amount of choice within that, but we will sort of look like this.

Stabilising self

So, what stabilises all this ever-changing self within the field? First is *body*, as I have said. Ruella Frank has done a lot of work on how early patterns of movement, reaching, crawling, walking, are laid down in the body in a sequential way to form how our body is now. Therefore, there is a way in which our autobiography can be read in the way we move, give, receive, walk, lie, sit—you can get a wealth of information. However, I want to point to a different aspect of it now, which is the relational aspect. Hence, I would like to do another short experiment. Now, without changing anything, scan your body and notice any tensions in your body; do not get rid of them, just notice any tensions in your body. Now, what I suggest you do is exaggerate those tensions, not so much that you hurt yourself, but so that it moves your body into a certain position as you exaggerate those tensions. This exercise is called "return to Notre Dame". And when you have got that, could you walk around as that; notice how you walk, because this will be an exaggeration of something that you do, and also notice how you contact or do not contact other people . . . Now go to the other pole: open up and notice your walking and your meeting with other people now . . . All right, could you sit down, please.

So, one of the ways in which we stabilise ourselves is how we hold our body, in two ways. One is that with certain body posture we will experience ourselves in a certain ways; the other is that with a certain body posture we make certain kinds of contact, other people respond to us in certain sorts of ways, or we tend to attract people who will respond to people who are like us, so there is both an organism and environment aspect of that stabilisation.

The second stability is *memory*. We remember things about ourselves; we remember our autobiography on both a verbal and a non-verbal level. Thus, memory is, of course, an important part of my stabilising who I am.

The third stabiliser, which is so basic it is almost invisible, is the *physical and chemical structure of the field*. We live in a world that, in some ways, is physically very predictable. You sat down on a chair with a fair amount of confidence that the chair was not going to change to gas. This hall was here last night, it is here this morning, it will be here tomorrow morning, earthquakes excepted. Essentially, we live in a world that has a quite large degree of physical predictability in it. And that is a kind of world in which some stability can happen.

The fourth aspect is the *social environment*. You probably notice this because we are in a different kind of social environment at the moment, among people with different cultures, speaking different languages. So, I would imagine each of us experiences, to some extent, a disruption of that social field, which is one of the things that we come to events like this for, because it takes us away from the stability of our lives. Thus, one of the ways in which my self is stabilised is that I live in a comparatively stable environment. My family is a refugee family, and the experience of refugees is of discontinuity and instability of a sense of self. There was a piece of research done in London to see whether black people were diagnosed as schizophrenic more often then white people. The aim was to see whether there was racism, whether cultural norms were not being taken into account. What actually came out of this study in Lambeth in South London was, no, black people were not diagnosed more often, but people from refugee or immigrant backgrounds—whether black or white—were diagnosed schizophrenic more often, and when you included second generation immigrants, the figure they found for psychosis was 75%. Now this is not just about people being diagnosed because the culture was not understood; it is, to my understanding, about this dislocation of sense of self when the social environment is not stable. So, we have all these things that provide stability.

Illusion

Next bit: this is not true; what I have just said is not true, it is an illusion, and I want to point now to the illusion. Read what you have been writing now, just read about a sentence of that, have a look at your writing, or just look over at someone else's piece of paper. Do you see the flow of a sentence? That is an illusion: we do not read s-t-a-b-i-l; what we do when we read is to scan backwards and forwards very fast, and what emerges from that miasma of letters, shapes, and combinations is the recognition of a sentence. It appears that we are doing something stable and linear, but we are not. Consciousness has been shown, through all the brain research that has been happening, not to be continuous, is not done in a linear, processing way. The sense of continuity is imposed on it; awareness is not continuous. We are shuttling backwards and forwards, in exactly the same way as when we read the letters, between looking, internal feeling, listening: we know that, because when a heavy lorry goes past, we notice that we have been listening because we hear it. Do you see what I mean when I say we impose the unity? The unity is something that we create that is not there in the original physicality of it.

So, let's look at each of these. Body: go back to where we started, the first experience of "body looms large", "hallucinatory", Perls, Hefferline, and Goodman call it, "passive, scattered, irrational" (1994, pp. 159–160). Precisely what we are talking about. It is only at the next stage that we and the physicality of the field relationships impose increasing amounts of stability on it. Thus, with body, there are stabilities, but the sense of the flow is imposed after the fact. Memory: we know that memory is not a tape recording; memory is a construct. If you look at the colour of Ellie's T-shirt here, could you just have a look at the colour now, close your eyes and remember the colour. We do not see that colour, we have no receptor for that colour. It is not that we have a brain path that takes in that colour, we construct that colour, and, in remembering, we construct it again. We know that memory is not stable; we know that when remembering something at different times in different psychophysical circumstances we remember it differently. Researchers talk about state-dependent memory, learning, and behaviour. We have in Britain rugby football clubs, the members of which get drunk and sing songs, and what was discovered was that if somebody learnt a song when they were drunk, they would not remember it so well when they were not drunk. They would be in a different psychophysical state, but when they were drunk again they would remember it. I am looking for funds to continue this research with some good whisky . . . But, at an extreme, people have different sets of memory–learning–behaviour, and we talk about dissociative personality or multiple personality. Your experience now would differ from an experience of yourself and your memories in a different part of life: if you are doing sport, for example, or if you are with your family. If a policeman stops you when you are driving your car, your experience of yourself and the memories you bring to it would be very different. So, a question that is important for me in therapy about memory is—even taking away the fact that memories can be misleading, can be made up and not to do with what actually happened, even if it were completely accurate—with a lifetime of memories, why this memory now? What is being stabilised, what sense of self, what activity of self is being stabilised by the client bringing this memory now? Alternatively, if I remember something about the client that the client told me, what is it that is important for me that I bring this particular memory of the client now?

So, again, there is an apparent stability caused by memory, but those stabilities can be, and usually will be, a number of different stabilities. Usually, in most people, the different senses of self will have knowledge of each other; there is not a wall between them. In some people, there is a wall between them, a created wall. So, it becomes very clear to me, on a memory level, that the illusion is that the sense of what makes us, of what stabilises self, is not stable. This is the paradox. The sense of what we experience as our stability is not stable. The self that I experience myself stably to be now is not the sense that I experienced myself stably to be yesterday. It is an illusion.

The physical and chemical predictability is reasonably stable. It does tend to bind it altogether.

The social environment again is not stable: most people will be different at work and at home, at the sports club, with their children, and with their parents. There will be a number of different stable social environments and they all have a similar sense of stability, familiarity, a sense of comfortableness, but they are all different. Do you understand what I'm saying?

Therapy

One of the things about therapy is that it puts us in the refugee situation, if you like. It puts us in a situation where we are in a culture that is different to the culture which we are normally in. The way the therapist responds, the way the group norms build up, are different. So, already our stability is being questioned. What is more, the attempts that we all make in those situations to bring it back to the known become obvious, as long as the therapist does not become confluent with them. So, if the therapist is not confluent and fits in with the things that the client does to try to bring us back to their social norms, then it becomes very obvious to the therapist and to the client how they do the illusion, how they create this sense of stability. Does that make sense, what I'm saying? So, I want to say something more about confluence here. Perls, Hefferline, and Goodman (1994) talk about the normal aspect of confluence: "We are in confluence with everything we are fundamentally, unproblematically or irremediably, dependent on: where there is no need or possibility of a change" (p. 232). It is worth continuing this quote, as it illustrates what I have said before:

> A child is in confluence with his family, an adult with his community, a man with the universe. If one is forced to become aware of these grounds of ultimate security [which Philip is going to talk about], the 'bottom drops out' and the anxiety that one feels is metaphysical. (ibid.)

So, if we are in a situation that is unproblematic for us, then we can afford to be confluent with all this stability. I have come across people who had a good, supported, happy, contactful childhood—it does exist. What then happens, very often, is that they stay quite close to their families geographically, they live down the road, they are in contact with them all the time, they feel supported by them, they are less adventurous, but they do not need the adventure. The extent of their confluence is not demanding confluence, they can do other things, but they do not need to move very far away because it is not problematic for them.

Where people come into therapy is when those confluences, those stabilities, are no longer unproblematic. At this stage, they need to face that metaphysical anxiety, and there is a need for the therapist not to go along with, and recreate, the confluence, because the clients are coming because the confluence does not work. Now, as Michael was pointing out yesterday, there is a real balance between how to do that so that you do not just hide what the client is coming to seek, and at the same time you do not shove the client into a different world. That is where contact, dialogue, and awareness, and the therapist's own personal therapy, all have their part. In a sense, it is more debilitating for the client if the therapist moves into a confluence and makes that confluence invisible, than if the therapist shoves, because the client is not then getting the change or the possibility of moving to a new stability that they are actually coming for. So, my preference, if I am going to err, is to err on the side of non-confluence rather than the side of confluence. The client is here needing something, there is something in the confluence that the client is willing to put themselves through therapy, with the time, the money, and the metaphysical anxiety that it entails, in order to change. I think I want to leave this here and take maybe ten minutes of initial questions, and then do a demonstration.

Questions and comments

Q: When you said about stability being an illusion, the content of memory is unstable, but the skill of the memory, the ability to remember, is not.

Peter: The ability to remember is stable but the content is not stable. If we did not have that ability, we would not have our sense of stability, absolutely. And yet, what we remember is not as stable as it looks.

Q: There are facts: let's say my father is an alcoholic, this is something stable.

Peter: What you are saying is that there are facts, absolutely, but what is remembered is not facts. What is remembered is specific events connected to the alcoholism. For some people, what would be remembered is the lively singing, for other people, it would be the angry alcoholic. So it is important to remember that it is not events in themselves that are being remembered, but it is emotionally charged experiences of those events. For some people, what would be remembered would be the father working twelve hours a day and the only way he can sleep is by drinking; that would be another way of remembering the same thing. So, the anger might be towards the system, or the boss who works father to the extent that he cannot live his life without that, or a family situation that is intolerable, or whatever.

Q: I didn't understand it quite completely, you talked about the first body that loomed. Can you talk more about that?

Philip: Will another way of saying what you said be that because we are living tensely, as if in an emergency, we don't go to a relaxed place, and so we don't often experience the body looming? We shorten forecontacting. I noticed that when we walked around, we were almost all tight in a variety of places, and, being tighter, we prevent ourselves from allowing our full body to loom.

Peter: Yes, and then we see our body as very much a fixed final entity.

Q: And when you were speaking about the unborn child, that is not the case.

Peter: Unborn children can be quite purposeful, as well as scattered. I don't know whether the autobiographical thing happens or not at that stage, different people say different things. Certainly, at the level of the purposeful, they can be with their kicking, beating in time, remembering, all sorts of different functions are happening, masturbating—we now know through scans that foetuses masturbate. Purposeful things happen.

Q: I would like more detail—you talk about Daniel Stern. You talk about "self", "emergent self". Daniel Stern is always making the very clear distinction between sense of self and self. He is always talking about sense of self. Is this distinction for you unimportant or not? If you included this distinction, would it make this any different for you?

Peter: I think I am talking about both at various times, and I am not being totally clear about which I am talking about. The different sensings involved in each of these different aspects of self make up our total sense of self, but sense of self is not the same as self. The self is activity, it's in the activity. We sense that the body acts in various different ways and we develop a sense alongside the activity and then the sense alters the activity and they sort of dialogue with each other because our sense of self changes the way we function in each of those three boundaries. Therefore, it changes our sense of self, which then changes self-activity—you can't really separate them. There are feelings and then there are selfings: they are not actually separate, that's what I'm saying.

Lilian: When you are talking about social interaction, would you include any historical perspective, life story, would you include this in social environment?

Peter: I would include historical social environment in memory. The social environment I am talking about is the current social environment. We would then be bringing memories, specific memories, to specific social environments, which would stabilise those social environments for us. But history I would include under memory, rather than social environment.

Michael: So when you speak of illusion, you don't mean an illusion that needs to be dispelled, but you mean that these things don't have the apparent continuity and solidity that they seem to, and if they become overly solid and continuous we are into the problems of, for example, fixed character. I just wanted to put it for a moment in my own language and think of them as the necessary fictions by which we live, and, in a sense, are aesthetic activity and our capacity to give more to what otherwise would remain scattered and irrational and rather chaotic. Like an artist continuously forming and reforming our experiences. You could say you can never step into the same memory or the same body twice. Each time it is a remaking or remembering. We give form to the experience.

Peter: It is a creative act each time.

CHAPTER TWENTY-FOUR

The mind and the senses: thinking in Gestalt therapy*

This is another paper trying to make sense of a theme muddied by both Fritz Perls' sloganising and the more recent wholesale dismissal that he had anything at all of interest to say. In this article, I explore around the theme of the therapeutic uses and abuses of thinking. Where does thinking help and where does it hinder?

I n this chapter, I enquire about the place of "thinking-about" in Gestalt therapy, when it supports the therapeutic process, and when it becomes a deflection from the process. I discuss the differences between *awareness* and *egotism*, the limitations of the paradoxical theory of change, and the implications of neurological considerations.

> "*Body* and *Mind*: this split is still popularly current, although among the best physicians the psychosomatic unity is taken for granted. We shall show that it is the exercise of a habitual and finally unaware deliberateness in the face of chronic emergency . . . that has made this

---

*First published in 2011, in *British Gestalt Journal*, 20(1).

crippling division inevitable and almost endemic. (Perls, Hefferline, & Goodman, 1994, p. 17, original italics)

"But the *why* at best leads to clever explanation, but never to an understanding . . . The *why* gives only unending inquiries into the cause of the cause of the cause of the cause of the cause of the cause. And as Freud has already observed, every event is *over*-determined, has *many* causes; all kinds of things come together in order to create the specific moment that is the now. Many factors come together to create this specific unique person which is *I*. (Perls, 1969a, p. 47, original italics)

Introduction

Gestalt therapy has had a shifting view of thinking in our history. From the earliest days, when Perls and Goodman were proposing a new way to approach psychotherapy, psychiatry, and psychology, to the Californian days, when all theory was "elephant shit", to a re-emphasis on thinking following from a reconsideration of both psychoanalytic and cognitive–behavioural therapies: somehow, my sense is that we have been following fashion, making over-general statements such as "we must include thinking if we are to be holistic", or "all thinking-about is wrong", but rarely going back to our first principles in a field approach to contact and self. It has often been left to our friends from outside Gestalt therapy, such as Stern (2003), to point out what we have to offer in a fresh way with his distinction between explicit (verbalised, symbolic) and implicit (non-verbal, non-symbolic) knowing:

This new view of implicit knowing poses a major problem for traditional psychoanalysis. This is because implicit knowing is not dynamically unconscious and thus is not withheld from consciousness by resistances . . . The concept of resistance or repression does not apply here. (Stern, 2004, p. 119)

What has also not happened, in my opinion, is a proper *chewing* of the subject of thinking in therapy, asking *why* Perls decried thinking-about and whether there is truth in his critique, or *when* it might be useful to make thinking figural and when not. In this chapter, I will try to clarify our terms and suggest how this provides a guide to the therapeutic usefulness of thinking-about in Gestalt therapy.

A quick guide to my argument

The mode of change in Gestalt therapy is an opening to new, previously inhibited ways of contacting the world, in which the client experiences him/herself in relation to others in a new way, and relaxes the habitual inhibitions to both contact and awareness that previously limited the clients self-actualisation. Such a change is not facilitated by withdrawing from the contact moment into thinking-about. Indeed, if the paradoxical theory of change (Beisser, 1970) were fully accurate, we could say that all that was needed was to stay in the contact moment. Thinking-about would then always be a way to avoid following the flow from the now to the next, from the limited present to a more open future. However, the paradoxical theory is not always an accurate statement of Gestalt theory (Philippson, 2005); there is sometimes a need for a planned approach to therapy, and, in some circumstances, the thinking-about can support the experimentation that allows such change. For example, as therapy progresses, clients become familiar with their own growing edges, and can discuss with the therapist possible experiments to explore these edges, leading to a collaborative approach, rather than an experiment as something suggested by the therapist and "done" by the client.

Self-awareness, self-consciousness, and egotism

A first priority must be to clarify our terms, since I believe there is considerable confusion in our field about our basic terms, particularly about *awareness*. I have come across quite a few examples of Gestaltists using "awareness" as a synonym for thinking-about: for example, "The client became aware that she was habitually tense", or "The therapist was aware that the client tended to be confluent". Now, this is not what Perls, Hefferline, and Goodman term "awareness": "Awareness is characterized by *contact*, by *sensing*, by *excitement* and by *Gestalt formation*" (Perls, Hefferline, & Goodman, 1994, p. xxv). "Note, however, that the awareness is not a thought about the problem but is itself a creative integration of the problem" (ibid., p. 8). This distinction goes back to *Ego, Hunger and Aggression* (Perls, 1992/1947), in the discussion of the difference between "self-consciousness" and "self-awareness". "The term 'self-conscious' is not a bad one. It indicates a retroflection, the fact that one's attention is directed towards one's self and not toward the object of one's irritation or potential interest." (Perls, 1992[1947], p. 307).

> It is important to avoid confusing self-consciousness with self-awareness. Unfortunately there is no word conveying the meaning of self-awareness that does not also suggest that in self-awareness, too, retroflection takes place. This, however, is not the case. (ibid., p. 308)

In the slightly different language of Perls, Hefferline, and Goodman, the term that is used is *egotism*. Like all the other "interruptions to contact", egotism is not to be understood as inherently pathological or problematic. Each one is described, written about from a perspective of normal functioning and of neurotic functioning, where the understanding of neurotic functioning is where choice has been given up in favour of unaware and fixed limitations to contacting. In particular, for egotism, the description is "... a slowing-down of spontaneity by further deliberate introspection and circumspection, to make sure that the ground possibilities are indeed exhausted ... before he commits himself" (Perls, Hefferline, & Goodman, 1994, p. 237). The authors continue with a description of the normal function of egotism: "Normally, egotism is indispensable in any process of elaborate complication and long maturation" (ibid.)

The description of the neurotic use of egotism is also significant:

> Neurotically, egotism is a kind of confluence with the deliberate awareness and an attempted annihilation of the uncontrollable and surprising ... He wards off the surprises of the environment ... by seeking to isolate himself as the only reality: this he does by taking over the environment and making it his own ... Such an 'environment' ceases to be environment, it does not nourish, and he does not grow or change. (ibid.)

So, verbalisation and explicit symbolised thinking is, for me (and I would argue also for Perls and Goodman), egotism rather than awareness, and the question is when the use of egotism in Gestalt therapy conforms to the description of "normal egotism" and when to that of "neurotic egotism".

Egotism in therapy

If the aim of Gestalt therapy is to restore contactful engagement informed by organismic self regulation, a physical moving towards an other that holds our interests and needs in the moment, we must ask ourselves what processes within a therapy session could fit the description of "elaborate complication and long maturation", because these would be the times when normal egotism would have a place. To me, it seems clear that the therapy situation actually has, of its nature, very few such processes. There is no set task to be achieved, there are few rules to mould our actions around, and there are few conflicting demands inherent in the therapeutic engagement. At the same time, there is a high value placed on the spontaneous, the "uncontrollable and surprising", rather than the controlled and habitual. In these circumstances, it is difficult to see where there is merit in a move to the symbolised or verbalised rather than engagement between therapist and client (with words, where used, as tokens of engagement rather than description, discussion, or talking-about). This is the essence of Fritz Perls' criticism of such activities in therapy. Neurotically, we could say that the client, and maybe also the therapist, is staying at a level where they have control and are not going to be surprised.

Self theory

"Self", in Gestalt therapy, is relational, a simultaneous identification of what is self and alienation of what is other (ego functioning) in the ground of the contact situation we now find ourselves in (id functioning) and of our symbolisation of whom I take myself to be (self-concept or personality functioning). Personality can be seen as a mixture of assimilated commitments (to relationships, activities, etc.), and values that organise and deepen our contacts, and defensive introjects and ego ideals that disrupt and limit our contacts to what is deemed safe or acceptable to others. As opposed to cognitive–behaviour therapy, which aims to adjust behaviour by addressing personality functioning cognitively: "use reason and reality-testing to challenge dysfunctional thinking" (Neenan & Dryden, 2004, p. 27), Gestalt therapy encourages a focus back to the "id of the situation" (Robine) and choiceful ego functioning to allow a contact to form that is fully geared to now, and which, in turn, allows new assimilations to personality functioning.

In verbalisation/egotism, the fullness of relational self is not available: what is addressed is personality functioning. This is true of both normal and fixated egotism, and is not necessarily problematic. The sensory and proprioceptive engagement that is central to id functioning, and the deepening engagement with the chosen figure of interest that is central to ego functioning, are replaced by "introspection and circumspection".

Looking again at "elaborate complication and long maturation"

Yet, there are aspects of Gestalt therapy that are longer term and complex, and where it is not clear that "the ground possibilities are exhausted". In these circumstances, there will be a need to slow down, to move away from making full contact too quickly, because it is likely to be a contact that is not of-the-moment, but is imported from elsewhere.

My critique of Beisser's paradoxical theory of change is relevant here:

> Looking more closely at the requirements of the phenomenological method also points out the problem that the paradoxical theory cannot be simply applied to situations where the client is sensorially out of contact with the 'where', and taking her experience of the 'who' from some fantasy world, maybe a replay of childhood, maybe a world where she can follow her whims because she is evil, or has no responsibility because she is so weak . . . The other assumption behind the theories of self-regulation and paradoxical theory of change is that the client's neurological development can support the self-regulating and growthful responses. (Philippson, 2005, pp. 14–15)

Maintaining the therapeutic relationship

The most obvious of these is the maintenance of the therapeutic relationship itself. Like any significant relationship, the relationship between therapist and client can be a difficult one, complicated by the interaction between the client's expectations and the therapist's conception of therapy, not to mention the more personal aspects involving transference and countertransference. If the relationship is to be as horizontal as possible, there is a need to be able to discuss "What are we doing together? Why do you do this, which does not seem useful (or even seems hurtful) to me?"

The "ground possibilities" to be found here are the understanding of what we are doing together in a way that allows us to work together as co-explorers of the client's self-actualisation in the world. If the client has been in therapy before, it could include an understanding of how this present therapy is similar and different to his/her previous experiences, both in relation to what is required from the client and what is required from the therapist. Can we engage in conflict? Can we touch? Can the client refuse to say or do something—and can the therapist? Can the therapist self-disclose?

Extending possibilities

The other complex factor is the ongoing "life-space" of the client. For Goldstein (1939) a vital part of our self-actualisation is the world we actualise to be ourselves in. We form ourselves in relation to that part of the environment we make figural. And one way in which we maintain a fixed experience of ourselves in the world is to (sometimes drastically) limit the world we engage with to that which is familiar, however painful and self-damaging. Such a limitation is also brought into the therapy room in the client's perspective and figure formation. There will often be many patterns in place to avoid facing a larger perspective on self and environment. By definition, the "ground possibilities are not exhausted", or even acknowledged or brought into awareness. The useful course of therapy with clients who maintain themselves in a very fixed world must involve experiments in engaging with the world outside the habitual limitations, both within the therapy session and beyond.

The experiments in awareness in the "self help" part of Perls, Hefferline, and Goodman engage with this need to extend the ground possibilities: doing things differently from usual, reversing normal patterns of behaviour, relating to your body in a different way. I find discussion of possible experiments to do in sessions or between sessions is a much more horizontal way of doing this than for me, as a therapist, just to hand out "homework". Often, the client can get a sense of how such a suggestion fits with a blind spot. In terms of Stern's distinction between explicit and implicit knowing, the explicit, verbalised thinking about ways to act leads to an implicit knowing that emerges from engaging in these new possibilities.

An example is a client who was scared to go to a sports club because s/he *knew* s/he would be embarrassed to do exercise in front of other people who were seeing his/her body. S/he went anyway, and was highly surprised to find that the embarrassment did not happen: the explicit "knowing" was contradicted by the implicit experiencing. Behind that change was a very important and unconscious implicit change. The client's response to a difficult history was an assimilation of observers as hostile and scathing, coupled with a desire not to see these shaming expressions. In now allowing sensory awareness of the actuality of how s/he was being seen, the client was risking seeing the painfully rejecting stares s/he was used to, and was, therefore, open to seeing the much more friendly present reality. As Stern wrote, this change in sensory engagement was never conscious, not because of repression or resistance, but because the engagement was energetic and surprising enough that there was no incentive to verbalise.

The neuroscience of extending possibilities

The discussion above points to a major theoretical difference between a Gestalt and a cognitive–behavioural approach, and, as Stern wrote, with a traditional psychoanalytic approach. The emphasis in the Gestalt approach is on implicit experience, not on verbalised or symbolised explicit understanding. This fits well with a modern understanding of how the two halves of the brain organise themselves differently. To quote Ramachandran,

> Thus the coping strategies of the two hemispheres are fundamentally different. The left hemisphere's job is to create a belief system or

model and to fold new experiences into that belief system. If confronted with some new information that doesn't fit the model, it relies on Freudian defense mechanisms to deny, repress or confabulate—anything to preserve the status quo. The right hemisphere's strategy, on the other hand, is to play 'Devil's Advocate', to question the status quo and look for global inconsistencies. (Ramachandran, 1999, p. 136)

From this perspective, which is shared by Gestalt therapy, the mode of effectiveness of cognitive–behavioural approaches is to encourage the client to temporarily act differently, giving an opportunity to experience new awarenesses and contacts from those around them. The breakdown point of this is likely to be if the client is living in an environment that will not actually contradict the pessimistic beliefs, but wishes to induct the client back into his/her role in the family, for example. The point is not to encourage the client to understand things differently, but to provide new experiences that the client can assimilate using his/her right-brain capacity, which then shifts the left-brain belief systems.

The advantage of the Gestalt approach is that the new experiences are first discovered in the relationship with the therapist, or within a setting therapist and client have worked out together is likely not to mirror their worst expectations. The therapist is quite truly on the client's side, and, even if things do not go well, the client is not on his/her own with the disappointment. If things become difficult in the relationship with the therapist, the latter takes part responsibility for what happened, rather than blaming the client.

Conclusion

There is much to appreciate in Fritz Perls' criticism of the emphasis on verbalisation and thinking-about/egotism in therapy. His criticism of basing therapy on explicit knowing, to the detriment of implicit knowing, is now taken up by influential people outside the Gestalt world (I have here focused on Stern and Ramachandran). The question of where such thinking/explicit knowing might be of use becomes one of looking at where, in the therapeutic encounter, there is a need to slow down contact and deal with longer-term, complex issues that arise in the therapy.

CHAPTER TWENTY-FIVE

I, thou, and us*

This paper discusses ways of group members using the language of "we", of the collectivity. This kind of language is usually discouraged or forbidden in Gestalt groups, leaving members unable to speak about group process, as if the whole was just the sum of the parts.

One solid barrier to getting Gestalt groups to look at their process—the whole range of their "here-and-now" interactions as individuals and as a system—is the Gestalt "rules", which say we should prefer to use "I" and "you" statements in our comments and exchanges.

Zinker (1977), in his summary of the "values" of a Gestalt group, includes the following: "Speak in the first person: first person statements enhance ownership of your feelings and observations", and "Make an effort to be direct with others (that is, don't speak about Jack to Mary; address yourself directly to Jack)".

The irony is that although Zinker is writing about group process, an overstrict acceptance of these "values" (I think "rules" is more honest) means that the—often indirect—comments about the whole

*First published in 1992, in *Gestalt: Working with Groups*. Manchester Gestalt Centre.

group, *us*, are made unacceptable. If the preferred way of speaking is to use "I" and "you", then many statements that can only be made using "we" and "us"' are not made. So, the whole area of group process that focuses on the group as a whole is ignored or distorted.

In groups we have attended, we have both experienced this:

Peter: We seem to be getting sadder and sadder.
Susan: You mean *you're* getting sad. Can you own that?

In other words, Peter's "we" statement is seen as a disguised "I" statement, a *projection* of his feelings on to the group.

Or, alternatively,

John: We're avoiding the issue of who's leading here.
Mark: Who is? You mean I am?

In this case, the "we"-statement is seen as a covert "you" statement, and Mark sees John as *blaming* him.

In both cases, the point of the original statement is lost. It simply is not the case that all "we" statements can be translated into "I" or "you" statements without loss of meaning. If a "we" statement is read as an "I" statement, then I often appear paranoid; if it is read as a "you" statement, I often appear critical. A valid Gestalt observation, that people sometimes use words like "one" or "we" to avoid taking responsibility for a statement about themselves, has been turned into a rule. The effect is to reduce all *group* process to "I–thou" or *interpersonal* process. The hidden philosophy here is the (unGestalt) one that in groups "the whole is equal to the sum of its parts". So, "We are sad" means "I'm sad and you're sad and he's sad . . ." We believe, in contrast, that in a group, a system, a *Gestalt*, the whole is greater than the sum of its parts—the extra involving the principles of organisation of the system that form the group/system/Gestalt identity. Statements about group leadership, group conflict, group atmosphere, group norms, etc. are not simply collections of statements about what is happening to individuals at that moment.

Exclusive insistence on the "I–thou" mode of speaking in groups runs the risk of losing the whole dimension of "us-ness"—*intimacy*—that makes each group unique. It ignores the relationship of the individual to the group, and those facets of the individual's experience and behaviour that exist *only because* she is now part of the group system.

The logical conclusion of insisting on an "I–thou" way of speaking in groups is to deny that group process exists at all. (Similar reasoning lay behind Mrs Thatcher's recent claim that there is no such thing as society . . .) If I am I and you are you, and we are totally responsible for ourselves, then how can I ever influence you? We commonly talk of "making" people upset or angry, or "getting them" to do things; on this view, *you* do not make me upset or angry; I *choose* these feelings all on my own.

Now, everyone knows that in real life—and even in Gestalt groups—we *do* occasionally manage to annoy or upset or move each other.

People influence each other. What can happen in a group is that we learn to recognise *our* part in the interaction, and come to see ourselves more as "agents" than "patients". This does not mean that we cease to be influenced.

So, let us get back to talking about "us", the group, as well as about "me" and "you". One good way to help people become aware of "whole group" process is to have them make statements beginning "I am the group and I . . ." This helps people identify with the group *as a whole*.

Sally: I am the group and I'm afraid to say anything. I don't feel safe as the group and I don't trust myself . . .

Peter: I am the group and I'm feeling excited. I think something's going to happen, and that's a bit scary as well . . .

This exercise might seem paradoxical in the light of what has been said, but is not. It "bridges the gap" between "I–thou" and "we" statements, and helps people identify with, and home in on, *group* atmospheres and issues.

What it comes down to is that, yes, what I say about "the group" *is* a projection, *and* that this does not mean that it is not a valid perception (and in fact *all* perceptions are also projections—to the extent that Enright (1980) has coined the term "perjection"). Once stated, its validity can be explored by others. Meanwhile, we are constantly learning about the way we influence, and are influenced by, our environment, learning which in itself will help us to change the way we interact with our environments outside therapy.

CHAPTER TWENTY-SIX

Individual therapy as group therapy*

This is an attempt to develop the field orientation of Gestalt therapy into the idea that we are always working with a whole relational field, not just with an individual. This perspective is sometimes more important than at other times. A trap can be to support the individual client in a way that causes disruption in their family, so that the client ends up less supported than in the first place. Of course, sometimes the disruption is necessary for any movement to happen, but at other times, it is just a shifting around of an unbalanced power structure. These days, I do not offer couple or family sessions with my clients.

"The human organism/environment is, of course, not only physical but social. So in any humane study, such as human physiology, psychology, or psychotherapy, we must speak of a field in which at least social–cultural, animal, and physical factors interact. Our approach in this book is 'unitary' in the sense that we try in a detailed way to consider every problem as occurring in a social–animal–physical field. From this point of view, for instance, historical and cultural factors cannot be considered as complicating or modifying conditions of a

---

*First published in 1992, in *Gestalt: Working with Groups*. Manchester Gestalt Centre.

simpler biophysical situation, but are intrinsic in the way any problem is presented to us."

(Perls, Hefferline, & Goodman, 1994, pp. 4–5)

The theme of this chapter is that all individual therapy is also group therapy. If I sit with an individual client, that client is not only presenting him/herself, but also the entire field of his/her interactions:

- family (parents, lover, children);
- community (neighbourhood, work, friends);
- culture (family, neighbourhood, national, world).

As the client progresses in therapy, so the client's interaction with his/her environment changes (in fact, in Gestalt terms, the two statements are synonymous). Changes in the individual mirror, and are mirrored in, changes in the environment. A lasting change in the individual can only go hand-in-hand with changes in that individual's environment. These environmental changes happen in one of five different ways (I will give examples from the family environment).

1. The environment rejects the individual and continues roughly as before. A family might switch roles around to replace the function of the individual as, for example, the "problem", or the "sick person", or the "person who looks after us". Sometimes, holding the "scapegoat" at a distance will be enough for the family to maintain business as usual.

2. By a mixture of compliments (on "how you used to be") and threats ("You'll be sorry"), the environment can reinduct the individual into previous ways of living. What the therapist sees in this situation is a client saying, "All this therapy is fine in theory, but doesn't apply in the real world."

3. The individual client can go away from therapy and dump his or her stored anger on others (e.g., parents, children, bosses) in the name of expressing feelings. This might lead to family rejection, or problems at work, or even abusive behaviour towards children. If the client has the role of being the "problem person" in the family, this role would be strengthened by such a reaction.

4. The environment can also change to incorporate the change in the individual. This can happen very beautifully and spontaneously, as interpersonal problems seem to vanish, where once they were overwhelming: parents start showing their affection for their grown-up children; children stop "attention seeking" behaviours as they discover they are getting more attention anyway; work teams start functioning smoothly, and the previous splits no longer seem so important.

5. Sometimes the individual therapy client and his/her environment reach a compromise. For example, a twenty-five-year-old "child" leaves her parents' home to live independently. She maintains contact with her parents, however, and chooses to accept some of the culture this involves (being seen as a child at times, accepting that her parents will put energy into their own conflicts rather than into their relationship with her). She has chosen out of a realistic assessment of what kind of relationship is available to her, preferring this to no relationship at all.

If individual therapy does not take into account the therapy of the whole environment, it is much more likely that the more destructive of these interactions will take place: that is, the individual will be rejected by (or will reject) those who formerly were closest to him/her, or the individual will find her/himself slipping back into old patterns that fit more comfortably into others' expectations. Either way, the therapist's splitting of the individual–environment field will very probably be mirrored in the client's own process.

So, what are the ways of working with the whole field while doing individual therapy?

1. As I have discussed above, working with the individual inevitably *does* affect that individual's environment. Sometimes, shock waves go through the environment just from the individual's decision to go into therapy. People perceive themselves to be under scrutiny, and react with soul-searching, guilt, and sometimes decisions to change stuck situations.

2. It is usually useful to "chart" the process of the environmental field around the client, to check out how others are reacting to the client's process, and how the client is responding to those reactions. This often becomes an important part of therapy, as the

client risks relating differently with parents, partner, children, friends, people at work, authority figures—and they learn to act differently towards the client.

As well as discussing or role-playing these interactions, it is often interesting to "sculpt" families or situations. In a group, this can be done by psychodrama. In individual therapy, it can be done via a drawing, dialogues with cushions, or other kinds of sculpt. I have a pack of cards that I find very useful—the client chooses one card to represent each family member ("family" being interpreted loosely). The client then sculpts the family using the cards. One of the beauties of using cards is the many different ways of expressing similarity, difference, comparison, and positioning. There are suit, colour, card value, court cards, gender of Jack, Queen, and King, positioning beside and positioning on top. For example, which family members are the same suit as the client? Often, the family will fall into two suits, one mother's suit, one father's suit. Is somebody "between" the client and somebody else? Why is mother a King and father a Queen?

By one, or a combination, of these methods, the individual client is encouraged to see themselves as part of an environmental system.

3. I offer to run family or couple sessions (or sessions with ex-lovers) including individual clients.

I do not find difficulty in these circumstances with issues of "who has my first loyalty?" I come to the situation with the strong belief that loyalty to the individual client *is synonymous with* loyalty to the client's environment. This fits in well with the Gestalt focus: I am not trying to *fix* the client's situation (potentially at someone else's expense); I am working with *awareness*, which operates at the contact boundary between me and my client, and between my client and her/his environment. I believe that this will allow for the best self-regulation for the client *and* the environment.

The only potentially destructive aspect of working with different people in a couple or a family or a group of friends is if I get caught in a bind of confidentiality. I know that John is having an affair with Jenny while acting jealously towards his wife, Jan. Meanwhile, Jan is having an affair with . . . This does not only happen in soap operas! My rule is that I am always open to see husbands, wives, lovers, parents, children, either together with the client or separately—but I will not guarantee to keep confidentiality. Neither will I gossip about one to the other. Exploring issues around this rule is often enough in itself to unlock a situation clamped rigid by secrecy. I have never had a problem about this way of working since I stopped guaranteeing confidentiality—the problem once again becomes one for the client and his/her environment to resolve. And a surprising number of people do take up the option: ex-lovers, parent and grown-up child, people in conflict.

4. We can bring other people into the therapy situation by using empty cushions, with the client exploring different ways of relating to the other and her/his fantasies of their reactions (mixed with her/his own fears).

While we are doing this, once again I get a sense not only of the individual and the person on the cushion, but the feel of the *kind of interactions* that take place within that family, or whatever. Is there a lot of pleading, guilt-tripping, energy or lack of it, is it isolated from the community, are the expectations success or failure? This level is often at least as important as the individual level. The client is then exploring not only new ways of relating to the individual, but, *on behalf of the family*, exploring new ways of that family being in the world.

5. I want clients to clarify and separate expression of historic anger (to be expressed in the therapy room) and expression of here-and-now feelings (to be expressed to the person concerned). I make clear to the client that anger is a *contact* emotion, aiming towards improving contact. This is the dilemma for many children, when they express anger towards parents and, rather than ending in a more contactful relationship, their parents withdraw and denounce them as "bad". Later on, they want to sort out their relationship with Mum and Dad, and immediately feel overwhelmed with fear that anger will destroy that relationship. This might be partially true. Some parents will still not accept any expression of anger towards them, even more so thirty years' pent-up rage.

Once the historic rage has been expressed in therapy, I encourage clients to *negotiate* new relationships with those around them, especially parents, lovers, and children. It might not be possible to achieve a totally straight relationship, and I see it as quite valid to make compromises for the sake of a relationship that is important to me, *unless* that relationship requires that I give up a large proportion of my selfhood.

Gil Boyne (Workshop Presentation, January 1989) has rewritten the last two lines of the Gestalt Prayer very beautifully: "If we meet as loving adults, that'll be wonderful; / If not, I'll accept that too, because that's the way it is."

6.   I try to achieve a minimal distinction between therapy and the outside world. This is one of the reasons I prefer working with groups rather than individually. However, even in individual therapy there are choices that can be made. I avoid great emphasis on confidentiality, safety, and protection as "issues" in themselves. Rather, I want the client to be clear what her/his personal wants and needs are. What is the danger against which you need protection? What kind of protection can I provide? Who might it be important that you tell about yourself? Are you using issues of protection as an indirect way of getting me to confirm that you are helpless? I confront ways the client messes up the relationship with me and with others in a direct, caring, yet not overprotective manner. I want to communicate at the same time that he/she will not be destroyed by confrontation, and that I will not hurt him/her, not out of therapeutic choice, but because why the hell should I? If the client is working on very early memories and is in a regressed state, I am gentle because I do not get pleasure out of hurting people, not because I have introjects of "protection".

How far can I take this approach?

The only real limit to this approach is: what connections are fully present in the here-and-now for me and my client? How far can I introduce questions about "What is my place in the nation, world, universe . . .?" without sounding like a second-rate mystic? Whatever level we explore must connect with my client's (and my) own experience. I shall give some examples.

Example 1

Martha has been working on issues relating to abuse and neglect as a child. She has become aware of, and expressed, rage to her parents. Then:

Martha: They weren't all bad, you know.

Peter: Tell me about them.

Martha: Mother's parents were violent and distant. Her mother was always angry. My father's mother was very powerful; father didn't have anything to say for himself when she was about. It was just like he was with mother.

Peter: Abusive behaviour often is handed down in this way. We're working to exorcise a demon, but not a demon called mum or dad. This demon is passed on from generation to generation until someone says, "The buck stops here." Your anger is on behalf of all those who suffered from the demon.

Next session:

Martha: I talked to my mum, said what we'd talked about, the demon and that, and she talked about her grandparents. We felt closer than we've been for years.

Example 2

Jim has been working towards acknowledging his homosexuality.

Jim: But people won't accept me if I'm openly gay.

John: That'll sometimes be true.

We go on to discuss anti-gay prejudice, AIDS fears, how gay people can be accepted for themselves even if their sexuality is frowned on, gayness in other cultures: Ancient Greek, American Indian, and other positive gay images.

John: And you have choices. To be prepared to be openly gay doesn't mean you have to say it in the first sentence when you meet someone. You might want to, as a political statement, and it's a choice.

Jim: I guess I saw it as all or nothing. Come to think of it, I don't even know whether you're gay or straight.

John: I'll tell you if you want to know.

Jim: I realise it doesn't really matter to me.

Example 3

Karen presents herself as depressed.

Karen: I feel very small and insignificant.

Peter: There's a big important universe out there, and then there's you.

Karen: Everything will go on just fine without me. I may as well not be here.

Peter: You're the left-over cog from when the universe was made.

Karen: Yes, like I was an "afterthought" in my family, ten years younger than my brother. No one really had time for me.

Peter: They didn't want you around. And neither did the rest of the universe?

Karen: No they didn't . . . Well, I suppose I didn't give them much chance.

Peter: So the cog says to the universe "Keep out"!

Karen: (Laughs) Something like that!

Example 4

Phil is worried about his son *Mark*, eight years old.

Phil: He says to me, "I hate you" and runs away. I don't know what I've done, I'm not violent or anything.

John: How do you feel when he says that?

Phil: Angry, sad.

John: What do you do or say to him?

Phil: Nothing. He wants to be on his own.

John: Be Mark.

Phil (M): I hate you dad. Go away.

John: How do you feel, Mark, when you say that?

Phil (M): Angry, sad, lonely.

John: What do you want from dad?

Phil (M): I don't know. I want him to leave me in peace.

John: And yet you're lonely. What would happen if he came closer instead?

Phil (M): I feel frightened. Maybe he'd hit me.

John: Is that what you want?

Phil (M): Well, maybe it's what I deserve.

John: For . . .?

Phil (M): For saying I hate him.

John: Anything else?

Phil (M): For pushing him away and making him angry.

John: So you push him away, otherwise he may hit you for pushing him away . . . What if he hugged you instead?

Phil (M): I'd cry. I'd be cross with dad for making me cry.
John: So, Phil, what do you think?
Phil: I think I need to hug him.
John: He'll be frightened, angry, and struggle.
Phil: Yes, well, we have to start somewhere!

Next session:

> *Phil:*   The little tiger really fought me, but we ended up hugging, both of us in tears. Mother thought I was being cruel, but I kept on and Mark said, "It's OK mum".
>
> *John:*   Mark got what he wanted and was scared to get . . . Now be mum!

(Now the locus of the conflict has shifted to the relationship between the parents. We need to work through all these shifts for therapy to be more than moving the conflict around. I might have sessions with the whole family, or might work with Phil and his wife, or just with Phil. Whichever way, I work with the whole family.)

* * *

Ethically, I am responsible not only for the therapy I do with the individual, but the therapy I do with the whole field. My goal is not to shift problems around, but to catalyse exploration and change in the environment at all levels towards greater contact and flexibility.

This may seem grandiose, and some parts of our environment are less open to change than others, but my experience is that change *does* happen in surprising places when this approach is taken.

It is also important ethically to differentiate what I have been saying from attempts to *manipulate* the environment. Therapy is a *contractual* undertaking. My client is my client. However, it is important to remember that the environment *is* affected, and that we cannot just disclaim response-ability for that (or its feedback effect on our client). Gestalt therapy fits this understanding well, with its emphasis on person-in-environment, and its avoidance of providing ready-made answers to the client. What we do is help the client—and, through the client, help his or her environment—to pose the questions that lead to fuller awareness of how they interact.

CHAPTER TWENTY-SEVEN

Why shouldn't we interrupt?*

This paper was part of an ongoing discussion between myself and my long-term co-therapist and co-author John Bernard Harris, aimed towards finding our own style and understanding of group psychotherapy. In general, our preferences lean towards allowing impulses to be brought to awareness and followed, even if this is messy, rather than queued up, retroflected, and lost in order to provide more tidiness. So, as well as allowing interruptions, we allow movement around the room, more than one process happening at once (as long as there is the possibility of support for it all) and sub-grouping, sometimes in two rooms, where the whole group is too big an arena for some exploration at some times.

One of the debates within the Gestalt world is on whether the term "interruption to contact" is an appropriate one, or whether the term should be renamed in a way that would more positively connote what is happening. For example, the Polsters (workshop presentations) speak of "self-regulation at the contact

---

*First published in 1995, in *Topics in Gestalt Therapy*, 3(2).

boundary" and Wheeler (1991) speaks of "moderating contact", or "styles of contact". The aim is to remove any sense of "the client is doing something wrong or resisting here", and explore from a purely phenomenological perspective what the client is doing.

I have great sympathy with these views: they follow in an honourable tradition, which I shall argue goes back to Perls, Hefferline, and Goodman (1994), and takes in the "enlightening Gestalt" of Enright (1980), the debate in the American *Gestalt Journal* around "Boundary processes and boundary states" (Swanson, 1988), and my own paper (Philippson, 1990). All of these point out, in various ways, the importance of all the ways in which we regulate our contact. I have written elsewhere (Philippson, 1991) of my disquiet that some of those writing on this theme do not seem to have been aware of the previous writing, and that they misread Perls, Hefferline, and Goodman about Perls' and Goodman's views, understanding them as pathologising "interruptions". In fact, they view interruptions, or resistances to contact, as "creative adjustments" of the organism. However, this chapter focuses on a somewhat different aspect of this, one that has great bearing on the way we work with Gestalt therapy groups.

My question is "What do we *lose* if we dismiss interruption or resistance as a negative process?" Of course, most of us have been told in our childhood that we must not interrupt others. It is certainly not polite behaviour. It is often incorporated in a "Don't interrupt" rule (either overt or unspoken, or part of a wider "Be polite" rule, which I shall discuss later) in therapy or other groups. Such a rule does have some advantages. It is a way of preventing some group members (who speak louder or are less polite than others) from pulling the conversation towards themselves and away from others. People can finish their statements without having to simultaneously parry other people's interjections. These are group issues that do have to be dealt with in some way.

However, a rule about not interrupting is a blunt instrument with which to deal with such issues. Its advantage *and* disadvantage is that it is impersonal, and limits a wide variety of responses in order to avoid naming the processes of specific group members who are acting disruptively. I am wary of group rules and norms that even-handedly outlaw types of activity to prevent some people using them disruptively. This is particularly true in groups where the learning is to be transferred to other situations where people will transgress these nice norms (e.g., they will interrupt each other), so that, in the end, group members think "That was very pleasant, but of no use in the real world." There are other situations where the possibility of interruption is an important part of the activity of the group. One of these is obvious: to interrupt a continuous interrupter.

However, what I am particularly thinking of is the Gestalt concept of *dental aggression*: the biting off of manageable chunks of what the environment offers, and chewing it to extract the nourishment, making it part of myself, and excreting the non-nourishing. This is the contactful use of interruption: self-regulation at my contact-boundary, as the Polsters say. In contrast, the uncontactful interruption of people who interrupt to pull the attention towards themselves is a similar process to that adopted by anorectics who gain a sense of power over their environment by closing their mouths to nourishment from outside and simultaneously provide food for others.

Thus, in a group, I will experience a stream of contact possibilities from my environment. If I do not find a way to regulate these contacts, the best I can hope to do is to swallow them whole (introject them) or isolate myself from them. If I allow myself to interrupt, I can regulate the flow of what people are saying to me. If I allow myself to be contactfully interrupted, I can be sure that I am making real contact with those I am speaking to, rather than rattling on to people who do not understand or do not agree. What I deny myself is the possibility of inducing confluence, so that my listeners' critical faculties are washed away by my eloquence. So, if I am teaching theory, for example, I tell people that I *want* them to interrupt me if they do not understand me, do not agree with me, or want time to digest further what I am saying. My preference for people reading this (or any) chapter is that you do not read it all at once, but critically, a bit at a time.

Does what I say accord with your own experience? Is it useful to you, or mere verbiage with the aim of attracting attention to myself (of course, it could be both). If someone is speaking in a therapy group, is s/he actually making contact, or "interrupting in advance": saying something to attract attention and deny it to others? Is the speaker making hostile comments towards other group members, feeling secure in the knowledge that the group norm is not to say anything until s/he has finished? If either of the latter, would any interruption of mine be in order to enhance contact or to grab the attention for myself? These are the sorts of question that it is useful for group leaders (and members) to pay attention to.

The injunction "Don't interrupt" is given in childhood with the specific aim of facilitating introjection. Children interrupt when they disagree, or when they are uninterested—that is, out of contact with what is being said to them. If they learn to keep quiet at such times, either the child's response will have been replaced by the parent's or teacher's view, or the child will have made a show of hearing, and then will act as if the contact has never taken place (which, in a sense, it has not). Sometimes, introjection from parents is necessary (e.g., "Don't run across the road"): ideally, this will be as a temporary measure, until the child is able to understand for him/herself how to cross a road safely. Here again, my conjecture would be that children who are allowed to interrupt in the service of improved understanding and contact would learn to make better sense of their world (including road safety) than those who swallow their understanding at second hand in large chunks.

Thus, in a Gestalt group, people are discovering new possibilities for contact, and, unlike in a psychodynamic group, are giving this priority over "inner work". It then becomes less obvious that it would be wrong for a group member to interrupt another group member's "work". The questions would be more: "Is this an attempt to enhance the contact with the group member who is speaking, or an attempt to disrupt it? If so, what is going on here? Is this some parallel process to the one the speaker is talking about? Are the speaker's boundaries firm enough that s/he will be able to respond to the interrupter, or do I as group leader need to step in?" Once again, in being aware of all these possibilities, I am again reminded of the flexibility and subtlety of Gestalt therapy, and its potential for allowing learning and growth in a comparatively uncontrolled or "not nice" environment.

I suppose the larger issue is the theme I alluded to earlier: *politeness*. One of the defining aspects of a Gestalt group (or individual therapy) is that there is no requirement to stick to polite behaviour. It is more clarifying to let the process develop naturally, always *with awareness*, and discover what is thereby being shown about the participants in the process. Thus, interruption, hostility, resistance for the sake of resistance, scapegoating, conflicts over who will take time when, are all potentially fertile processes. The Gestalt approach is that there are no "innocent victims" here. What is it about *this* person that s/he is chosen as the scapegoat, or is frequently interrupted, or does not find the time to speak? Does this happen in other contexts as well?

Now, this scapegoating or marginalisation of a group member is potentially very destructive, confirming in the group member an image of how s/he is (less important, no good, etc.), and maybe also confirming for other group members that their needs are more important than anyone else's. The factor that decides whether this approach is therapeutic or destructive is the degree of awareness of the group. There needs to be a culture, fostered by the therapist, that group members both commit themselves to the processes of the group, and simultaneously stay curious about these processes. It is this curiosity that prevents confluence with the group process, and allows people to learn from whatever occurs, rather than riding a rollercoaster to the end of a ride, wherever that is. Part of the awareness, which must be held by the therapist, is that some people at some times are more fragile and less able to interact or conflict than at other times. This will be part of the context of any group interaction. Thus, some people will need temporary protection from interruption or some forms of conflict, and this can be explicit, rather than some blanket rule.

The important point in all this is that these issues—when to be polite, when to interrupt, when to allow for someone's inability to engage in a particular kind of contact, how to get time for yourself in a competitive situation—are all part of living in the world, and proper areas for therapeutic exploration. Groups conducted in this way will be less comfortable than more polite groups, but awareness from such a group can be immediately transferred to other situations. The group does not become a nurturing "charmed circle" where people can do things that (both before and after therapy) they would not be willing to do in the world outside therapy.

Right, I've finished this—you can all speak now!

REFERENCES

Alexander, R., Brickman, B., Jacobs, L., Trop, J., & Yontef, G. (1992). Transference meets dialogue. *Gestalt Journal*, *XV*(2): 61–108.

American Psychiatric Association (1987). *Diagnostic and Statistical Manual of Mental Disorders, Third Edition, Revised* (*DSM-III-R*). Washington, DC: American Psychiatric Association.

Argyris, C. (1986). Skilled incompetence. *Harvard Business Review*, *64*(5): 74–79.

Bateson, G., Jackson, D. D., Haley, J., & Weakland, J. (1972). Towards a theory of schizophrenia. In: G. Bateson (Ed.), *Steps to an Ecology of Mind*. New York: Ballantine Books.

Beebe Hill, R. (1979). *Hanta Yo*. London: Futura.

Beisser, A. (1970). The paradoxical theory of change. In: J. Fagan & I. L. Shepherd (Eds.), *Gestalt Therapy Now* (pp. 88–92). New York: Harper & Row.

Bergantino, L. (1993). Recollections of a young whippersnapper. *Gestalt Journal*, *XVI*(2): 91–94.

Berne, E. (2010). *Games People Play: The Psychology of Human Relationships*. London: Penguin Books.

Bion, W. R. (1961). *Experiences in Groups*. London, Tavistock.

Breuer, J., & Freud, S. (1895d). *Studies in Hysteria. S.E., 2*. London: Hogarth Press.

Buber, M. (1965). *Between Man and Man*. New York: Collier Books.

Carroll, L. (2000). *Alice in Wonderland*. New York: Harper Festival.

Clarkson, P. (1992). *Transactional Analysis Psychotherapy: An Integrated Approach*. London: Routledge.

Cornell, W. F. (2003). The impassioned body. *British Gestalt Journal, 12*(2): 97–104.

Damasio, A. (1999). *The Feeling of What Happens: Body, Emotion and the Making of Consciousness*. London: Heinemann.

Davidove, D. (1991). Loss of ego functions, conflict and resistance. *Gestalt Journal, XIV*(2): 27–43.

Davis, D. R. (1987). Transference. In: R. L. Gregory (Ed.), *The Oxford Companion to the Mind* (p. 781). Oxford: Oxford University Press.

De Bono, E. (1973). *Lateral Thinking: Creativity Step by Step*. New York: Harper Colophon.

Delany, S. R. (1996). *Trouble on Triton: An Ambiguous Heterotopia*. Hanover, NH: Wesleyan University Press.

Dublin, J. (1977). Gestalt therapy, existential-Gestalt therapy and/versus "Perls-ism". In: E. W. L. Smith (Ed.), *The Growing Edge of Gestalt Therapy* (pp. 124–150). Secaucus, NJ: Citadel Press.

Enright, J. (1980). *Enlightening Gestalt*. Mill Valley, CA: Pro Telos.

Erickson, M. H. (1980). *The Collected Works of Milton H. Erickson on Hypnosis* (4 volumes), E. L. Rossi (Ed.). New York: Irvington.

Erskine, R. (1995). Shame and self-righteousness. *British Gestalt Journal, 4*(2): 107–117.

Fagan, J., & Shepherd, I. L. (1970). *Gestalt Therapy Now*. New York: Science & Behaviour Books.

Fanon, F. (2001). *The Wretched of the Earth*. London: Penguin Classics.

Fanon, F. (2008). *Black Skins, White Masks*. London: Pluto Press.

Frank, R. (2001). *Body of Awareness*. Cambridge, MA: Gestalt Press.

Freire, P. (1996). *Pedagogy of the Oppressed*. London: Penguin.

Freud, S. (1916–1917). *Introductory Lectures on Psycho-analysis. S.E., 15–16*. London: Hogarth.

Friedman, M. (1990). Dialogue, philosophical anthropology, and Gestalt therapy. *Gestalt Journal, XIII*(1): 7–40.

From, I. (1984) Reflections on Gestalt therapy after thirty-two years of practice: a requiem for Gestalt. *Gestalt Journal, VII*(1): 4–12.

Gleick, J. (1987). *Chaos: Making a New Science*. New York: Viking Press.

Goldstein, K. (1939). *The Organism*. Boston, MA: American Book Company.

Goodman, P. (1960). *Growing Up Absurd*. New York: Vintage Books.

Goodman, P. (1971). *Compulsory Miseducation*. London: Penguin.

Greenberg, E. (1989). Healing the borderline. *Gestalt Journal, XII*(2): 11–55.

Greenberg, E. (1991). Special: the diagnosis and treatment of narcissistic disorders. Gestalt Center of Long Island 14th Annual Conference Presentation.

Greenberg, J. R., & Mitchell, S. A. (1983). *Object Relations in Psychoanalytic Theory*. Cambridge, MA: Harvard University Press.

Groddeck, G. (1949). *The Book of the It*. London: Vision Press.

Harris, J. B. (1990). Structure and spontaneity. GRTA Conference handout.

Hillman, J., & Ventura, M. (1992). *We've Had 100 Years of Psychotherapy and the World's Getting Worse*. San Francisco, CA: Harper.

Hycner, R., & Jacobs, L. (1995). *The Healing Relationship in Gestalt Therapy: A Dialogic/Self Psychology Approach*. Highland, NY: Gestalt Journal Press.

Jacobs, L. (2003). Review of 'Self in Relation'. *International Gestalt Journal, 26*(1): 137–148.

Kennedy, D. (2003). The phenomenal field: the homeground of Gestalt therapy. *British Gestalt Journal, 12*(2): 76–87.

Kepner, J. (2003). The embodied field. *British Gestalt Journal, 12*(1): 6–14.

Kohut, H. (1971). *The Analysis of the Self*. New York: International Universities Press.

Kohut, H. (1977). *The Restoration of the Self*. New York: International Universities Press.

Kuhn, T. (1970). *The Structure of Scientific Revolutions*. Chicago, IL: University of Chicago Press.

Land, E. (1977). The retinex theory of colour vision. *Scientific American, 237*(6): 108–128.

Lao Tsu (1972). *Tao Te Ching*, G. Feng & J. English (Trans.). London: Wildwood House.

Lasch, C. (1979). *The Culture of Narcissism*. London: Norton/Abacus.

Lasch, C. (1985). *The Minimal Self*. London: Picador.

Latner, J. (1983). This is the speed of light: field and systems theories in Gestalt Therapy. *Gestalt Journal, VI*(2): 71–90. Also the debate on Latner's paper and Gestalt theory taking up the whole of Gestalt Journal *VII*(1) (Spring 1984).

Latner, J. (1998). Sex in therapy. *British Gestalt Journal, 7*(2): 136–138.

Lee, R., & Wheeler, G. (1996). *The Voice of Shame*. San Francisco, CA: Jossey-Bass.

Lewin, K. (1951). *Field Theory in Social Science*. New York: Harper & Row.

Lewin, R. (1993). *Complexity.* London: J. M. Dent.

Mackewn, J. (1997). *Developing Gestalt Counselling.* London: Sage.

Mahler, J. S., Pine, F., & Bergman, A. (1975). *The Psychological Birth of the Human Infant.* New York: Basic Books.

Marcus, E. H. (1979). *Gestalt Therapy and Beyond.* Cupertino, CA: Meta.

Masterson, J. F. (1981). *The Narcissistic and Borderline Disorders.* New York: Brunner-Mazel.

Mathys, M. (1995). A cross-cultural encounter. *British Gestalt Journal, 4*(2): 101–106.

Neenan, M., & Dryden, W. (2004). *Cognitive Therapy: 100 Key Points and Techniques.* New York: Brunner-Routledge.

Norwood, R. (1989). *Women Who Love Too Much.* London: Arrow.

O'Shea, L. (2000). Sexuality: old struggles and new challenges. *Gestalt Review, 4*(1): 8–25.

Parlett, M. (1991). Reflections on field theory. *British Gestalt Journal, 1*(2): 69–81.

Parlett, M. (1997). The unified field in practice. *Gestalt Review, 1*(1): 16–33.

Perls, F. S. (1947). *Ego, Hunger and Aggression.* London: Allen Unwin [reprinted Highland, NY: Gestalt Journal Press, 1992].

Perls, F. S. (1948). Theory and technique of personality integration. *American Journal of Psychotherapy, 2*(4): 565–586.

Perls, F. S. (1969a). *Gestalt Therapy Verbatim.* Moab, UT: Real People Press.

Perls F. S. (1969b). *In and Out the Garbage Pail.* New York: Bantam.

Perls, F. S. (1973). *The Gestalt Approach & Eye Witness to Therapy.* New York: Science & Behavior Books.

Perls, F. S. (1978). Finding self through Gestalt therapy. *Gestalt Journal, I*(1): 54–73.

Perls, F. S., Hefferline, R., & Goodman, P. (1994). *Gestalt Therapy: Excitement and Growth in the Human Personality.* Highland, NY: Gestalt Journal Press.

Philippson, L. (1855). *The Development of the Religious Idea in Judaism, Christianity and Mahomedanism: Considered in Twelve Lectures on the History and Purport of Judaism.* A. M. Goldsmid (Trans.). London: Longman, Brown, Green, & Longmans.

Philippson, P. (1990). Awareness, the contact boundary and the field. *Gestalt Journal, XIII*(2): 73–84 and this volume.

Philippson, P. (1991). 'Gestalt Reconsidered' again. *British Gestalt Journal, 1*(2): 103–106.

Philippson, P. (1993a). Pseudo-introjection. *Topics in Gestalt Therapy, 1*(2): 10–14.

Philippson, P. (1993b). Gestalt and regression. *British Gestalt Journal*, 2(2): 121–124.

Philippson, P. (1995). Two theories of five layers. *Topics in Gestalt Therapy*, 3(1): 11–23.

Philippson, P. (1996). A note in response to Richard Erskine on shame. *British Gestalt Journal*, 5(2): 129–130.

Philippson, P. (2001). *Self in Relation*. Highland, NY: Gestalt Journal Press.

Philippson, P. (2004). The experience of shame. *International Gestalt Journal*, 27(2): 85–96.

Philippson, P. (2005). Paradox—strategic, naïve and Gestalt. *International Gestalt Journal*, 28(2): 9–17.

Philippson, P., & Harris, J. (1990). *Gestalt Therapy: Working with Groups*. Manchester: Manchester Gestalt Centre.

Polster, E. (1991). Response to "Loss of ego functions, conflict and resistance". *Gestalt Journal*, *XIV*(2): 45–60.

Polster, E. (1993). Individuality and commonality. *British Gestalt Journal*, 2(1): 41–43.

Polster, E., & Polster, M. (1974). *Gestalt Therapy Integrated: Contours of Theory and Practice*. New York: Vintage.

Prigogine, I., & Stengers, I. (1984). *Order Out of Chaos*. New York: Bantam Books.

Quiller-Couch, A. (Ed.) (1939). *The Oxford Book of English Verse, 1250–1918*. Oxford: Clarendon Press.

Ramachandran, V. S. (1999). *Phantoms in the Brain*. London: Fourth Estate.

Reynolds, D. (1985). *Playing Ball on Running Water*. London: Sheldon Press.

Reynolds, D. (1986). *Even in Summer The Ice Doesn't Melt*. London: William Morrow.

Roberts, A. (1999). Digging up the bodies. *British Gestalt Journal*, 8(2): 134–137.

Rogers, C., & Ryback, D. (1984). One alternative to planetary suicide. *The Consulting Psychologist*, 12(2): 3–12.

Rogers, C., & Stevens, B. (1973). *Person to Person*. London: Souvenir Press.

Rossi, E. (1986). *The Psychobiology of Mind–Body Healing*. New York: Norton.

Rutter, P. (1990). *Sex in the Forbidden Zone*. London: Unwin Hyman.

Sartre, J.-P. (1978). *Being and Nothingness*. New York: Quokka.

Schiff, J. L., & Day, B. (1970). *All My Children*. New York: Pyramid.

Schore, A. (1994). *Affect Regulation and the Origin of the Self*. Hove: Lawrence Erlbaum.

Schore, A. (2003). *Affect Regulation and the Repair of the Self*. New York: W. W. Norton.

Selvini Palazzoli, M., Boscolo, L., Cecchin, G., & Prata, G. (1978). *Paradox and Counter-Paradox*. New York: Jason Aronson.

Staemmler, F.-M. (1997). Towards a theory of regressive processes in Gestalt therapy. *Gestalt Journal, XX*(1): 49–120.

Staemmler, F.-M. (2009). *Aggression, Time, and Understanding*. Santa Cruz, CA: Gestalt Press.

Stern, D. N. (1985). *The Interpersonal World of the Infant*. New York: Basic Books.

Stern, D. N. (2003). On the other side of the moon. In: M. Spagnuolo Lobb & N. Amendt-Lyon (Eds.), *Creative License: The Art of Gestalt Therapy* (pp. 21–35). New York: Springer.

Stern, D. N. (2004). *The Present Moment in Psychotherapy and Everyday Life*. New York: W. W. Norton.

Stevens, T., & Mulsow, M. (2006). There is no meaningful relationship between television exposure and symptoms of attention-deficit/hyperactivity disorder. *Pediatrics, 117*: 665–672.

Swanson, J. L. (1988). Boundary processes and boundary states. *Gestalt Journal, XI*(2): 5–24. Also the debate which takes up the rest of that volume and some of *Gestalt Journal XII*(1).

Tobin, S. (1982). Self-disorders, Gestalt therapy and self psychology. *Gestalt Journal, V*(2): 3–44.

Waldrop, M. M. (1993). *Complexity*. London: Viking Press.

Wheeler, G. (1991). *Gestalt Reconsidered*. New York: Gardner Press.

Wheeler, G. (1995). Shame in two paradigms of therapy. *British Gestalt Journal, 4*(2): 76–85.

Wheeler, G. (1997). Self and shame: a Gestalt approach. *Gestalt Review, 1*(3): 221–244.

Wheeler, G. (2000). *Beyond Individualism, Toward a New Understanding of Self, Relationship, and Experience*. Cambridge, MA: GIC Press.

Wollants, G. (2008). *Gestalt Therapy: Therapy of the Situation*. Turnhout, Belgium: Faculteit voor mens en samenleving of course.

Yontef, G. (1988a). Comments on "Boundary processes and boundary states". *Gestalt Journal, XI*(2): 25–35.

Yontef, G. (1988b). Assimilating diagnostic and psychoanalytic perspectives into Gestalt therapy. *Gestalt Journal, XI*(1): 5–32.

Yontef, G. (1992). Considering 'Gestalt Reconsidered': a review in depth. *Gestalt Journal, XV*(1): 95–118.

Yontef, G. (1993). *Awareness, Dialogue and Process*. Highland, NY: Gestalt Journal Press.

Yontef, G., & Tobin, S. (1983). A dialogue on theory: number 2. *Gestalt Journal, VI*(1): 54–90.

Zinker, J. (1977). *Creative Process in Gestalt Therapy*. New York: Vintage Books.

Zinker, J. (1994). *In Search of Good Form*. San Francisco, CA: Jossey-Bass.

INDEX